Claire Scobie worked for the *Telegraph Magazine* and won the Catherine Pakenham Award as Best Young Woman Journalist of the Year. She now writes for numerous publications, including the *Daily Telegraph*, the *Independent*, the *Glasgow Herald*, the *Age*, and the *South China Morning Post*. After living in the Indian sub-continent, she moved to Australia in 2002. *Last Seen in Lhasa* is her first book.

Praise for *Last Seen in Lhasa*:

'Truly wonderful . . . not only a deeply moving and inspiring account of a friendship but also an enthralling insight into a vanishing world.'
Mick Brown, author of *The Spiritual Tourist*

'[Through reading *Last Seen in Lhasa*] I learned about the simple daily life of the Tibetan nun, Ani. It is like a silent conversation, influenced by her silent nature. She lives from cave to cave under the light of our sun and moon; she eats the same food every day but it gives her a rich mind to taste life; without need for an expensive mattress, she dreams peacefully on a yak skin. Claire Scobie's refreshing book shows how people can see their lives differently. How much time do we have to waste chasing material things, living an easy life with good food and comfortable sleep?' Xinran, author of *Sky Burial*

'Claire Scobie brings a great eye and a great heart to this wonderful story of place, friendship and spirituality. This is an inner journey as well as an outer one, but the detail, subtlety and surprises of the outer journey make her experiences of Tibet utterly compelling.' Stephanie Dowrick, author of *Choosing Happiness*

For my parents,
whose journeys inspired my own

LAST SEEN IN LHASA

The story of an extraordinary friendship
in modern Tibet

Claire Scobie

RIDER

London · Sydney · Auckland · Johannesburg

1 3 5 7 9 10 8 6 4 2

First published in 2006 by Rider, an imprint of Ebury Publishing
This edition published by Rider in 2007

Ebury Publishing is a Random House Group company

The Random House Group Limited Reg. No. 954009

Addresses for companies within the Random House Group can be found at
www.randomhouse.co.uk

A CIP catalogue record for this book is available from the British Library

The Random House Group Limited makes every effort to ensure that the papers used in our
books are made from trees that have been legally sourced from well-managed and credibly
certified forests. Our paper procurement policy can be found on www.randomhouse.co.uk

Mixed Sources

Product group from well-managed
forests and other controlled sources
FSC   www.fsc.org Cert no. TT-COC-2139
© 1996 Forest Stewardship Council

Printed in the UK by CPI Cox & Wyman, Reading, RG1 8EX

ISBN 9781846040061

Each friend represents a world in us, a world not born until they arrive, and it is only by this meeting that a new world is born.

Anaïs Nin

We close ourselves off from Eden in order to live the common-sense life and then find ways of escaping from that when it gets too mundane . . . We fear ecstasy because it is too demanding, requires too much discipline, too much surrender. Occasionally we touch it – through meditation, dance, celebration and ritual and we are lit up, we become truly alive. Then we return to the solid world and die again.

Theolyn Cortens

Not all who wander are lost.

J. R. R. Tolkien

CONTENTS

Please note

All Tibetan words are spelled phonetically in English in order to make them easier to read. The political climate in Tibet remains unpredictable. On Ani's request I have neither disclosed her spiritual name, nor that of her nunnery in order to protect her identity. I have also changed most of the names of any Tibetans mentioned.

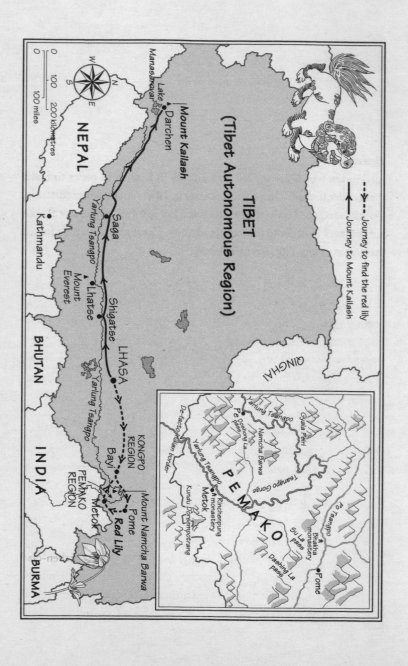

CHAPTER 1

The Pass of Sharp Stones

I DON'T know how I know Ani as I do. I know how I met her. I know how old she is and that at the age of twenty-two she ran away from home to join a nunnery. I know she is the fifth of nine children and grew up in a large black tent spun from yak hair. I know how at ease I feel when I am with her. Why we were thrown together is a question I have yet to find an answer to. Some would say fate, others dismiss it as chance.

My lasting memory of Ani is crossing a mountain pass in south-east Tibet. Usually one step ahead, Ani strode purposefully with a gnarled staff in her hand. The sleeves of her fuchsia-pink blouse billowed. Her straw hat sagged from the monsoonal downpours. She steered me steadily along the path, only slowing down when we wound upwards. The higher we climbed, the more rugged the landscape, the thinner the air. I became short of breath, my lungs straining with each step. Ani started to feel dizzy and to keep us on track we held hands tightly. At that moment nothing separated us from the spirit of existence.

The landscape resembled a living Stonehenge with lichen-clad boulders and giant rocks. In the distance was a glacier, its dirty minty-blue snout pointing down the mountainside. By a river, a sculpture of burnished amber rocks gleaming under the crush of glacial melt, there was a mule that had sunk to its knees and died. As we approached the summit of the pass, snow crunching underfoot, I picked buttercup-yellow primulas and electric-blue poppies – an offering of gratitude for our safe passage. Side by side now, Ani and I fell into step. Her knees were troubling her – she suffered from arthritis. I could barely feel my legs, numb with cold.

Finally the top of 'the pass of sharp stones' came into view, marked with faded prayer flags. The wreckage of an army helicopter lay scattered near more skeletons of mules. The local porters were slumped near their bamboo baskets laden with luggage. There were cairns of stones, greying *khatas* – ceremonial scarves – to placate the temperamental mountain deities and I placed the bunch of flowers among them. My head was spinning from the altitude, which was 13,500 feet. Bowing her head, Ani tied a *khata* at the windswept altar as she said a short prayer. With the wind buffeting us and barely able to stand, after a brief pause to catch our breath, we tumbled back down the other side.

This image remains singed in my mind: the sheer physical exertion of the climb through a wilderness barely touched by the modern world, the camaraderie between us and knowing that without Ani at my side, I'm not sure I could have made it.

We were in Pemako, a region geographically unlike anywhere else on the barren Tibetan plateau, one of the most forbidding and little known places on the planet, with a history lost in the thickets of myth and folklore. Accessible only on foot, Pemako (pronounced Pem-ack-oh) lies nestled among the Himalayas between Tibet and north-east India. With a tiered eco-system that extends from snowfields to evergreen forest before plummeting to subtropical jungle, it is home to bears and snow leopards, long-tailed monkeys and Bengali tigers. Pygmy blue flycatchers swoop and dive, fire-tailed sunbirds hover above flame-coloured orchids.

In 1992 the Chinese authorities granted a Western group permission to visit, the first in over half a century. Seven years later the valleys were again closed and there are no signs they will be reopened. As far as I know, I am the only English woman to have set foot in Pemako, 'the Promised Land of Tibetan prophecy. . . hidden behind misty barriers where ordinary men do not go'.[1]

I had first gone to the mountains that border Pemako in search of a rare red lily. Little could I have predicted how that flower would interweave my destiny with a woman eleven years older than myself, who lived differently to anything I had ever known or believed still existed. Ani spends her days on pilgrimage, walking from holy site to sacred mountain, her life solely devoted to a higher purpose. What defines me bears no relevance to Ani. We do not speak the same language nor do we share background, life experience or belief. In order to understand her, I realised I needed to adopt a new mode of perception. For this I tried to define what Ani is: by birth a nomad, by nature a wanderer, by nurture a pilgrim and by choice a nun.

I enjoy the company of others; Ani seeks out solitude. I'm intellectual, I think in words; Ani is mystical, she rests in the spaces between the words. I can't bear the cold. Ani lives in the coldest house imaginable and, if she must, will sleep out in the snow on plastic sheeting with a sheepskin for warmth. She has no money and eats the same indigestible meal – *tsampa* – three times a day.

And yet, improbably, over the years as I have travelled back and forth to Tibet our friendship has taken seed. As I have become more aware of what happens to a people when a country is occupied and freedom is denied, each of my seven journeys has been, in a sense, part of my own pilgrimage. Each stage has allowed me to discover a deeper truth. Friendship requires patience. It takes time to build trust, especially in a country where foreigners are mistrusted and political oppression is a daily part of life. For Ani to travel with me and invite me into her home took considerable risk. But for Ani to open her inner world to me – the vanishing world of a wandering hermit – took rare and singular courage. She is the last of a generation, a lone woman in pursuit of perfection, in search of enlightenment.

CHAPTER 2

The Search for the Red Lily

In the days before leaving on my first journey to Tibet in search of the red lily I was filled with a sense of apprehension. I had a tightness in my chest and a fear that I would be unable to breathe, that I would suffer altitude sickness. On the plane from Kathmandu to Lhasa, the Himalayan range sprawled as far as the eye could see. When I came eye-level with Chomolongma, 'mother goddess of the universe', better known as Mount Everest, my anxieties melted away. Her angular peak glistened like the pleated headdress of an Egyptian sphinx and for a brief moment seemed within grasp, until the plane swung sharply left into a wide gorge. Below the tributaries of the Yarlung Tsangpo River shimmered like plaits of tressed jade. There was a flash of metallic grey: one of the few tarmac roads connecting Gongkar airport with Lhasa.

Inside the terminal, the ceilings were high, the facilities basic. Propaganda posters of Chinese and smiling Tibetans in traditional costume plastered the walls. Officials jumped to attention. Soldiers with machine guns loitered. Waiting for our party was a pale moon-faced Chinese man with a shock of black hair. It was Tang Wei, our Chinese guide, who greeted everyone with a broad smile of tobacco-stained teeth and a firm hug. Outside waited Sherpas from Nepal, David Burlinson, owner of the travel agency who had organised the trip, and two Tibetan guides sporting baseball caps, Tashi and Tsering.

Besides us there was one other group of Westerners led by a tall American with an unkempt beard, a bandana carelessly tied around his neck, a man who Ken Cox, our group leader, pointed out as Ian Baker, one of the few Westerners to have explored Pemako.

Walking out of doors I was immediately struck by the intensity of the light; the sunshine was blinding and threw every detail into sharp, almost psychedelic relief. The sky was a rich velvety cobalt blue; the air, sparse and crisp. We were at an altitude of some 11,500 feet and to my relief, I had no difficulty breathing. There was merely a faint headache, a slight pounding in my temples as if I had drunk two glasses of champagne on an empty stomach. If anything, I felt curiously elated.

Our convoy of two four-wheel-drive Land cruisers and one truck drove in the opposite direction to Lhasa, following the Yarlung Tsangpo downstream through the region of Kongpo. Known in Tibet as 'the purifier', this river begins life as a trickle from a glacier around 650 miles west at Mount Kailash, and fills with snowmelt from the northern slopes of the Himalayas. Tibet is literally the fountainhead of Asia, the source of ten great river systems providing millions – an estimated 47 per cent of the world's population – with their daily water.

Our plant-hunting expedition was timed for early June when alpine flowers awaken from an iron-hard winter to trumpet the start of summer. A month later the monsoon begins, roads turn to mud and avalanches block mountain passes. We had to be prepared for kaleidoscopic weather and a climate of four seasons, not in one day, but in one hour. Such substantial rainfall could serve to make Kongpo most inhospitable. For plant-hunters, it is an organic nirvana with swathes of primeval forest and peaks much higher than Mont Blanc still unclimbed. Back in 1950 Frank Kingdon Ward, the late British botanist who is credited with having collected 23,000 plants, would walk back to his camp with armfuls of new species.

Scarlet Pimpernel, Orange Bill, Yellow Peril: each flower sounded like a character from a book, each with a quixotic story to tell. Every spring they bloom in the Himalayas. Some reach over fifty feet, while others are barely knee-high. I was no plant-hunter nor particularly intrepid but when I was invited to join the hunt for the rare red lily, I could not resist.

It had all begun the year before on a chill November day in 1996, when I was standing ankle-deep in mud in a field in Scotland. I was visiting Glendoick Gardens, a rhododendron nursery, run by a friend, Ken Cox. Typically wearing cotton patchwork trousers with a thin navy blue jumper, Ken offered to take me on a tour of the grounds. Walking into a miniature Himalayan garden, his blue-grey eyes, framed by long eyelashes, darting from plant to plant, Ken explained that he, his father Peter, and grandfather Euan had brought the seed of many of the plants from the East.

After accompanying the well-known plant-hunter Reginald Farrer to Burma in 1919, Euan Cox had become one of the great garden writers of his age. As a toddler Ken had inherited the plant gene, displaying a precocious talent for memorising plant names. Now director of the family firm, he spent his summers leading earnest plant-hunters to China and Tibet in search of flowers not yet plucked or recorded, hybridised or patented, plants that were still new to science.

As we strolled along sinuous paths, I looked around at the towering bushes of rhododendrons, azaleas and hedges of juniper, trying to imagine what they would look like in Tibet. Or, for that matter, what Tibet would look like.

'I'm going back to Tibet next year in search of a rare flower, the little red lily,' Ken said, sitting on a wooden bench. '*Lilium paradoxum* has never been introduced to the West. It is to lilies what duck-billed platypus is to reptiles or amphibians. There's nothing else like it. The shape of the flower, the size, the colour – all are different. This time I'm determined to find it.' He paused, searching my face. 'Why don't you come? You could write a story about it.'

I had no idea there were places in the world still unexplored, places where someone like me – unfit and afraid of heights – could go. By the time I left Scotland to fly back to London I'd made up my mind to join the expedition. Months of uncertainty lay ahead. Other willing plant-hunters needed to be found to make up group numbers. Official permission from the Chinese had to be granted. South-east Tibet still remained off-limits and four permits were required from four different offices: Foreign Affairs, Military, Tourism and, most importantly, the secret police, known as the Public Security Bureau (PSB).

With such a brief flowering season, plant-collecting in Tibet is always a gamble. I had no assurances that I would locate my floral grail and in June 1997, when we finally set off, it was to be a long drive before I could start looking for the lily, on two mountain passes that cross into the remote region of Pemako.

Situated about 400 miles east of Lhasa, Pemako is located in lower Kongpo, where the Yarlung Tsangpo plunges off the Tibetan plateau into a tangled knot of Himalayan peaks. In only twenty-four miles the river level drops from 9,600 to about 1,000 feet as it makes a nearly 180-degree turn to run south-west into Assam, carving out the world's deepest, most impenetrable gorge. At its lowest point the Tsangpo Gorge plunges to 17,658 feet: over three times the height of the Grand Canyon.

On our journey, days passed jumping in and out of the four-wheel-drive jeep as eccentric, somewhat fastidious plant-hunters spied unusual flora. At times, they were blind to all else, like ducks on a pond: head down, tail up. Nights were spent in soulless hotels with bathrooms but no water. Outside were terrible toilets, concrete like the rest of the Chinese-built towns. In restaurants with red velvet-clad walls, reminiscent of a Parisian brothel, occasionally with a large picture of Chairman Mao staring down, the ice began to thaw among my eclectic travelling companions.

Over dinner, the conversation between the dozen plantsmen and women from England and America would meander around sex, bowels and plants. Blonde, long-legged Amy Denton, a PhD student from Seattle, would describe flowers as the exquisite genitalia of the plant world, 'so much more attractive than our own'. Anne Chambers, a fine botanist painter from Glasgow, rhapsodised about her favourite plants, the lime-green and yellow *Arisaema flavum* with curling tongue-shaped petals and the dark maroon *Cypripedium*, a six-petalled slipper orchid that resembles a perfectly proportioned gonad. (The word itself 'is derived from the Greek *Kypris pedion*, which translates as "the genital region of Aphrodite".'[1]) The wise-looking elder of the group, Tony Cox (no relation to Ken), seventy-five, a retired customs official, sat quietly in the corner, suffering a touch of altitude sickness.

The drive was punctuated with regular military checkpoints and incidents with erratic, louche-looking Chinese policemen: one, blind drunk at nine in the morning, was found poking through our luggage; another in plainclothes pointed a gun at Tang Wei's head after a dispute escalated in a restaurant. On day five we reached Bayi, a military town in the middle of nowhere, where our group reported to the Section of Alien and Entry-Exit Administration at the Public Security Bureau for papers to be rubber-stamped.

An ugly functional town, Bayi – literally 1 August, the founding date of the People's Liberation Army – is the sort of place one wants to leave on arrival. Rainbow-coloured motorcycle rickshaws touted for business along wide empty streets, figures in khaki-green uniform climbed in and out of jeeps. Our convoy crossed a bridge with another military checkpoint, before a steep ascent up to a pass, where yaks ran like scared rocking horses with ankle-length furry skirts, and only then did we leave Sino-Tibet and enter into another world – the Wild West of Asia and the heart of Kongpo.

Unlike much of Tibet, Kongpo is densely forested with higher rainfall and a wetter climate. Ethnically and linguistically distinct, the province has long been influenced by its proximity to the indigenous tribes from Burma and Assam who have migrated into the eastern Himalayas, and over the centuries intermarried with Tibetans. Historically the rulers of central Tibet have regarded the inhabitants of Kongpo with suspicion. Reputedly the locals poison their enemies, indulge in incest, even cannibalism and are well versed in the black arts. Once a stronghold for the shamanistic and animist Bon religion – worshipping the spirits in nature, mountains and trees – that pre-dates Buddhism and was formerly known as Black Bon (now as New Bon), it is this that may have 'added to [Kongpo's] reputation as a region of darkness in the eyes of the Buddhist'.[2]

On the long drive east, I cast my mind back to the series of events that had brought me to Tibet. It was undoubtedly the red lily that proved to be the final impetus I needed to leave my secure London life and become a freelance journalist. Crucially, I had to persuade my editor at the *Telegraph Magazine,* where I was working, to commission an article on the hunt for the rare red lily on a freelance basis. My editor agreed, telling me, 'You better find it.' After handing in my notice at the magazine I dutifully amassed a bundle of research on all aspects of Tibet. While I should have been reading about the current political situation, I was much more interested in the yellowed cuttings about the intrepid botanist Frank Kingdon Ward, in whose footsteps we would be following, or, rather, going where he had not.

Kingdon Ward, wiry, with pronounced lines in the centre of his forehead and bushy eyebrows, always dreamed of becoming an explorer. Enduring the toughest conditions, he would spend months alone, scrambling up and down mountainsides as he relentlessly collected plants, photographing and surveying the land. The hardships, dangers and the paltry amounts he earned from some twenty-five books mattered little, for he was utterly bewitched by the wild temperate gardens of south-east Tibet. I wondered, as I read, if I would be cast under the same spell.

Before I left England for Tibet, I made a visit to Eastbourne to meet

Ward's second wife. She lived in a spotless flat, the shelves crammed with a collection of films on nature, science and astronomy, reflecting her own life-long interest in exploration. She had fine silvery hair set in a classic perm, blush-pink cheeks and sharp eyes. I had brought a map of south-east Tibet to show her the route our plant-hunting expedition would follow.

'Oh gosh,' she said. 'It makes my fingers tingle. Snow should be teeming down when you go.' Her eyes twinkled as she talked about her ten 'marvellous years' married to Frank. He was a man who, despite four gold medals and fifty years of plant-hunting, 'was very hard on himself', without 'the slightest conception of what a great explorer he was'.

They had met at a lunch party in 1944 in Bombay where Jean's father was a judge in the Bombay High Court. Three years later, when she was twenty-six and Frank sixty-two, they were married in Chelsea, and five days after that were en route to Manipur in north-east India. 'My parents were worried for me,' said Jean, an only child. 'But they did accept the marriage with good grace, despite Frank's superiority.' For ten months the newlyweds lived in a mud hut, setting their watches by the sun. Over the years Jean learned to endure sleeping in bedding so wet that every morning she would wring it out.

We walked slowly to a local pub near Jean's apartment block and over half a pint of beer, she relived her plant-collecting days as 'a botanette'. (One of Frank's favourite lilies found in Manipur in 1946 was later named after his wife, born Jean Macklin, *Lilium mackliniae*.) The most frenzied season was October when the seeds were drying, she explained, taking a sip of beer. 'You were always unpacking and packing these damn packets of seeds. Some, like lily seeds, were dry anyway; others, like magnolia, were very oily.'

'When you were travelling in Tibet,' I asked, impressed by her fearlessness, 'did you ever experience any discrimination as a woman?'

'None whatsoever,' she said sharply. 'You won't find any difficulty at all. Women are treated equally.'

Before her arrival Frank's medicine kit was hopelessly inadequate, she recalled. 'There was quinine, aspirin, a starter and a stopper. But he just carried on.' In 1954, after being ill for some time, a senior doctor at the Tropical Hospital in London refused to give him a health certificate for the Colonial Office because his blood pressure was too high.

'If he wanted to go on another expedition, even with blood pressure of 250, who was I to stop him?' she said. 'It was none of my business. I was fully aware that he might drop down dead and amazed that he didn't. We got away with it.'

Four years later, aged seventy-three, Frank died suddenly. They were living in a bedsit in a Cromwell Road hotel in London, having never owned a home or garden of their own. That 'was part of the beauty of it, one was pretty free', said Jean, who would later move to Norway after meeting her second husband Albert Rasmussen.

'And after those trips to Tibet at a young age, did it feel like other experiences in life couldn't compare?'

'Oh yes,' she conceded. 'Nothing's been as good since. I loved my time in Norway too, but those ten years with Frank were quite unique. I think I was very very privileged.'

Now that I was in south-east Tibet, I was beginning to appreciate Jean's enthusiasm for this remote corner of the world. Since the Victorian era when the race to discover unknown plants began in earnest, reaching its zenith in the 1920s and 1930s, thousands of ordinary British garden plants – rhododendron, magnolia, primula and, of course, lilies – have originated from the Sino-Himalaya.

Our thirty-three-year-old group leader, Ken Cox, was equally enthusiastic about the botanical cornucopia still waiting to be discovered in Kongpo. Lean, engaging and seemingly immune to the cold, Ken would bound up the mountains, combing the slopes for unusual flowers and simultaneously deliver a monologue on the existentialism of gardening: 'in a constant state of growth and deterioration, a sort of compression of the futility of life'. He was passionate about all plants, but particularly the red lily. Since he had first read about it in the meticulous field notes of two British plant-collectors, Frank Ludlow and George Sherriff, this elusive flower had captured his imagination.

In their 1947 expedition, Ludlow and Sherriff hoped to cross into the region of Pome in Kongpo via the Su La pass – 'virgin country to the botanist' – and sent two of their local guides on ahead to secure a safe passage from the irascible local headman, the *dzongpen*. The pair of servants returned with over twenty rhododendrons and several new species, including the red lily. They also brought bad news. The *dzongpen* refused to give them any assistance in the matter of food and transport until he had seen the expedition's passport. 'This action,' wrote Ludlow in his diaries, 'has now ruined the whole of our plans for collecting on the Su La range because once refused, there is no second chance.'[3]

In 1956 the single specimen collected would be described in the *Bulletin of the British Museum* as a 'dark purplish-red' lily, growing one to two feet high. The classification affirms that there is 'no information about the poise of the flower in the living state', and, what's more, that it is a 'species apart'.

'From what I've read, Ludlow and Sherriff were clearly very excited about this lily,' said Ken, clearly very excited himself. 'So here's a plant that's been known and written about, there's even a specimen of it in the British Museum Herbarium, but it's never been introduced. You do your detective work to solve the puzzle and find the plant.' He clapped his hands. 'That's what gives you the thrill.'

The guitar riffs of Pink Floyd flooded our car – Tang Wei was an ardent fan of rock music – and, leaning forward in his seat, Ken went on: 'It's a historical game. You can't get the lily – the weather, the Chinese, the Tibetans, the fact that it's disputed territory by the Indian and Chinese governments. Everyone gets in the way. As a plant-collector it's my goal to find a mountain range that people haven't been to before. The Tibet-India border area is *it*. It's a place on the map that you can point a pen to and say no-one has been there.'

It was during Ken's 1996 expedition to the same region that a mountaineer named June Ross spotted a 'flash of red' growing high on granite scree on the Dokar La. She cautiously climbed towards it, and succeeded in photographing the flower and picking one bloom before the loose rock-face gave way. When Ross arrived back at the camp 3,000 feet lower down she showed Cox the flower.

'Unmistakably,' Ken told me, 'this was *the* red lily.'

'But what's so special about it?'

'Lilies are flamboyant, feminine, sexual, larger than life and, like orchids, are the most evolutionary advanced of the plant world. This particular lily, as the Latin name implies, is a paradox. It's not quite a lily as its leaves grow in a distinctive whorl around a long slender stem.' He paused for breath. 'But a lily right at the bound of lilydom, kind of halfway between a lily and a *Nomocharis*.'

I stared at him blankly.

'The *Nomocharis* is a closely related *genus* to lilies. They're tiny things, smaller lily-like bulbous plants peculiar to these mountains. At one point the *Nomocharis* was included in the lily *genus* and then someone took it out—' He checked himself as my eyes glazed over. 'This is the sort of thing that happens in taxonomy.'

'Right,' I said. 'The fact that it's so rare, does that mean it's worth a lot?'

'The commercial value isn't huge, perhaps £20 at most but lily-collectors would be on the phone: rich, pedantic, monomaniac lily-collectors. The lily could become a really great parent and breed a fantastic race of new lilies.' He paused, thinking about this. 'Or it could be genetically incompatible with all other lilies because it's quite isolated. We don't know.'

'So if the seed was successfully collected, it could with some coaxing grow in a Scottish nursery?'

'Yes. When a new plant is discovered two people get credit. So the red lily,' he added, a touch wistful, 'would be discovered by Ludlow and Sherriff, introduced by Cox.'

Continuing further along the Sichuan Highway, we passed a prison where a group of inmates, their ankles manacled in chains, were digging a trench with an armed officer standing guard. The image could have been from a Second World War newsreel of a prisoner-of-war camp. Later I would discover that this was probably Powo Tramo Prison, notorious for its brutal treatment of inmates.

The road unwound before us like a corkscrew from 11,500 to 6,500 feet down to the village of Peilung. Renowned as one of the worst stretches of road in Tibet, precariously hewn into the hillside and frequently washed away by landslips, corpses of trucks lay scattered down the steep riverbank. The climate turned humid, and temperate rainforest clothed the slopes. Wild strawberries and bushes of brambles grew with sweet tangerine-coloured fruit, similar to a raspberry. Less appetising were the leeches, which I discovered when taking a pee. Mid-stream I leapt up in the air as half a dozen thirsty bloodsuckers shot towards my exposed flesh, much to the hilarity of the plant-hunters who were foraging for subtropical exotica that grew in the foliage.

While I found my botanical companions entertaining, they were a world apart from the Tibet that I was eager to explore. Over dinner in the steaming mess tent they would casually break out in Latin, quibble about the merits of etymology and have feuds over taxonomy.

Over a week into the red lily trip, I was getting restless at seeing Tibet only through the prism of a car window. I was not alone. Unrest was growing among the group, with complaints at the rudimentary conditions. 'Bed tea' brought to the tent every morning by our polite Sherpas counted for little when the bedding was damp, the rain never ceased and the loo was a hole in the ground surrounded by a tarpaulin. One day after a bone-shaking drive and frustration at the changing itinerary – snow still blocked the passes where the alpine flowers were growing – dissent became mutiny when one irate plant-hunter threatened to throw rocks at another, who responded with angry curses. Amy, the blonde student, sat in the crossfire looking distinctly unwell and had to hop out of the car every ten minutes with diarrhoea.

Not long after, on one exceptionally rowdy evening, I went outside after dinner to cool down by the river. The clouds were heavy, the forest thick. Some monks approached: two old men and two young boys wearing luminous yellow hats peered into my face. They were on a pilgrimage to Lhasa and held out their hands for a donation. When I offered 10 renminbi, their eyes glinted like stars.

Earlier that day I had seen something that had stopped me in my tracks. Two pilgrims in their mid-twenties, around my age, were prostrating along the road. Wearing worn plastic aprons, flat wooden gloves and kneepads, with their hands in prayer position, they bent, kneeled and laid themselves full-length, their forehead touching the ground, then rose again. As I watched them my familiar rational world fell away. They displayed a depth of faith that I had never encountered, one that would take them to Lhasa, prostrating all the way.

The deeper we journeyed into Kongpo, the more intrigued I was by the integral relationship between Tibetans and their land. There was a collective belief grounded in the power of nature, revered and feared in equal measure. Sacred markers were scattered everywhere: Buddhas carved on rocks, prayers flags strung across mountain passes. To the pilgrim, writes Keith Dowman, 'The landscape becomes a treasury of symbols. . . [to] provide a constant source of comfort . . . A reminder of the goal of the path.'⁴

For some years I had been looking for a deeper spiritual foundation for my own life, in reaction to the materialist ethos of society that placed such a high value on outward success, on money, on 'doing' rather than simply 'being'. I was curious, open and at times hungry for what spiritual teachings offered: wisdom, clarity, inner serenity and a profound equanimity with whatever hand life dealt. Now that I was removed from my normal London routine, among the hypnotic silence of the mountains, something inside me was ignited. The singular combination of wide horizons, the searing light and the wildness of this strange land was bewitching. In the words of Edwin Bernbaum: 'By awakening a sense of the sacred, making us aware of a deeper reality, mountains connect us to the world and make our lives more real.'[5]

Out of the darkness the gleaming white teeth of Tashi, one of the guides, appeared.

'Having a good time?' he asked. 'First time to Tibet?'

I nodded.

'You like flowers like the others?' Tashi motioned towards the mess tent where raucous laughter was erupting. The nightly game of bridge was under way.

'Yes. I'm looking for a rare lily. It's a sort of flower—' I stopped, taking one of his Panda cigarettes. 'Where are you from?'

'My father was from Kham but I live in Lhasa.' He squatted on his haunches. 'You know how Buddhism came to Tibet?'

'No,' I said, guessing he was going to tell me.

'It was like this. How you say, a giant ogress she mated with a monkey. They had two children, one boy, one girl. They were the first Tibetans. Stupid, ignorant, very sinful.' He took a long drag on the cigarette. 'Then much later, in the eighth century, King Trisong Detsen invited Padmasambhava to come from India. He flew on a lotus and rescued the country from demons. We call him Guru Rinpoche, he's like a second Buddha.'

I didn't look convinced.

'This is true,' he insisted. 'This is how the Tibetan people were born. Tibet was a very bad place before Buddhism came. If you pray to Buddha, he save you. I see you have a photo of Green Tara, Buddha of Compassion.'

I turned my mind back to the year before when I'd been given the photo of Tara, said to be the first woman to reach enlightenment, who vowed that she would always be reborn in a female body. It was unexpected. I was in a Scottish hotel, writing an article on a weekend of the paranormal when I had fallen into conversation with Gordon Smith, one of the guest speakers. Known as the 'psychic barber' he is now recognised as one of Britain's foremost mediums. He insisted I take the photo of Tara. Writing the words of her mantra, *Om Tare Tu Tare Ture So Ha*, on the back, he said knowingly, 'It will help you on your journeys.'

It is an arresting image of an emerald-green goddess with pouted scarlet lips, floating cross-legged on a peach lotus above a tranquil landscape of mountains and a family of deer. Since arriving in Tibet, the photo had become something of a talisman.

Dragging myself back to the moment, I found Tashi still talking. 'I see sometimes you say her mantra. You should take the Tibetan name Drolma which means Tara.'

'How do you pronounce it?'

'You say it like Drohh-ma.'

'I like that,' I said, repeating it softly. 'Drolma, Drolma. That can be my name in Tibet.'

He looked at me hard, weighing me up. 'Big problems now in Tibet. Once there were 6,000 monasteries in my country. Now only 400. It makes me sad, very sad, but what can we do? Who can we tell? No-one will listen.'

The following afternoon I visited my first Tibetan monastery, where Frank Kingdon Ward had stayed in 1933. The ruins of the original building stood stark on the steep, barren hillside; the new buildings were half the size. The view remained: 20,000-foot mountains with fluted cliffs and the Ata Kang Glacier towering over silvery-aquamarine lakes. The pyramidal peak, known as Dorje Tsengen, 'so sheer that no snow lies on its south face', wrote Ward, lorded above the lakes.[6]

Juniper smoke wafting towards me from an open brazier, I approached an old monk who was sitting on a woodpile outside the monastery. His robes were thickly greased with *dri* butter (from the female yak), his face like an ancient map of the world. Through the Tibetan guide Tashi, the monk told me about his life, speaking as he turned his string of speckled amber prayer beads in a deliberate, methodical manner.

At the age of nine Phuntsok joined the Geluk monastery. When he was thirty-three, in 1959, he said, 'the Chinese army came and all the monks ran away. Much of the monastery was destroyed and we all hid in the forest.' The following year the monks were joined by twenty-five local Tibetans armed with guns. They left their forest refuge to fight the Chinese, 'to protect what was left of our monastery'.

Outnumbered by the army, the rebels were all killed or captured. Phuntsok was one of those caught and spent the next twenty years in jail in Chamdo, some 250 miles to the north. For the first decade, he said simply, 'the conditions were very strict, then things got a bit easier.' After his release in 1982, there was a period of relative religious freedom, and he was told the Chinese government would give money to rebuild the monastery. When nothing materialised, he and some monks went on pilgrimage to Lhasa to raise funds. In the late eighties the temple was built with help from local villagers, desperate to have their monastery back. Too remote for high lamas from Lhasa to visit, our group were the first foreigners to see the new building.

'Before 1959,' Phuntsok said, gesturing to the ruins behind, 'it was much bigger, with herds of yak and sheep. Today there are only twelve monks and one young boy, the cow-herder. I'm eighty, the oldest here.'

The old monk answered my questions without hesitation. Pasang, one of the drivers, hovered nearby, finally motioning Tashi to stop talking and for us to leave. While there was seemingly nobody else around and we were far from any obvious police or military presence, in my naivety I hadn't realised that by having such a conversation I was endangering not only the monk, but also the guide and driver.

Ken had brought a photocopy of a photograph of the monastery taken by Kingdon Ward in 1933. Shortly before leaving, he gave it to the monk, whose face lit up. Holding the piece of paper between gnarled fingers, Phuntsok studied the picture intently. He doubtless had not seen an image of the monastery of his youth before its destruction. It was a poignant gesture and even the most cynical of the group were touched. As we left, Tony Cox, usually stoical and reserved, was close to tears. Puffing on his pipe, he said, 'I hope you continue to enjoy this view. Such a beautiful view.'

When we drove away, the old monk watched us go down the twisty track, his presence lingering in the car afterwards. Everybody was moved to silence. Later that day, mulling over what had happened, I felt a wave of guilt that I had placed the Tibetans at such risk. Tashi took me aside and suggested it was better not to mention the conversation with the monk to Tang Wei, our Chinese guide, who, sick with flu, had not accompanied us for several days. Meeting the monk and hearing his story, told with dignity and courage, with no trace of blame or anger, had a profound effect: it gave me a searingly authentic insight into that dark passage of history when Mao Tse-tung ordered his armies to 'liberate Tibet'.

At breaking light the next day, our first serious search for the red lily began south of Pome (pronounced Pom-may) up to the Dashing La pass. Ascending the trail, the local porters we had hired complained that their loads were too heavy and sat down on strike until more money was promised. Only then would the bedraggled men begin again, their flimsy Chinese army pumps sliding in the rain. The logging trail cut through forests of picea, spruce and junipers over 200 years old, with soft shell-pink *Rhododendron uvariifolium* growing in abundance in the foliage.

On our track through the Tolkienesque forest, everything dripped. Underfoot was soft and springy moss. Tree trunks, spongy to the touch, littered the ground. Ferns were coiled in clumps, their slimy heads like sea horses dipped in black oil. Lichen hung like cobwebs spinning the elfin forest together in a pale green net. When we stopped for lunch with

Ken, I noticed a movement in the undergrowth and spied a red panda. About two feet long, this rare and endangered raccoon-like animal, with a dark russet and white face and a thick bushy striped tail, took pause to stare before disappearing.

The following morning, the day had finally arrived when we would be tramping across potential red lily country. The weather was predictably awful and, in sleety rain, only a few of the stalwarts climbed up towards the Dashing La. Cutting steps in the snowfields, we ascended into a natural alpine garden at 12,000 feet. There were scats of musk deer and we were told that black bears and Bengali tigers still roamed. When the clouds began to clear, allowing a crack of visibility, our party climbed towards those promising patches of barren scree where the lily might grow.

Within a few minutes, my footsteps set off an avalanche, curdling my insides. A glimpse of sun and both the blushing red flowers of a waxy *Rhododendron forrestii* and an avalanche burst into life. The glaciers groaned and moaned as if crying out to each other across the valleys. These eerie sounds caused by the ice retreating and advancing made the mountainside seem peculiarly animate and I could appreciate why, among the crags, Tibetans believe deity-protectors or *suma* still dwell. It is said that the great Tantric master Guru Rinpoche (Padmasambhava in Sanskrit) subjugated many of the natural spirits and elemental demons of the Bon religion, transforming them from malevolent forces into the pantheon of Buddhist protectors.

The louder the roar of the avalanches, the faster my heart pounded. When I looked up, I could see peaks lost in cloud and curtains of mist rolling in. I retreated. The others cautiously advanced to a natural rhododendron garden, but found no red lily.

We arrived back at camp to find panic. There had been an unforeseen visit by the PSB, apoplectic at having climbed up a trail in the pouring rain for three hours. We were told there was a problem with the permits and were ordered to report to the Pome station (far back down in the valley) the following day. Tang Wei warned us that in these parts the police make their own rules and that, in the worst case, we could be escorted back to Lhasa.

At sunup, the camp was dismantled and the group walked back down the logging trail to Pome. I talked to the guide, Tashi, who had taken me into his confidence since my conversation with the old monk. In his mid-twenties, his wide flat face, turned-up nose and cheeky grin lent him a mischievous air. His hair was greased back, and mirrored sunglasses hid espresso-coloured eyes. Wearing loose beige trousers and a dove-grey woollen tank top, he looked more like an American preppy student than a Tibetan tour guide.

'Have you been to Lhasa yet?' he asked.

I shook my head.

'It's changing fast. There are too many Chinese. Tibetans are frustrated. We're unable to work, unable to speak or move freely. We feel trapped,' he complained. 'At night my friends and I roam around Lhasa looking for fights with the Chinese or we go round in a group on motorbikes trying to stir up the police.' He smirked. 'The best game is throwing mud at Chinese girls. Too much make-up, too high heels.'

'Don't you get into trouble?'

'Sure, I've been beaten up, I've been in fights.' He shrugged. 'People use knives, not fists. One time my old girlfriend was in tears begging me to stop. I couldn't help myself. Too much anger in here.' He tapped his heart.

'Perhaps things are better out of the city,' I said brightly. 'Your land is so beautiful.'

'What use is beauty' – he gave a brittle smile – 'if our people are not free?'

At Pome, another one-dirt-road town lined with seedy restaurants, the group ordered bowls of greasy noodles while Tang Wei was summoned into the police station. The head officer, a portly Tibetan with square black sunglasses that half obscured his flaccid pasty face, a cluster of gold stars on his shoulder, was expecting us. When Tang Wei appeared nearly an hour later he was smoking furiously.

From the moment he entered the station, the head PSB officer humiliated him, Tang Wei exclaimed, flicking his mop of black hair. 'The police demanded that I hand over all our films and cameras. I paid some money and asked them to call my PSB friend in Bayi to talk some sense to them.'

Tang Wei's *guanxi* (connections) at Bayi ensured that the Pome police retracted their decision to confiscate our film but could not dissuade them from kicking us out of the region by nightfall. We were forbidden from going up the Su La pass, where I had hoped to find the red lily. Our permits were torn up as null and void. In a ruse, the police also warned Tang Wei that an escaped and dangerous prisoner was on the run.

Officials in Pome want a quiet life and foreigners, especially those walking around mountains on the frontier with India, are a hassle. Since the 1962 Indo-China War, when Chinese troops flooded across into Assam, the border regions have been in dispute. Later I learned that one of our head porters had tipped off the Pome policemen – perhaps in return for a backhander – leading to a crippling fine for all the other porters who had carried our luggage. Knowing their impoverished state, I felt concerned about the financial effect of our trip on the men we'd hired. It was hard not to stifle a loud groan as we drove out of the district.

After the Pome police forced us to abandon our search for the red lily, Ken decided we should attempt an ascent up to the top of the Doshong La pass, described by Frank Kingdon Ward as a 'rhododendron fairyland'. Used by the local Monpa tribes during the summer months as one of the main trade routes into Pemako, it would take us two gruelling attempts to reach the summit of the 13,500-foot snow-covered pass. On reaching the top I felt ecstatic. Through the swirling mist and cloud I caught glimpses of the trail that crossed over the Doshong La into 'the hidden land' of Pemako. I had an urge to keep on walking, as if an invisible thread, a force stronger than myself, were pulling me into the thickly forested valleys below. Not finding the rare red lily proved to be one of those fortunate life-altering events which would bring me back to Tibet much sooner than I imagined, and through which I would meet Ani.

CHAPTER 3

Monsoon in Kathmandu

O N our return to Nepal it was with some trepidation that I contacted my editor with the news that I had failed to find the red lily. He was unimpressed, and told me that if the story was going to be published, he wanted to see a picture of the flower. Ken had a hunch that Ian Baker, the American whom we had seen at Lhasa airport and who lived in Kathmandu, could be leading an independent expedition to Pemako later in the year. Since 1993 Baker had returned yearly as explorer and pilgrim in his quest to penetrate the depths of Pemako, described by the eighth-century mystic-saint Guru Rinpoche as 'a celestial realm on earth'.

When I called Baker and told him about our plant-hunting trip and the skirmish with the Pome police, he sounded concerned, but not surprised. In a gravelly American accent, he told me that the following month he would be leading a party over the Su La pass, where I hoped to find the red lily, on a month-long pilgrimage through Pemako. He continued, 'Only today did one group member unexpectedly pull out. Why don't you take his place?'

It seemed like a sign, some sort of propitious omen. As far as Baker knew, I would be the first English woman to visit Pemako. While he assured me that he did have the correct permits to cross the Su La, I knew there was a risk that the Pome police would turn us back for a second time and I would fail to find the flower. I agonised over the cost – over £3,000 – I fretted at my unfitness, but within a day I made my decision. If outwardly it was again the red lily that gave me the excuse to join, inwardly there was a deeper longing. The feeling of standing at the top of the Doshong La had haunted me and I wanted to know what lay beyond on the other side of the pass. An invitation to a hidden land would, I imagined, be a journey into the unknown, a journey of the spirit.

Six months before, when I was still living in London, I came home late from work one day, exhausted, to an empty flat in Brixton. My mind was spinning from the magazine story I was working on. I leafed through the mail. A phone bill, a bank statement, a newsletter written by Swami Nishchalananda Saraswati, director of the yoga ashram in Wales I had recently visited. Idly I started to read: *Sannyasa* in Sanskrit 'is the tradition of "Complete Surrender" to relinquish expectations and surrender to the Unknown'.

My legs trembled under me as if I were going to faint. I felt this tremendous pull to the floor and lay down in the semi-darkness. The word 'surrender' occasioned such trepidation that I stayed inert for a long time until, gingerly, I began to read on:

'Surrender requires a descent of Consciousness which can be called Grace.' Every person 'will have their own definition – "Surrender to Destiny", "Surrender to the Divine or God" . . . Contrary to common belief, *Sannyasa* is not a rejection of everyday life but a fulfilment of it. It is more concerned with abandoning that which is unreal – our delusion as well as habits, expectations, name, fame and our sense of separateness from others.'

Afterwards I tried to make sense of that whole episode and understand why the word 'surrender' triggered such a startling response. It was like being given an invitation to trust in life itself, to have faith that without markers or a guide I would always find my way. Sometimes it is only in unfamiliar terrain that the sound of the inner voice guiding our search can be heard. I knew that among the peaks of south-east Tibet something had been awakened: the seeds of a new current in my life had already been planted. Intuitively I recognised Pemako to be the next stage of the journey – a chance to step out into the unknown, not only physically but within myself.

My editor agreed to hold the red lily story, wishing me better luck second time round; in the intervening weeks I stayed in monsoon Kathmandu. I wandered the streets deserted of tourists and drank sweet *chai* with bored shopkeepers. In preparation for the pilgrimage ahead I trawled spiritual bookshops and read the texts of enlightened teachers. *The Bhagavad Gita, The Foundations of Mysticism* by Lama Govinda, *At the Left Hand of God*, about an *aghori* – an Indian Tantric master – who lived in cremation grounds and slipped seamlessly between the worlds of life and death. One night I dreamed about Guru Rinpoche, the Tibetan mystic-saint. I also, somewhat curiously, had a vivid premonition of travelling with a Tibetan nun across Tibet.

I found out what I could about Pemako, but, as so few Westerners have explored the region, there was little more than a footnote in the guidebooks. Literally 'land of the heavenly lotus' it's described in Gyurme Dorje's *Tibet Handbook* as 'only for pilgrims and explorers of great stamina and physical endurance'.

The northern reaches of Pemako lie in Tibet, in lower Kongpo, with the southern part spilling into Arunachal Pradesh in India. The only way in and out involves climbing over a snow-clad mountain pass; some passes are too high to be accessible, and local tribes frequent only a handful during the summer months. Straddling a disputed border with India, Pemako is also a 'special military region', guarded fiercely by the Chinese army and local police.

A month before our departure date, I received a fax from Ian Baker, the group leader, with a rough itinerary. 'According to revealed texts ascribed to Padmasambhava, Pemako's unique geomantic energies serve as a catalyst on the spiritual path,' he wrote. 'Generations of Tibetan pilgrims seeking enlightenment and political refuge have found inspiration and sanctuary in Pemako,' a place where the physical and spiritual worlds overlap.

'Participants should be prepared inwardly as well as outwardly for perennial rain, leeches and snakes . . . and should have a deep and genuine commitment to the spirit of pilgrimage. As one lama said, "the pilgrimage through Pemako is not easy but if you can view hardships with equanimity, the land itself transforms mundane perceptions into luminous awareness."'

Baker then gave an extensive list of the equipment we would require, including a *khukri* or machete for bushwhacking, ropes for rappelling, gaiters and, not least, a collapsible umbrella. He also included an outline of our journey, which aimed to reach Pemashelri, the 'lotus crystal mountain'. It was clear that once we were in the valleys our exact route would remain vague. It appeared Pemako was a nebulous place, a spiritualscape where legend merged with truth.

Pemashelri lay somewhere south of Namcha Barwa, until 1992 the highest unclimbed mountain in the world, its razor-sharp pinnacle standing at 25,436 feet. It is between the peaks of Namcha Barwa and Gyala Pelri (23,891 feet) – the two summits standing like sentinels barely thirteen miles apart – that the Yarlung Tsangpo River thunders south, squeezed between sheer walls of rock into the heart of the Tsangpo Gorge, where early twentieth-century explorers speculated that a giant waterfall existed.

For Baker it was the search for these legendary falls, and both their geographical and spiritual significances, that brought him, an accomplished climber and Buddhist scholar, repeatedly back to Tibet. Since the seventies, Baker had lived in Nepal, immersed in a spiritual beatnik counter-culture. He was described by one college friend as 'Part Merlin, part Merry Prankster who was at the centre of a bohemian fringe that fused intellectual curiosity with a bacchanalian party spirit . . . [like] a character from another century'.[1]

Ian suggested that I should seek advice from one of the few lamas to have made pilgrimages through Pemako, and who was living in exile in

Kathmandu. One afternoon I therefore paid a visit to Bhakha Tulku (a *tulku* is a reincarnated spiritual teacher) who was waiting to emigrate to America. The abbot received me sitting on a throne-like wooden chair in his large house, richly decorated with Tibetan hangings and religious icons. As an abbot in the Nyingma school of Tibetan Buddhism, which allows *tulkus* to marry, his demure Tibetan wife waited upon him. I sat awkwardly cross-legged in front of him on the floor. Dressed in cream robes, with a curling silver-grey moustache and wispy beard, Bhakha Tulku had the air of a kindly wizard.

When I told him about my foiled search for the red lily and how the head of police expelled our plant-hunting group from Pome, the *tulku* roared with laughter. 'Most leading positions in Tibet are in the hands of the Chinese. The head policeman in Pome is Tibetan, known for his stubbornness and hatred of foreigners,' he said, then he paused, a frown knitting his brow together. 'But I think I know this plant you describe. I've seen an unusual dark red flower on the trail over the Su La pass.'

In 1994 Bhakha Tulku was prohibited from walking in the grounds of his own monastery, situated on the edge of the Pemako valleys, and was driven to leave his ancestral home, accused by the authorities of spying for the American government. The head of police, it appears, was threatened by the abbot's highly revered status in his community. Shortly after he left Tibet – and surely no coincidence – extensive and illegal logging of the ancient forests around Bhakha monastery began. (This is despite 'an unconditional logging ban' throughout Tibet following the 1998 floods of the Yangtze River in China. This national disaster, causing millions downstream to be displaced and up to 10,000 killed, was directly attributed to the decades of deforestation in Tibet. From 1950 to 1985 Tibet's forest cover was reduced by 46 per cent, causing irreparable damage to the plateau's fragile eco-system.[2])

At the age of thirteen, Bhakha Tulku first visited Pemako with his mother, a devout Buddhist, who led the family there several times on pilgrimage. 'It's very hard. You fall over in the mud all the time,' he told me. 'There are leeches, snakes and the sound of tigers at night.'

At one rain-sodden camp, a group of Khampa pilgrims began to chop down the wooden pilgrim shelter for a fire. The local villagers became angry. Knives were drawn. 'Suddenly there was a huge roar like an earthquake and we saw this giant tiger leap from one valley across to the other,' he recalled. 'Everyone immediately forgot about fighting and prostrated full-length on the ground.'

Fixing me with his hawkish eyes, he lowered his voice. 'The tiger was a manifestation of one of the guardians of Pemako. You mustn't speak angrily and don't disturb the spirits,' he cautioned, adding with an enigmatic smile, 'Say *Om Mani Padme Hung* and you'll be OK. You're young, you can walk.' Buoyed by his parting words, I felt renewed strength and left feeling oddly serene.

Some weeks later on the eve of the departure for Tibet, with no real idea where I was going or where this pilgrimage would end, beneath my cheery bravado I was terrified. I returned to Bhakha Tulku's house to meet Ian Baker and the other group members – four Herculean American men and a German woman – for a Buddhist fire ceremony. The abbot led the elaborate ritual, asking that we be protected and all obstacles – both physical and spiritual – be removed from our journey. The flames leapt high, and the room filled with pungent smoke from burning juniper. The pilgrimage into the 'hidden valleys' had begun.

CHAPTER 4

Meeting Ani

A DAY later, while our equipment and luggage were being loaded into four-wheel-drive jeeps for the long drive to south-east Tibet, I noticed a small, robust woman with a round face. It was Ani, the dreadlocked nun, who was joining our group as an unofficial spiritual guide. Anxious not to be forgotten, she had arrived the day before on a bus from her nunnery. She parked herself next to our blue Dongfeng lorry and was wringing her hands expectantly. At her feet lay a cloth knapsack and a thick sheepskin coat; on her head she wore a battered straw hat, which seemed to hover a few inches above her hair.

I was startled by her warm cranberry cheeks, which matched the colour of her *chuba* (a full-length Tibetan tunic). Bright-eyed, the bridge of her nose crinkled when she smiled, her lips curving into a heart-shaped arc. I noticed how her tiny hands mirrored my own, except that my palms are soft with faint creases, while hers had grooves etched deep. She was wearing a blouse of dark fuchsia with wide sleeves. On the cords around her waist hung a talisman; on her slender wrists were bracelets engraved with sacred symbols. The jewellery and clothing gave me the impression that Ani was not a nun but rather a lay woman. And yet, instantly, I could tell she was a woman apart.

'I'm Claire.' I reached out to shake her hand.

'Care-see,' she replied, her brow puckering as she attempted to pronounce my name. 'Care-see. Carrr.'

Ani spoke no English. I knew no Tibetan.

'Call me Drolma if it makes it easier,' I said, giving her my new Tibetan name.

'Drolma, Drolma,' she said in a lilting voice and nodded. '*Tashi delek.*'

For Tibetans, the inhospitable terrain and sense of enigma heighten Pemako's status as one of the most powerful places for a pilgrim to visit. While the dangers are great, so are the boons. The extreme weather conditions contribute to the risk, as do the trails that follow knife-edge ridges. These days few Tibetans visit Pemako: the distance, inaccessibility and, most of all, the brooding presence of the Chinese army deter even the hardiest pilgrim. Those who do are usually Khampas from the eastern region of Kham, known for their strength and courage. It's rare to find anyone from Lhasa embarking on such an arduous journey.

But Ani was not easily dissuaded. After spending seven years at her nunnery, at the age of twenty-nine Ani set out on what would become a life-long pilgrimage, receiving blessings and asking for alms along the way. An essential Tibetan Buddhist experience, pilgrimage for a monk and a nun especially is considered one path to Buddhahood: the first steps towards the promise of enlightenment. One of Ani's first destinations – and surely one of the most arduous – was to Pemako, where she spent thirteen months, dividing her time between silent meditation at the main monastery, Rinchenpung *gompa*, and journeys within the valleys.

'One night meditating at Rinchenpung,' she would tell me later, 'is like a hundred days practising in other sacred places outside Pemako.'

Given her unique knowledge of the area and, in Ian Baker's words, her 'mastery of esoteric yogic practices' the American had invited Ani, a woman who 'exemplified the spirit of pilgrimage'. Baker impressed upon all the six Westerners that walking through Pemako demanded a deep commitment and respect for pilgrimage. In his early forties, dressed in a khaki shirt and waistcoat, with an unkempt beard and tousled hair, Baker cultivated the air of a beleaguered explorer. With his intense eyes flickering in the mid-distance, I sensed that nothing went unnoticed.

The other Americans in our team were Hamid Sardar, a Harvard-educated Tibetologist and Ken Storm Jr, a bespectacled Minneapolis businessman, both of whom had been with Baker on several expeditions to Pemako; and two brothers from Arizona, Gil and Troy Gillenwater. Then there was Waltraut Ott, an earnest German Buddhist, Ani and myself. Sonam, the Tibetan tour guide and a team of Sherpas from Nepal, all dedicated Buddhists, who would cook and set up camp en route, joined us.

We would set out from Bhakha Tulku's *gompa,* one of the major monasteries of the Pome region. Situated on the southern bank of the Po-Tsangpo River, to reach the *gompa* we had to cross a bouncy wooden suspension bridge adorned with colourful prayer flags. Beyond lay a path through old-growth forests to the base of the Su La pass where I hoped to find the lily.

On the first night at Bhakha monastery I shared a dormitory with Ani and I watched her make three quick prostrations with her hands clasped in prayer before she lay down on the narrow wooden bed. She fell asleep within minutes of her head touching the pillow she had fashioned from her knapsack and slept curled up on her side like a child, her face buried in the sleeves of her tunic. 'I feel drawn to the Tibetans, especially Ani,' I wrote in my journal. 'She intrigues me most, she's like a shining light. It should be *her* story I write.'

The following morning our group took over one of the upstairs' rooms in the monastery and we spent hours re-packing and checking equipment. Gil and Troy Gillenwater had come prepared with twice as much luggage – and food – as everyone else. I watched in dismay as they spread out packs of power bars, tins of pâté and smoked oysters. They had Gore-Tex socks and Gore-Tex gaiters, blow-up cushions to sit on and crampons to scale cliffs. After casting an eye over their pile, mine looked rather forlorn: one pair of cheap waterproof trousers, one pair of cheap gaiters from Kathmandu, a few packs of cashews, and a couple of slabs of Dairy Milk.

The Gillenwater brothers were an entertaining and unlikely pair – successful property developers, Buddhist-seekers and outdoor extremists, who in 1994 had accompanied the American, Richard Fisher, rafting down part of the Yarlung Tsangpo, known as 'the Everest of white-water'. (In 1992, Fisher had been one of the first modern explorers to penetrate the Tsangpo Gorge.) A year later, with their brother Todd, the Gillenwaters joined Ian Baker on a pilgrimage through Pemako and were the first Western party to reach the sacred mountain Kundu Dorsempotrang in the heart of the valleys. Early on, all three brothers swam in a pool considered by the local tribes to be inhabited by *nagas* – snake-like spirits – who, if disturbed, can cause severe illness.

'Gee, we were as sick as a dog on that trip,' said Gil, his head shaved like a US marine and his piercing blue eyes bloodshot. 'It was absolute living hell, the hardest thing I've ever done . . .'

'That night, and for the next week we were all throwing up and having to climb 5,000-foot mountains,' Troy, his younger brother, continued in a rumbling American drawl. 'It was each man for himself. It sucked.'

'Why did you come back then?' I asked uneasily.

'We wanted to really appreciate it, ya' know, not have bad memories. The Pemako jungles are one of the toughest, most formidable places for hiking. At the same time, it's an awesome magical place where ordinary Western logic breaks down,' replied Gil, struggling to zip up his case. 'Claire, Pemako is somewhere that binds people for life. You can never know, can never begin to imagine, the effect a journey to this place will have until much later.'

Taking a deep breath, I smiled feebly, feeling hopelessly inexperienced. I decided to take a break from the testosterone-fuelled atmosphere and explore Bhakha *gompa*. Wandering around the gardens, where vermilion dahlias danced in summer bloom, I passed a wooden drop toilet with no door. A monk sitting bolt upright bowed his head politely as I walked by.

The original sixteenth-century buildings were destroyed in the Cultural Revolution and the new temple was under construction. Inside, candles flickered under freshly carved Buddhas. At the far end on a table was a photo of Bhakha Tulku, the abbot of the monastery who I had met in Nepal. The photo showed a man wearing a finely embroidered ceremonial hat, his heavy-lidded eyes in trance. Now at his monastery, I was aware of the gaping hole he had left. His monks were rudderless without their master at the helm, his local community deprived of their venerated teacher.

As I came out of the temple I was assailed by a strong smell, a potent blend of sweet oiliness and blue-veined cheese, with a touch of beef stock. It was Ani, holding a new pair of small-size walking shoes, a gift from Waltraut. To go with them, I gave her two pairs of thick socks.

'*Tuk je che, Drolma-la.* Thank you, Drolma,' she said, her head tilting to one side like a timid robin.

Watching her walk away with a light step, I noticed Ani's girlish mannerisms, at odds with her age, which by the faint lines across her forehead I guessed to be around thirty-five. Her eyes were the colour of roasted chestnuts, the black eyebrows set wide apart. It was a benevolent open face that seemed to invite everything – and everybody – in.

Outside, rain drizzled. As if expecting the group's arrival, a motley gaggle of porters were waiting on the lawn in front of the monastery. With no other means of carrying supplies over the mountain passes, for generations the local tribes – Monpa and Lopa – have been used as human pack-horses by Tibetan chieftains and Buddhist lamas who first colonised the area and today by the Chinese military. Many of the porters were required to carry salt and petrol for the army for 50 renminbi a day during the summer months. Their clothes were army cast-offs, their hunting rifles old Chinese models.

Arguments over wages were part of the ritual and, as in an Indian bazaar, each side limbered up for the contest. The Monpa porters had upped their daily rate from 50 to 80 renminbi in the knowledge that, if refused, it could be days before more appeared like stealth out of the forest. While Baker and Sonam, the Tibetan guide, beat the price down a rainbow appeared in the direction we would be taking. It was the third in three days and in Tibet rainbows are always viewed as auspicious.

After lunch, Sonam left with twenty bottles of beer for the police in the nearby town of Pome, where the irascible headman who'd ousted our plant-hunting group from his province held office. It was a tense afternoon. There were no assurances that the police chief would grant us permission to cross the Su La. Until 1931 the kingdom of Pome was ruled independently and still today, far from the tentacles of Lhasa's jurisdiction, the Tibetan and Chinese PSB make their own rules. At dusk Sonam returned with a tipsy smile. We would depart the following morning.

Our provisional route, once we had crossed the Su La, would be to follow the Tsangpo south for several days until we reached a village where we could cross the river via a metal cable strung high above the foaming waters. If the cable was no longer in operation we would need to continue until the bridge below Metok, the only major settlement in the region, also a Chinese army post. As our permits did not cover Metok, this could cause problems with the local PSB, but if there was no other means of crossing the wide river it was a risk we would have to take. There were various meditation caves and a hermitage at Mandeldem to visit, but the main destination was Pemashelri: exact co-ordinates still unknown. We had three weeks to complete the journey on foot and would emerge on the south-west side of Pemako and cross over the south side of the Doshong La out of the valleys. On the plant-hunting trip I had ascended the north side of the Doshong La and it was from the snowy summit that I caught my first glimpse into the valleys of Pemako.

With night creeping in, I found Sonam in the cosy kitchen of the monastery, furnished with trestle tables and where a roaring log fire burned. He confided he was anxious about the trip. 'I have a permit for the Su La but people, especially Ian, want to go places where even the locals are forbidden. If we go to closed areas' – he lowered his voice – 'it will be me and my travel agency who'll pay the price.'

Carrying a Thermos flask of butter tea, a bowl of *tsampa* – ground roasted barley flour – and slabs of *dri* butter, Ani helped a monk to set the table, then sat down with her wooden bowl. She mixed the *tsampa* and tea, and added butter and sugar, moulding it into a gooey mixture.

'*Pa*,' she said, offering me a doughy ball. '*Shimbo du*. It's tasty. *Za, za.* Eat, eat.'

Taking a bite, I tried to force my face into a smile, not easy with my mouth full of sweetened sawdust. I persevered, washing it down with butter tea, a not entirely unpleasant soupy drink. Ani roared with fruity laughter at my expression. Sticking her tongue out and blowing loud raspberries, she lifted up her bottom and gestured vigorously with one hand as if going to the toilet.

Sonam chuckled. 'She's saying be careful, *tsampa* can give you diarrhoea. Better you eat *inji* [Western] food.'

Ani took off her straw hat and curled up in a lumpy spiral were her jet-black dreadlocks which poured from her head like a fountain, lending her a wild and powerful presence. She scooped up some of the butter and smeared it through her heavy, coarse hair, which fell below her waist. Before I could resist she also rubbed some into mine, telling me it was good for my hair. Close-up the butter smelled awful, like meat stew. I asked her, with Sonam translating, about the significance of her dreadlocks.

'When I first became a nun I did special practices and had to keep my hair long. It's called "meditation hair".' She paused, thinking this over. 'I follow the Karma Kagyu lineage and before the Cultural Revolution there were many long hair practitioners. These days the tradition is no longer kept.'

'When did you start to grow your hair?' I asked.

'I can't remember.' She gave a little shrug. 'But I've only had my head shaved twice in my life.'

'Are the dreadlocks important?' I pressed, sensing they were keepers of history and secrecy.

'I lost my comb and had no money to buy another.' She fidgeted, avoiding the question. 'I didn't want to bother with brushing my hair, that's all. So I let it get thick.'

(As in the Indian *sadhu* tradition, a person on meditative retreat will not waste time worrying about non-essential activities, such as combing or cutting hair, and then, since all life is practice, not cutting it at all to maintain its 'power'.)

'My hair helps me look like a common lay woman,' Ani continued. 'Then I'm not harassed by police who make it much harder for nuns and monks to travel on pilgrimage.'

'Are there many nuns like you with long hair who wander from place to place?'

'No.' She shook her head vigorously. 'There are very few with long hair in central Tibet. I don't remember ever meeting another nun like me in all my years on the road. People say to me, "You have long hair but you wear red. Are you a nun?" They think I'm a Khampa nun so often they don't help me or let me stay. They're worried if they do, more Khampas will follow—'

'Why would they be?'

'Khampas have a bad reputation in Tibet,' explained Sonam. 'As thieves.'

'Other times people don't believe I'm a nun at all.' She sniffed, a little annoyed. 'Then they don't respect me, they just think I'm a lay woman. Then it's most important to practise compassion.'

'You always travel alone?'

'Usually. If I'm with other nuns they cry and can't bear the troubles on the road.'

'You never get frightened?' I took a sip of my butter tea. Now rather congealed, it was hard to force down.

'I'm scared of thieves or dogs, but I've never had a problem.'

Ani stood up and swirled the Thermos flask of tea in a clockwise direction, pouring us all another round.

'I'm tough like my birth sign,' she declared. 'I was born in the third month of the Tibetan calendar, in the Year of the Iron Ox [1961].'

'Where do you sleep?'

'When I'm on the road, outside villages so people don't trouble me. I put stones down on a piece of plastic and sleep with a blanket.' She blew on her tea, cooling it down. 'If I can I find a cave, then I'll spend time on retreat and do my spiritual practice. I feel very content in a cave rather than a house,' she said, her eyes brightening.

'Close to here I spent one year in a cave and from the entrance could see Mount Namcha Barwa. It was comfortable and dry inside, with plenty of firewood from a peach tree. The only bother were fleas from previous pilgrims. In summer they would bite when I was meditating,' she said with a laugh. 'But I liked staying there. It opened up my mind, I felt free from any unhappiness.'

I shook my head in astonishment at Ani's matter-of-fact manner, trying to imagine myself in her shoes – only begging for food, sleeping rough and stepping out with just one small bag on pilgrimage. No fanfare, no ceremony and no friends. It would take considerable resolve, I thought, to strike out alone, to forge a path where others did not tread.

She met my gaze, her face flushed from the fire.

'*Nga kyipo du Pemako ne.* I'm happy to be back in Pemako. It's where you can advance spiritually much faster than in other places. Pemako's like both heaven and hell.'

At first light the next day, our party started out from Bhakha *gompa* to begin the crossing over the Su La. I was finally on the threshold of 'red lily territory'. Dynamite blasts shuddered through the valley: the sound of construction for another logging road. In parts the sacred forest of hemlock and fir resembled a battleground. Colossal trees lay strewn like dead soldiers; a sapper from Sichuan loped past, his hands encrusted with black viscosity like congealed blood. An old lama in robes appeared like an apparition, sock-less but wearing a golden red crown. He shook hands casually and continued on his way, not in the least taken aback to encounter Westerners on the trail, the first since 1913.

Our group quickly became strung out, with the fittest – Ani and the Gillenwaters – up ahead. I had fallen to the back, grumpy and out of shape. Ken Storm, a fan of Frank Kingdon Ward with a passion for the Romantic poets, who was the only group member to share my enthusiasm for the red lily, had marched in front, promising he would scour the slopes for the elusive flower.

Once out of the forest, everywhere became sky and space, the air filled with the scent of spring. As the path narrowed up a steep gully, I scrambled over boulders and soon sounded like a steam engine running out of steam. I stopped every ten minutes to catch my breath and scan the scree with binoculars for a flash of red, beginning to doubt if I would find the lily. Vegetation became sparse, snowfields loomed ahead. I had all but given up when I heard a yell and ducked, assuming it was rocks falling.

'Found it. Found it,' echoed down the mountainside. I puffed towards Ken Storm, who proudly pointed to seven blooms of *Lilium paradoxum*, clinging to a vertical cliff face, which I fell down several times as I tried to photograph them. The six-petalled flowers of a dark carmine colour were studded with raindrops. Each blossom trembled in the breeze. They were elegant, a bell-like flower of poise and grace with slender stems and, at intervals, whorls of feathery leaves. It felt almost sacrilegious to pick one, but I did, carefully wrapping it in tissue paper. I had agreed to show Ken Cox the flower on my return. When Ken Storm showed it to some of the local porters they explained that the roots of the red lily were used for medicinal purposes and as a cure for fever. Cox was delighted to know that I had found the flower. With none in seed, I could not be the one to introduce the red lily to cultivation, so it has yet to be propagated in the West and for now, at least, still grows untrammelled and free. Some months later my story, 'The Hunt for the Red Lily', appeared in the *Telegraph Magazine*.

Thrilled at finding the lily, I soldiered on to the top of the 13,000-foot Su La pass. With rain sluicing down, snow crunching underfoot, it became an effort of will to find my way. Shivering and sweating, my heart racing from the altitude, I felt an unexpected exhilaration. On the pass, where the separation between worlds is thin, the boundary between the elements, the earth and myself seemed to dissolve. I breathed with the wind, I heard the sigh of the land. It was as if the veils of ordinary perception lifted and for a moment I grasped the interconnectedness of all life, spun together in a weave of consciousness, uniting everyone and everything.

On the other side of the mountain, not far ahead, I spied the pink chequered tunic of Ani. Flushed with excitement, I careered down to find her helping Sonam, the guide, who had damaged his knee tendons.

'*Ga le, ga le*. Slowly, slowly,' said Ani, steadying his arm.

She walked in front, I stayed close behind.

'My two protectors,' said Sonam, with a weak smile, the colour draining from his face.

Ani called two of the porters to help. Two young bow-legged men approached, wearing the old-fashioned Mao blue jacket with trousers to match. They were short and stocky with wide foreheads and huge chests (their lungs stretch to one and a half times the capacity of low-altitude races to accommodate their extreme physical lifestyle).

'We use medicine first,' said one porter, opening his silver amulet box. He took a handful of blessed orange barley seeds and rubbed them on Sonam's knees whispering prayers. I don't know if they helped, but Sonam's mood improved even if the pain didn't. Somehow the porters succeeded in piggy-backing Sonam in a relay race, first taking their heavy loads in bamboo baskets and then carrying the limping guide until he could struggle on.

'How far is it?' Sonam winced.

'A couple of hours maybe.' The porter shrugged.

I soon learned that in Pemako time is measured in days not hours. Three hours became six, the path disappeared into snow banks and down a glacier. We descended 5,000 feet, the height of the Grand Canyon, and after dark, bruised and battered, Ani and I arrived in the damp yak hut where the others were already bedding down for the first night in the valleys.

CHAPTER 5

Into the Hidden Valleys

IN Tibetan Buddhist lore Pemako is one of the foremost of 108 'hidden lands' (*beyuls*) which in the eighth century Guru Rinpoche prophesied would serve as a refuge when the world succumbed to the dark forces of moral decay and environmental degradation, when 'the law of Tibet will break. Chinese, Mongols and the barbarians of the borderland will wage war [and] an ocean of blood will be formed.'[1] In the mythic tradition of Guru Rinpoche, who is regarded by the Nyingma order, the oldest Tibetan Buddhist sect, as a second Buddha, it is said that as a legacy to the Tibetan people, *terma* – 'revealed texts' – were left throughout Tibet for future generations.

'The main reason for concealing *terma* was a fear that the doctrines would, in time, fade or become adulterated,' writes Span Hanna. '*Terma* were concealed in rocks, mountainsides, trees, temples, images, lakes and even in the sky' to be revealed by lamas, known as *tertons* or 'treasure-finders', through dreams or in meditation.[2]

In 1986, on a pilgrimage at Bon Ri mountain in Kongpo, Hanna, an Australian, witnessed a *terton* in action. During a ceremony by a large boulder, a middle-aged Tibetan woman called Khandro Khachi Wangmo ('Powerful Lady of the Dakini Realm') stripped to the waist to 'assure that no trickery was involved' and then with her *phurbu* – ritual dagger – struck the rock. Hanna watched in amazement as the Tibetan woman removed slabs of stone and, 'reached into a cavity, and removed a small seated figurine. . . and a thunderbolt sceptre or *dorje*'. Hanna was then told, 'The objects themselves are not in the rock' but can 'become physically available through the rock'. The treasures 'remain in another realm guarded by beings called "*terdak*"'. [3]

Such bewildering accounts can be as confounding as the notion that a 'hidden land' may remain closed, even invisible to the uninitiated. In Buddhist theology 'hidden lands' contain outer, inner and secret dimensions and it's only those with heightened perception or 'Buddha vision', who can enter, who can even see the gateway concealed in the landscape. Some are in the jungle, others in 'the midst of the snow mountains', explains the Kagyu lama, Tai Situ Rinpoche, the principal teacher of the seventeenth Karmapa, the head of the Karma Kagyu school. 'There will be a particular person or persons who will unveil [the hidden lands] . . . Some are specially beneficial during the time of famine and war; some are very particular to the time when people need spiritual inspiration, spiritual benefit.' [4]

It was only in the seventeenth century that the 'hidden land' of Pemako first became known, after two Nyingma 'treasure-finders' revealed *terma* texts believed to have been left by Guru Rinpoche himself. Incurring the wrath of the Monpa tribes who lived in the valleys and resented the incursion of pilgrims, ambushing and killing zealous Buddhists with poison-tipped arrows, the visionary lamas persisted and during the eighteenth century Pemako was formally opened as a place of pilgrimage. With time, the Monpa who practised animism would be converted to the Nyingma school.

The *terma* texts, written in a cryptic, arcane language which only a realised lama can decipher, say that somewhere in the valleys, behind a waterfall, lies a portal into an earthly paradise. Known as Chime Yangsang Ne – literally 'the innermost secret place of immortality' [5] – entrance would only be granted to those with sincere faith and the requisite karma. (Tibetans adhere to the laws of karma – the belief that whatever you experience, positive or negative, depends on past actions.)

By the mid-nineteenth century Pemako was a magnet not only for devout Tibetan pilgrims. As the race to survey the world's blank spaces gathered pace, British explorers became intrigued by the region as they tried to chart the course of the Yarlung Tsangpo, the central, defining feature of the landscape. Around 1,200 miles long, this river, the world's highest, runs parallel to the Himalayas, collecting the snow from the entire length of the range before it disappears into the *terra incognita* between India and Tibet. Surveyors were mystified at how the Tsangpo could drop over 8,000 feet in twenty-four miles before becoming the Brahmaputra, India's vast holy river.

For centuries, Western expeditions had attempted to reach Tibet and the 'forbidden city' of Lhasa. Few succeeded. Encircled by mountains, forming a natural boundary on all sides, Tibet lords over central Asia. In the south are the Himalayas; the Kunlun ranges guard the north and beyond are the desolate saltpans of Tsaidam. The west is flanked by the Karakoram mountains of Pakistan and eastern Tibet splinters into high peaks and plunges into thick forests. If the physical hardships were not enough, any efforts by explorers to infiltrate were constantly thwarted by Tibetan stubbornness and well-organised prevention. Tibetans did not want uninvited guests to set foot on their land, which covered an immense area larger than Western Europe.

'Tibet was not only a political entity, it was foremost a civilisation, covering the whole of the Tibetan-speaking world,' writes Tibetan historian Tsering Shakya.[6] Ethnic Tibet once stretched over a huge area extending into western Nepal, Ladakh and Sikkim in northern India. Today China refers to Tibet as only the central province of the Tibetan Autonomous Region (TAR); the eastern regions of Kham and Amdo are referred to as Sichuan and Qinghai respectively.

In the late nineteenth century any British expedition sent from India to reach Pemako also had to contend with the hostile and warring Abors of northern Assam, who had no qualms about massacring any foreigner daring to encroach on their turf. On one occasion the Mishmi tribes, infamous for their poisoned arrows, murdered two French missionaries, Fathers Krick and Bourry. Nonetheless the 'riddle of the Tsangpo' continued to be the subject of intense speculation, on a par with trying to find the source of the Nile. Explorers were intrigued by a local legend that told of huge waterfalls that 'would rival or even surpass Niagara'. Even as late as 1911, the year two British officers on a quest for the 'falls of Brahmaputra' were murdered on the Assamese frontier, 'the question of the identity of the Tsangpo and Brahmaputra Rivers' remained unanswered.[7]

Two years later, two British officers, Captain Henry Morshead and Lieutenant Colonel F. M. Bailey – who had accompanied Colonel Francis Younghusband's 1904 march into Lhasa, the first major expedition by a Western power into Tibet – disappeared for six months on a mission to map the course of the Yarlung Tsangpo. They concluded that the thundering torrent was indeed the same river as the placid Brahmaputra and that it turned back on itself in a giant arc, before cascading into a series of impenetrable gorges. They failed to find any substantial waterfalls.

In 1924, inspired by this cause célèbre, the botanist Frank Kingdon Ward and his companion Lord Jack Cawdor resolved to collect plants along the remaining fifty miles of the gorge and solve the waterfall riddle 'which had been a geographical mystery for half a century'.[8] They forged a trail for forty-five torturous miles until they were trapped by walls of rock with occasional glimpses of the river far below. Forced to give up, they never disproved the Tibetan legend that tells of seventy-five falls, each guarded by a water spirit.

Ward would later tell the Royal Geographical Society that apart from a forty-foot waterfall, which he named Rainbow Falls, it was unlikely that any larger falls existed in 'the remaining 5 miles'. As he wrote: 'What happened next, we could only guess, for the river, after hurling itself through the gap, rushes headlong into a gorge so deep and narrow that one could hardly see any sky overhead; then it disappeared.'[9] His expedition would bring to a close the mystery of the inner gorge, relegating the lost waterfall once more to the domain of myth. It was to remain unsolved for another seventy-five years, until the challenge was taken up by several American explorers, among them Ian Baker.

In *The Riddle of the Tsangpo Gorges* Kingdon Ward described Pemako as, 'the Promised Land of the Tibetan prophecy . . . a land flowing with milk and honey, where the crops grew of their own accord'.[10] His account, like those of other early twentieth-century explorers such as F. M. Bailey, would in time be spun by the British novelist James Hilton into the myth of Shangri-La. Tibet has long occupied a shifting, illusory realm in popular Western culture and Hilton drew upon the enduring tales of this mysterious land, where lamas could fly and monks withstand sub-zero temperatures, existing on air alone.

In 1933 *Lost Horizon* was first published about a utopian valley where immortals live in perfect harmony according to ancient wisdom, in pursuit of the highest ideals of art, philosophy and science. It captured the public imagination at a time when the West needed to escape from the grim reality of Depression and approaching war, a time when people wanted to believe a place of innocence still existed. Four years later, *Lost Horizon* was immortalised in Hollywood with Frank Capra's eponymous screen version. This archetypal quest for a preview of heaven on earth is central to mystical traditions across the world. It is the search for bliss, for an unchanging state of existence that can never be tarnished.

The reality in Pemako is, however, much more complex than Hilton's 'valley of the Blue Moon'. While described 'in the guidebooks revealed by the treasure-finders as a pure-land paradise of Buddhas', writes Tibetan scholar Keith Dowman, Pemako's 'natural environment is especially hostile and unforgiving'. It can appear closer to 'a realm of hell'.[11] This was borne out in the 1960s when Tibetans, especially Khampas from the east, following Guru Rinpoche's prophecies, fled the advancing Chinese armies in a desperate bid to escape to India. They believed they would find sanctuary and be miraculously protected from death in Pemako's labyrinthine valleys. Many never made it. Unable to cope with the sticky heat, untold numbers perished from malaria and disease.

©

On our pilgrimage through Pemako, the group of seven Westerners, Ani, the Sherpas and some thirty local porters, piled with luggage, would naturally separate and come together as we wound our way through the jungle, contending with leeches, biting moths, stinging gnats and, at first, constant rain. The slopes were lush with tropical vegetation, humidity thickened the air to syrup. At night the Sherpas would set up camp on precariously steep inclines, making simple meals on flaming paraffin stoves. I noticed Ani was always on hand, helping with whatever task was required, deferring to the Westerners with an expression of awe and bemusement.

I shared an insect-ridden tent with Waltraut, the German Buddhist, who believed she had an intimate connection with the wrathful Tantric goddess Vajrayogini – known as Dorje Phagmo in Tibetan – who was the 'patron' deity of Pemako. This scarlet goddess in a ring of fire is depicted with a sow's head – (a sow symbolises ignorance which the deity has conquered through wisdom). Our companionship was forced by dint of circumstance and, considering we'd never met before, was remarkably harmonious.

Nevertheless it was Ani whom I gravitated towards. In the beginning I can't pretend I was anyone other than one of the group for her. A few days into the expedition, with no hope of finding a shower, I asked Ani if she would mind helping while I bathed with a bucket of cold water. We had arrived at a village surrounded by whispering cornfields with an abandoned wooden army barracks in the centre of a grassy square, a faded Chinese flag atop. Behind the building, Ani and I found a secluded corner. Holding a towel around me did not prevent a gaggle of flat-chested, bony-shouldered girls trying to have a peek at my generous figure. (On two other occasions a male porter prodded my breasts in curiosity to see if they were real.)

Amid shrieks of high-pitched laughter, Ani shooed the girls away and then together we strolled down to the village pump to wash our clothes on the flat, smooth stones. Ani rubbed her blouse with the force of a baker pummelling dough, as she would scrub her face each morning with a worn flannel and cheap pink soap. At night to clean her teeth she used a combination of her index finger and an ancient orange toothbrush with bristles at all angles, but no toothpaste. I noticed her toiletries were carefully wrapped in a handkerchief-sized cloth. Mine took up half my rucksack. Walking back to the cluster of timber houses, Ani showed me which leaves to use as toilet paper and which to avoid; pointing out berries that could be eaten and those that were poisonous.

When we returned to the barracks where camp was set up, the Gillenwater brothers announced that they were going to split from the main group and trek upriver in an attempt to reach the legendary waterfalls hidden in the Tsangpo Gorge. Ken Storm Jr would follow soon after, leaving four Westerners in our party. If all went to plan, we would meet the others on the far side of the valleys. I was sorry to see the good-humoured brothers leave, because they were a levelling influence, less caught up in the competitive machismo that bristled between Ian and Hamid Sardar.

A tall balding man with dark brooding eyes, Hamid was brought up in Iran. As a young boy his father would take him hunting and on one occasion, recalled Hamid, they were walking through the forest when a giant bear appeared. His father took aim, the bullet whistling past his son's ear, and the bear fell dead only feet away. After the revolution in Tehran, Hamid's family moved to France where they lived in a chateau outside Paris, and then Hamid was sent to college in America, later studying Tibetan and Sanskrit for a doctorate at Harvard.

After Hamid met Baker in Nepal in the mid-eighties, both had become consumed by Tibet's 'hidden lands' and Hamid began to translate some of the Buddhist texts on Pemako. Uncompromising and fearless, Hamid was a diligent Buddhist practitioner of Dzogchen, a spiritual path known as the 'Natural Great Perfection', who relished telling me leech horror stories. On one Pemako trip, he said, he woke to find a swollen Tiger leech inside his mouth, gorging on his blood.

Inside the barracks, the walls plastered with outdated Communist propaganda posters – a glassy-eyed Mao, smiling Chinese and Tibetans hand in hand – Hamid was holding court over a philosophical conversation on the relativity of time and cyclic existence.

'So is it true that karma means that every thought ensnares us, every action leads to a reaction?' I asked, settling down with a mug of tea.

'Yes,' replied Hamid. 'But even loosening your attachment to thoughts makes you more open. It's a start to decondition yourself. Rather than become attached, watch the mental somersaults and your own reactions, let them be. Be the observer, the eternal witness.' He took a swig of tea. 'Until you've become more realised like Ani' – he paused, gazing onto the grassy field as she approached – 'you're continually creating karma. It's when you stop meditating that it – enlightenment – really begins. You can see it in Ani, you can see it in her grace.'

When Ani and I walked together along the trail she maintained a slow rhythmic gait, turning the plastic beads of her *mala* and murmuring, always murmuring under her breath. If I quickened, she would slow me down with a gentle touch on the hand. When my legs started to tremble like a pneumatic drill from exhaustion, we would collapse into laughter until we could both draw enough stamina to carry on. On more than one occasion when I slipped, she saved me from a nasty fall.

Ani's face changed continually. She possessed a curious blend of innocence with formidable strength. There was a quality I couldn't quite put my finger on – a calmness, a sense of inner certainty – and when I was with her I noticed something inside me relaxed. I softened. I found myself copying her, clumsily using my own sandalwood *mala*. It was a somewhat innocent notion that if I tried to do what she did, maybe I would become a little of what she was.

'Drolma,' she would say kindly, when I was lagging, 'remember to repeat Guru Rinpoche's mantra, *Om Ah Hung Benza Guru Padme Siddhi Hung.* It will give you strength.'

I learned to read her body language and we communicated with gestures, eye contact, broken words of Tibetan and, often, through an unspoken understanding. When Sonam, the guide, whose knees had recovered, was trekking alongside us, he would translate and details of Ani's life spilled out in a haphazard manner.

I learned that she grew up in a nomad encampment some two days' horse-ride west of Lhasa and until she was twenty-two lived in a black tent spun from yak wool, the size of three large rooms with a fire in the middle, sleeping on animal skins on the ground. From the age of six, she tended her parents' yak and sheep, which numbered over 150, taking them every day to the higher pastures alone or with one of her siblings. At first she found it monotonous, but with time she had grown to love the silence, the solitude.

Her father, Yongden, was a very honest person with hands 'like a brown bear' who treated everyone with equal respect; her mother, Lhamo, had a good figure with 'hands like a lady'. By nature a gentle, compassionate woman, she would at times find her daughter infuriating. 'When we went to the fields to work, I would stare up at the clouds,' recalled Ani, 'and tell Ama, my mother, "Each is a different Buddha, each travelling to a different place."' Lhamo would cuff her, telling Ani to get back to work and pull the wool hanging off the backside of the sheep. Ani refused. '"No," I'd tell her. "You wouldn't like it if someone pulled the hair from your head, it would hurt."'

By all accounts her early childhood was happy. 'I just played. I didn't know anything about the causes of suffering then.' Her parents, it would seem, sheltered her from the worst excesses of the Cultural Revolution, which began when she was just five years old and saw the wholesale destruction of Tibetan culture and religion. A time etched on the collective memory as 'when the sky fell to the earth'. [12]

When Ani's grandparents became the subject of vicious *thamzing* –

political struggle – meetings, her life turned upside down. Accused of being rich nomads at a time when name, fame and prosperity were targeted as enemies of the Proletarian Revolution, her maternal grandparents were taken away and tortured by the People's Liberation Army. When I questioned Ani further on this, she would not elaborate. I did not press her, sensing that I had not earned the right to know more about such a sensitive and, I imagined, unbearably painful subject.

Ani was more forthcoming about her decision to become a nun and one day, tramping along the narrow path through Pemako, she told me her story. Her mother, she said, didn't want her to get ordained. She tried to persuade Ani to marry the son of a local family. Ani steadfastly refused.

'The thought instantly made me feel unhappy and afraid,' she said. 'I kept telling my mother, "I want to be a nun."' A life in robes seemed uncomplicated compared to the endless physical toil that Ani's relatives endured: 'I always feel that to get married and live like lay people is a painful life. Young couples look happy before having a family but then children are like the weight of a plough on a yak's neck.'

Lhamo went to visit a local mystic to ask advice about Ani's future. Using a *mala* and a sheep knee bone to give a divination, the old woman told Lhamo that her daughter would be a good practitioner; otherwise her life would be very difficult with lots of obstacles. Ani only learned about the prediction later from a friend.

'My mother supported one of my brothers to become a monk, believing he would have a strong religious practice and rise to a high position,' Ani continued. 'To me, she said, "Women always change their mind. They're like clouds in the summer sky, always blowing, always changing."'

In the West, development is measured in terms of outward structure and technology. In Tibet studying the inner worlds is considered more important. The monasteries were the keepers of knowledge and also the guardians of dogma, power and wealth, with each of the four main Buddhist sects pursuing its own unique path of theological observance.

Nyingma, the 'old school', adheres closely to the teachings of Guru Rinpoche; Geluk, also known as Yellow Hats and the school of the Dalai Lama, emphasises scholastic pursuits and debate; the Kagyu or Black Hats, regards solitary retreat and experiential meditation as the most efficacious route to Buddhahood; and lastly the Sakya order focuses on monastic discipline and study.

Historically in Tibet, every family would offer a son to the local monastery and boys were urged to follow religious study. Nuns, however, had an ambivalent, second-class status in Tibetan society, and even girls with fervent spiritual beliefs would be encouraged to pursue a secular life. Some Tantric texts claimed females could attain enlightenment quicker than men; others described women as defiled and impure – because of their sexuality, menstruation and childbirth – whose defects included greed, hate and delusion.

One of the most common prayers for female Tibetan Buddhists was, and perhaps still is, for rebirth as a man. 'In the "Sutra on Changing Female Sex" the Buddha makes this clear,' writes Tsultrim Allione. 'You [women] should have such an intention . . . Because I wish to be freed from the impurities of the woman's body, I will acquire the beautiful and fresh body of a man.' [13]

(Ani would tell me some years later that she's never prayed to be reborn as a man in a future life, saying, 'It's the same for men and women to reach enlightenment. The only difference between them is sometimes women have a more fickle mind.')

About a year after the prediction given by the mystic, Ani ran away from home on the pretext of gathering medicinal plants. Leaving her jewellery behind, even the lump of turquoise which she wore in her hair, Ani took only her pearl earrings, her text of the goddess Tara and her steel bowl for *tsampa*. It took most of a day from the isolated valley where she had lived for all her twenty-two years to reach the nunnery which she'd visited once before, 'as part of the local dance troupe'.

'You were a dancer?' I said in surprise. 'What, like the Tibetan *cham*?'
'*Min, min.* No, no. This was during Mao's time. All the songs

were for the glory of Communist China – criticising the old Tibetan government, the landlords and our superstitious traditions and religion.' She paused for breath as the trail climbed steeply upwards.

There was little left of the nunnery that Ani had chosen. Only a roofless temple and a handful of rough stone shelters had survived the ravages of the Cultural Revolution. Seen as part of the feudal system, monks and nuns were particularly singled out for persecution at that time, subjected to acts of unspeakable cruelty, beatings and humiliation. Lamas were paraded through the streets wearing a dunce cap and then sent to harsh labour camps; nuns were forced to have sex with monks in public places. The revolution had ended barely seven years before Ani arrived at the ransacked nunnery. In such an unpredictable climate, choosing to become ordained was potentially fraught with political danger.

Five old nuns and four monks were living among the ruins. One of the nuns agreed that Ani could share her room, even though the young woman had nothing, not even *tsampa*, to offer in return.

'Two days later, my father arrived to take me back. An old lama told him, "To be born as a human being is the rarest thing. Only humans have the most precious fortune and opportunity to practise religion. Let your daughter stay." Then my mother came to take me home.' Ani pulled a long face, screwing up her eyes.

'Ama was very angry, telling me that one of her younger sisters became a nun and died at a young age. She threatened that if I didn't come home, she'd send some young men to drag me back.' Ani leaned on her stick and continued. 'The same old lama spoke to my mother: "Your daughter's a very nice child. If she's decided by herself to be a nun, don't change that decision. If you take her home, her life will be cut very short." I always felt grateful to him for his kindness and generosity.'

'What did you say to your mother?'

'I pleaded, "Ama-la, you don't need to worry about me. You don't need to bring me food or clothes. I can drink water in winter and eat grasses in summer." Finally she agreed. "We'll see how long you can last," she said. She left me a small bag of *tsampa*. I think she thought that when the food ran out I'd come home.' Ani paused, and then said at last, 'But I didn't. The old lama shaved my hair and I took my vows, pledging my allegiance to the Three Jewels – the Buddha, Dharma and Sangha.' Instinctively, she placed her hand across her heart.

'I returned the pearl earrings to my father and over the next few months ate nothing but a spoon of *tsampa* a day.' Rubbing her tummy, she grinned. 'I felt weak. My stomach grumbled. I didn't mind. I was happy.'

'You couldn't ask the other nuns for food?'

'I was too shy. When one of the nuns offered, I ate only a mouthful. Sometimes I collected nettles for soup like the *yogi* Milarepa or I was given *tsok* [temple offerings] made from *tsampa*. The old nun was kind, lending me her sheepskin blanket.'

'Did you miss home?'

'No. Six months later my father arrived with more supplies and by then, both my parents accepted that I would stay.'

Once Ani became a nun, she said, 'My father and I grew apart, each following our own lives.' Three years later, at the age of fifty, Yongden died from stomach and kidney problems. 'For over five months he was ill, blood coming out of his nose and mouth. We were very poor and had no medicine,' she said, looking away. 'I visited him once at home and then returned to the nunnery. I never saw him again.'

On her father's death, in Tibetan custom, lamas came to recite prayers from the *Tibetan Book of the Dead* and perform a ceremony to release his consciousness directly into the 'pure land', to pass quickly through the forty-nine levels of the Bardo – the intermediate state between life and death. Yongden was then given a sky burial. With little soil and few trees for cremation this is the preferred way for Tibetans to dispose of their dead. In an elaborate ritual with smoking juniper, the corpse is cut up with knives, the bones crushed, pounded and mixed with *tsampa*. Attracted by the pungent smoke and the odour of raw flesh, scores of Himalayan griffin vultures and lammergeyers, huge bearded vultures, gather around the charnel ground on the rocks, ready to swoop and feast on the body, leaving barely a few bones.

Grisly though it may appear from a Western perspective – where death is denied and sanitised – for a Tibetan to witness a sky burial is a profound lesson in life's impermanence. As it is believed the soul (or mind) has already left the body before it is dismembered, the body is seen simply as meat, to be offered to the heavens, for the benefit of all living beings.

Only men were permitted to witness her father's sky burial, said Ani sadly, who 'felt as if the sky had fallen into the land'. She stayed behind, saying special prayers that her father would take rebirth again as a human. 'The mind is like the wind, it comes and goes. Everyone must go to Yama, the Lord of Death and get reborn, and where they go depends upon the deeds of their past lives.'

☺

After over a week trekking, starting early until camp was set up every evening, a day of rest was granted at the village of Chutanka, perched on a ledge high above the Tsangpo River and home to the Lopa tribe. Led by the hypnotic sound of a bell, Sonam, Ani and I climbed past chocolate-brown houses on stilts with baskets of red chillies scorching in the sun up to a tiny timber monastery. Inside an elderly Lopa nun, her silvery hair cropped, her face sunken, turned a large prayer wheel. Each time it rotated, a high-pitched bell sang out and in its wake, I quivered like a tuning fork. We were offered peaches and roasted corn on the cob, and we sat down in the cool interior. Following Ani's lead I took a peach.

I'd been warned not to accept food from villagers for fear of being poisoned by a *dugma*. These poison witches, so it is said, still live in the valleys, brewing a lethal concoction of snake venom, rotten egg and herbs to kill their enemies. The tradition is reputedly passed from mother to daughter and it can take months before the victim dies. As they become weaker, the poisoner allegedly acquires all the victim's positive physical and mental qualities, so they target only rich, clever people. The practices are believed to originate from the descendants of the Mishmi and Abor warriors of northern India (the same tribes who had killed off some of the British officers intent on figuring out the riddle of the Tsangpo Gorge).

With Sonam interpreting, I asked Ani what she knew about the poison cults.

'I was told the poisoners are Monpas, usually women. I don't know any,' said Ani, biting into the small juicy peach. 'Before making a brew they take a vow. If the woman can't find a person to poison – by slipping it into their food or *chang* [barley beer] – so as not to break their vow, they have to give the mixture to an animal. Some say that you can tell where a poisoner lives because they have a black flag outside the house. I'm not sure.' She thought for a moment. 'I never heard of Mishmis. Do they have a tail?'

'What? A tail. I don't think so.' I laughed.

'I heard some tribes did.' She grinned back.

A basket of peaches later, Ani was bent double with cramps, giggling and groaning.

'Aa-ooo, aw-ooo,' she cried, clutching her stomach. 'I've eaten too many.'

'Ani-la, I hope they weren't poisoned.'

'*Min, min.* No, no. I was just being greedy.'

Back at the house of the Chutanka village chief, Ian and Hamid were sitting on animal skins on the dirt-encrusted floor. The room was dark, dust hovering in shafts of sunlight. Fat flies buzzed, and the smell of swine hung heavy – beneath the house was the family's pigsty. Tense negotiations were under way to hire more porters and find a cable crossing over the Tsangpo.

Baker was trying to find out if a trail existed on the other side of the river leading to a remote hermitage called Mandeldem. From there he believed a path might lead to the entrance of Yangsang Ne, the paradisiacal realm said to be behind the waterfall in the gorge. Taking this route would mean finding our way through an unmapped valley and then crossing a 17,000-foot snow-covered pass, the Nam La.

'The cable you've heard about is rusted,' said the chief, with feet spread-eagled like a duck. 'No-one has tried it in years.'

Ian persisted. The headman said that the hermitage had once been a place of pilgrimage for villagers from Chutanka. 'But now the way has grown over,' continued the chief. 'Trees would need to be felled and rolled down the mountainside to use as bridges as there are many rivers to cross. To get there would take four days, with poisonous snakes and leeches so thick you have to scrape them off with a knife.'

When the headman demanded 350 renminbi a day – over four times the normal rate for porters – adding, 'My men would die, I will not let them go,' it was clear the discussion was over. We would not be able to reach Mandeldem and would have to continue south and cross the river at Metok, which our permits did not cover.

I knew before we set out that our itinerary was fluid, and I now suspected that Ian Baker had invited Waltraut and me merely to 'defray' costs and was pursuing his own private agenda. In his book *The Heart of the World* published seven years later, Baker reveals his obsessive search to find Yangsang Ne, ruminating at length whether it's a physical place or a metaphor for a state of mind. When asking, 'several lamas for their theories about Yangsang's coordinates, no two had the same perspective, though all insisted that, like the Tantric power places (*pitha*) of ancient India, Yangsang was no mere metaphor, but an actual place, albeit not strictly geographical'.

I think that reaching Yangsang was only part of Baker's motivation. He was in an explorers' race to be the first to chart the last five miles of the Tsangpo Gorge. Each journey Baker made into the region was a step closer to that goal.

If I was not party to Ian's exact plans, I was aware that both he and Hamid regarded their extensive – and hard-earned – knowledge about Pemako as highly secret. I think that Ian particularly was wary that as a journalist I would exploit decades of serious exploration for the sake of one newspaper story. At the outset we made an agreement that if I did write an article, it would not include details of his previous journeys and he could check it before it went to print. (All of which I did when a piece was later published in *Condé Nast Traveller*.) Nonetheless as it became apparent to me on our pilgrimage that neither Ian nor Hamid wanted to share information – I was told by Waltraut that they thought I wasn't a serious enough pilgrim – I found myself turning towards Ani for companionship.

Over six feet tall, Baker was a commanding figure who spoke in high-faluting fashion, ruminating about esoteric theories. He had received teachings from countless lamas, spent time on retreat in caves and, as a committed Buddhist, professed to live by the Tantric principles between the light and dark, sacred and profane. In his words, he was drawn to 'erotic mysticism'.[14] Yet there was something impenetrable about the man who purposely, I think, fostered ambiguity. (The motto of his travel company, Red Panda Expeditions – 'confuse and elude' – neatly summed it up.)

If the group dynamics between Hamid, Ian, Waltraut and me were somewhat strained before the village of Chutanka, they unravelled further in the days afterwards. Waltraut began to complain that we were now on 'a picture pilgrimage' as hours passed at idyllic waterfalls while the two Americans asked the locals, especially the beautiful women, of whom there were many, to pose for photographs for a book they said they were preparing. In part Polynesian, in part Mongolian, with wide almond-shaped eyes and high cheekbones, the younger women were indeed exquisite and also admirably strong, carrying fifty-five pounds in their flimsy bamboo baskets like a bag of groceries.

Baker appeared to be particularly struck by the daughter of the Chutanka chief, whose thickly lashed eyes, olive complexion and slender build would not have looked out of place on a Parisian catwalk. Several years before, the teenager had fallen mysteriously ill, suffering from dizzy spells. The villagers believed she could be a *dakini* – a goddess incarnate.

After a heated argument between her parents and Baker, who offered more money, they reluctantly agreed their daughter could join us, on condition that she would not carry a heavy load and would be accompanied by her sister and brother. Despite Ian's concerted efforts to photograph her, she kept a wary distance, shadows of confusion often darting across her lovely face.

I was highly uncomfortable about how Baker had bought the 'dakini girl', as she was nicknamed, for the duration of the trek. Both Waltraut and I felt protective of her, raising the issue one evening around the campfire and telling Ian we didn't trust his motives. When he explained that some Tantric practices involved 'collecting the menstrual blood of a virgin at full moon', I found myself wondering if his spirituality wasn't a smokescreen for something else.

Ani was oblivious to any tensions among the Westerners, continuing to treat Ian with humility and respect. The porters were equally deferential towards the Americans, in awe of their extensive knowledge of Pemako, their passion and, I think, their belligerent toughness. Some of the young porters had been with them on previous journeys and took on a role almost as their personal bodyguards.

With the passing of days, Ani and I became friends with four of our porters, proud half-Monpa half-Tibetan cousins, and we would share lunch together. I traded my heavy chapati peanut butter sandwiches for tsampa, salt tea and chillies. Surprisingly, tsampa had become more palatable than sandwiches. They ate Tibetan-style, tossing the pa into their mouths followed by a whole dried chilli. I kneaded mine into a doughy ball and washed it down with black salt tea, which they insisted I drink in huge quantities.

Following their intuition, the four cousins scaled razor-sharp ridges with finely honed balance. Untamed like their landscape, they were as agile as the rare takins – a shaggy ox-like creature with horns – which they would hunt for food. Deeply reverential towards their natural world, viewed as sacred, the young men would often appear more spirit than matter.

The local tribes still practised an elaborately animistic form of Tibetan Buddhism. While walking they muttered mantras; in the evening around the campfire, the sky bursting with a billion stars, they read scriptures bound in saffron cloth, tracing their finger over the ornate Tibetan lettering. The men carried *gau* – amulet – boxes, well loved and smooth from touch, containing precious sacred objects and a photo of their personal lama. At night they slept on huge velvety palm leaves and, for protection, hung the *gau* boxes above to ward off evil spirits.

But life in the valleys, where even matches were a novelty, was far from nirvana. If the porters fell sick, it was several days' walk to the nearest hospital. I peered into one makeshift clinic in a village where a Chinese doctor was treating a queue of locals with an injection of antibiotics. He did not once change the needle. 'And if we are too ill to walk,' one porter said simply, 'we wait to die.'

CHAPTER 6

The Essence of Flowers

A NI belongs to both the Nyingma and the Kagyu schools – known as Ka-Nying for short (the mixing of those two traditions in Tibet is relatively common) – and can trace her line back to the tenth century. Her first guru, Drubwang P. Rinpoche, was a Drigung Kagyu lama – a sub-sect within the main Kagyu lineage – who was lionised in his community as an eminent *yogi*: someone who devotes their entire life to meditation. There were many stories about his 'great magical power'. Some monks were said to have seen their master 'floating as if walking, yet his feet did not touch the ground'.

Outwardly a *yogi* or *yogini* may look no different to a monk or nun. Some are householders who are permitted to marry, others celibate hermits. These mystics who broke away from the bricks and mortar of learning, who sought out the natural grottoes to devise a new language of the soul, one predicated not on scripture, rather on inner experience, are revered as the spiritual elite of Tibetan Buddhism, often referred to as the Vajrayana path – the 'Thunderbolt' or 'Diamond' Vehicle.

Vajrayana arose from a group of texts called Tantras and is the most esoteric form of Buddhism. Prone to misinterpretation, many of the practices and initiations are regarded as secret. In essence, Tantra aims to embrace all emotions, desires and experiences, however mundane, worldly or unpleasant, as opportunities for spiritual practice and growth. The advanced Tantric techniques ultimately allow the practitioner to rise above habitual mental patterns and attachments.

From her early twenties, until his death in 1988, Ani received teachings from P. Rinpoche who advised that, 'whatever you're offered to eat, you must eat; whatever you're given to wear, you must wear. If someone says something bad you must tolerate it in your heart. For without tolerance, there's no compassion.'

P. Rinpoche had died sitting upright in meditation. Only after several days did his body begin to shrink without decomposing. In Tibet this is a sign of an accomplished practitioner, who, at the time of death, manifests a 'rainbow body' where the five gross elements of the physical body are transformed into their pure essence – five-coloured light. (Sometimes the body shrinks or it vanishes completely, leaving only the hair and nails.)

At the Rinpoche's cremation, Ani recalls that rainbows appeared and some people heard celestial singing. She saw 'flowers – red, white, maroon – falling from the sky' which disappeared 'before they reached the ground'. These were auspicious omens, 'an ubiquitous sign of a saintly death in Tibetan hagiography'.[1]

After the death of her master, Ani continued to be given ad hoc instruction from his disciple, T. Rinpoche. With the passing of years and much time spent on retreat at her nunnery, a nagging restlessness grew inside her. Ani knew of the pilgrimage sites scattered throughout Tibet and wanted to visit them.

'It was an inner feeling, an instinct,' Ani would tell me. 'A lama didn't tell me to go. There was no vision and no dream – I've never had any significant dreams – I just started to go by myself.'

'Why did you come to Pemako?' I asked.

'For spiritual development. I didn't know much about the region before I came. I knew that the protector that guarded over Pemako was the same as my local deity, so I felt a natural spiritual connection with the place.' Ani arrived in the Year of the Iron Horse, 1990, and stayed for one year, one month and fifteen days. 'It was one of the happiest times of my life. A result of good human birth.'

The predicted rains had not come and as we continued south towards the Indian border, the sultrier it became. The sky, soft and spacious, deepened from buttermilk to cerulean; the sun cast a peachy-gold tint over the valleys. Ani and I often walked in silence, only broken by the sound of her muttering under her breath. I noticed how effortlessly she seemed to fall into this still quiet pool. She was clearly comfortable traversing her interior landscape; I could only tiptoe around my own.

Some days a sense of dream superseded reality; others an exhausted torpor set in and with it I found ferocious emotions would bubble up from nowhere, and then, just as quickly, subside. Physically gruelling, I had to draw upon every fibre in my body to cope with the rough terrain. But the sheer effort – up and down, down and up – had a cleansing effect and my usual meaningless mental chatter would subside. Occasionally I slipped into an empty, weightless and blissful space, until I tripped over a tree root or found yet another leech crawling down my neck. After picking off a dozen in one hour, I gave up counting.

Peak after peak appeared – Gyala Pelri, a dome of ice behind a puff of cloud, and then the glinting pinnacle of Namcha Barwa, known as the 'blazing meteorite'. One night camping on the edge of a village I was kept awake by rustling, only to find, the following morning, that our ground-sheet resembled a sieve: we'd set up camp above a killer ants' nest. They had devoured our tent like butter.

When boredom set in, I focused on my immediate world – and what an extraordinary one it was. Polka-dot butterflies as large as bats fluttered above furry centipedes. Giant olive-brown stick insects swooped low and shimmering emerald stag beetles, the size of a toy car, hauled themselves up tree trunks. Everything whispered and everywhere was green, a deep dizzying green. I would imagine that each step was on sacred ground, reminding myself that this was a revered place of pilgrimage and, with time, this engendered a new reverence and an immense respect for the effortless beauty around me; for the calligraphy of a flower, the divinity in a leaf.

The aromas were always changing: sweet-smelling grass, sticky rotting vegetation, freshly cut hay which transported me instantly back to England on a hot summer's day. It seemed like I'd been walking along this trail forever, yet it was barely a fortnight. Cut off from the rest of the world, with few reference points to my former life, sometimes I would need to remember home, as if to remember myself. I cast my mind back to the previous year, trying to piece together the journey that had led me to Pemako and to Ani.

It was when I was working as a journalist in London that a feeling of spiritual aridity, an aching emptiness inside, began to preoccupy me. I wanted to be successful but not at the expense of my dreams, of my deeper intuition. I started to feel distinctly uncomfortable in my own skin: I felt a fake. I took up yoga, looked for answers on the burgeoning shelves of the self-help industry, tried aromatherapy massage courses and studied the chakras – the seven energy centres in the body.

Then one day I remember having to look up the word 'compassion' in a dictionary. I wondered why I'd never used it – only to realise with a sinking heart that I'd genuinely never felt it, not true compassion, the selfless sort described in Buddhist teachings. Only later would I realise that this small moment would have far-reaching consequences on my own pilgrimage. 'First there is the personal restlessness . . . Then there is the need to feel something deeper than the surface glare of things,' writes Joan Marler, dancer and mythologist. 'For many women, going on a sacred journey means getting back in touch with what is sacred in the earth.'[2]

@

From time to time Ani and I stumbled across a profusion of scarlet-orange and hot-pink orchids. Delicately plucking a flower, she showed me how to suck the nectar from the stamen, then she fastened whorls of blossoms in her hair, swaying along the path like a Hawaiian beach girl. When the silence began to crowd in, and the path became dull, I played Pulp or the Chemical Brothers on my Walkman. Ani wanted to listen too, frowning at the hard plastic earphones before mimicking my dancing – her ebony dreadlocks spiralling, her arms flailing – and then for no reason we skipped, until we fell into the shade and fanned each other with palm leaves.

Hamid was also feeling the heat and one afternoon we found him by the path stripped to the waist. Covering her mouth with the back of her hand, Ani pealed with laughter, pointing at Hamid's very hairy chest before she squatted down and began stroking him like a puppy.

'What are you doing, Ani-la?' shouted Sonam as he approached. 'Ani, stop it. Nuns shouldn't do that.'

'It's OK,' I said in defence. 'It's harmless.'

'I don't care,' he retorted. 'Ani is *not* a street girl.'

With a noisy sniff and a slight pout, Ani started to rearrange her dreadlocks, re-coiling them in a spiral before firmly pulling down the straw hat. I was intrigued by Ani's relationship with her faith. She followed a path of asceticism, yet not to the exclusion of pleasure. There was nothing pious or ethereal about her. Far from her celibacy lending her the air of a person in denial, she could be bawdy and, unlike nuns - with a shaven head who can appear asexual, Ani exuded an earthy womanliness.

I wondered if this was because a significant part of her spiritual practice was to meditate upon the goddess Vajrayogini. In the tradition of Tibetan sacred geography, Pemako is visioned in the shape of Vajrayogini with the 'Tsangpo river as her blood [or life-force] and the mountain Kundu Dorsempotrang as her heart centre', explained Ani. 'Pilgrims go to different places in Pemako to visit different parts of Vajrayogini's body and receive special blessings.' Tibetan scholar Toni Huber describes the Tibetan inclination to perceive features of the landscape as animated, with specific contours, mountains and lakes representing a deity or animal as part of the 'folk religion'.[3] By imagining the land in such a way, the subtle energy body – and chakras – of the Tantric practitioner is brought into alignment with the goddess perceived to lie supine across the region. Depending on the pilgrim's level of realisation, this initiates a profound transformation of the psyche. On a more mundane level, to view the land in this way reduces the illusion of separation between what is within and what is outside, between human and animal, tree and stone. It gives rise to a profound experience of unity and inter-relatedness – an understanding that all life is sacred, all is connected.

'The *neys*, or sacred sites themselves, through their geological features and the narratives of transformation attached to them, continually remind pilgrims of the liberating power of the Tantric Buddhist tradition,' write Dunham and Baker. 'Over time pilgrimage guidebooks were written, giving instructions to pilgrims visiting the holy sites and accounts of their history and significance. These guidebooks, *neyigs*, empowered Tibet and its people with a sacred geography, a narrated vision of the world ordered and transformed through Buddhist magic and metaphysics.'[4]

The exact location of each body part of the goddess Vajrayogini with the topography of the Pemako landscape varies according to which pilgrim guide is referred to. According to one text her right breast is identified with the mountain Namcha Barwa, with her crown, or highest chakra, at Gyala Pelri. Rinchenpung is her navel and her 'secret place' is said to be over the Indian border in Arunachal Pradesh.

From the late eighteenth century Rinchenpung *gompa* became the focal point of pilgrimage in Pemako. Believed to be a powerful place where *dakinis* – literally 'sky dancers' – gather and illumination is effortlessly attained, it's associated with the wrathful incarnation of Guru Rinpoche who holds a scorpion in one hand, symbolic of fear that has been conquered. Situated in a lush valley, Rinchenpung monastery is built on a small hill, amid a jungle of rhododendrons.

It was there that Ani lived in a small cottage for one year, spending her time alone, meditating on the deity Khacho Wangmo, a form of Vajrayogini. It rained relentlessly and she was forever picking off leeches from her body. There were 'multicoloured birds – red, yellow, green and blue', biting flies, monkeys and deadly turquoise snakes. She ate simply – *tsampa*, bananas and oranges – and would hear tales about Pemako from the locals who frequently visited the *gompa* for chanting and ceremonies.

Together with Sonam, as we wound our way up to the county 'capital' of Metok – which means flowers in Tibetan – Ani told me about a rare practice she'd undertaken on the advice of a Khampa lama when staying in her hermitage.

Pemako is famous for its effusion of flowers and considered an especially potent place to perform *metok chulen* – literally extracting the quintessence of flowers – which refines one's subtle body (the network of invisible channels and centres through which energy passes), through prayer, visualisations, yoga and ritual. This is the first of several practices where the adept gradually reduces their intake of solid food until they are sustained purely by the essence, aiming to sever attachment to physical nourishment. The more advanced practitioner will live only on mineral and water essences, and eventually on air alone.

The miraculous qualities of the flowers in the valleys are described in detail in Padmasambhava's text, 'A Clear Mirror for Identifying the Five Special Plants'. Their properties include the gift of immortality and the ability to fly; their perfumed scent gives rise to feelings of bliss, purifying the body and heightening one's meditation.[5]

Before beginning *metok chulen*, Ani made a vow not to eat any food, barely drink a glass of water a day, and for three weeks to remain in silence. She collected flowers, grinding them with water into a small tablet. 'Over the weeks I became very thin and weak, my skin hanging loose, empty. In the end I couldn't sit because my ribs poked in my tummy,' she recalled. 'My whole body hurt, as if it was being squashed under a building. Even my mouth stuck together.' She clamped her teeth tightly for emphasis. 'The ground swayed beneath me and my whole body became light.'

Ani then went on to describe the visions she had – 'of beautiful trees, fruits and flowers in many different colours' – both within her mind and with her eyes open.

I asked if it was like paradise.

'Yes. Except there were three stages to it. The first twenty-one days I felt happy like a young girl. Then at the end when I began to eat a little *tsampa* gruel – I couldn't eat much or else my intestines would break and I could die – I felt suffering through the body like I was feeling the suffering of all people. This lasted for fifteen days.' She leaned on her gnarled staff. 'Then I started to be like normal, except my body felt very old, heavy and it was hard to move.'

'Do you think it helped you?'

'Yes, undoubtedly,' she replied. '*Metok chulen* is a way of purifying the mind. You see, Drolma, outward appearances aren't so important, it's the mind within that's precious.'

'Is that because the body isn't as solid as it appears?'

'The body's like a rainbow.' She prodded my arm. 'It's ephemeral.'

My confusion must have been obvious.

'Think of it like this,' she said patiently. 'The body is the guest of the land. It's like a temporary shelter to house the mind. When you die the bone goes into the earth, blood into water, the warmth of the body into fire and breath into the air. But the mind isn't finished and will come again and again in different incarnations. This is what you must respect and why it's important to practise religion and prepare for the next life.'

I could see Sonam was floundering.

'Do you believe such things, Sonam?'

'I don't know.' He gave a little shrug. 'I was educated in China. At school we were told there is no God.'

I'm not sure what I was expecting in Metok, but 'county capital' was a wild misnomer. Situated among paddy fields on high land above the

Tsangpo and barely ten miles from the Indian border, this was the final outpost. A decade earlier a road was built connecting Metok to Pome on the other side of the valleys. It rapidly became impassable, submerged by landslips during the monsoon and blocked by snow in winter. These days supplies could only be flown in by helicopter or carried by the legions of human pack-horses – raggle-taggle groups of Chinese army porters loaded with boxes of ammunition and *bai jiu* (a clear liquor made from grain) who walked like zombies, their faces a grimace of fatigue.

On arriving in Metok, Ani rested her hand on my arm. 'Rinchenpung is over there,' she said, pointing south towards dense jungle. Unfortunately there was neither the time nor inclination from Ian and Hamid to make a detour over a pass several thousand feet high to the *gompa*. Both had visited it before. As it became apparent that our party would not reach any of the holy sites intended – in part because of the slow march of the porters, in part the detour we made down to Metok to cross the river, and then there were the long photo shoots at enchanting waterfalls – a sense of palpable disillusionment was setting in among Hamid, Waltraut and me.

'Pilgrimage is only in your heart,' Ian insisted. 'From the Dzogchen perspective you just walk without any discrimination. If you don't get the *mana* – the vibrant energy from the power places or the monasteries – you have to experience and create it out of every moment.'

While I could sense that Ani was able to do this, never complaining, her boundless enthusiasm rarely flagging, for myself Baker's words rang hollow. In Metok karaoke blared at night and our squalid unswept dormitories, infested with bedbugs and rats, leaked. Dominated by an army barracks, to guard the disputed border with India, the 'capital' was little more than a few wooden shacks on stilts around a square. A place full of misfits: emaciated men, bored soldiers and overweight Chinese staring gormlessly into space. The town was epitomised by the view beneath the communal toilets – a heaving sea of maggots.

The PSB officer in charge promptly put our party under quasi house arrest because our permit was invalid. The next twenty-four hours slid by in a haze of *chang* drinking – the cause of Metok's rotten atmosphere. Sonam disappeared, clutching boxes of cigarettes, to schmooze with the police, and staggered in later that afternoon. I went 'shopping' and reluctantly traded my expensive 'hi-tech' boots, held together with elastic bands and sticky tape, for a pair of khaki-green army plimsolls. With my one pair of waterproof trousers falling apart, I was beginning to look (and smell) like a grubby porter girl. It was close to two weeks since the last shower. Following Sonam's diplomacy and a bribe, we were finally allowed to continue on our way.

The incident with the PSB in Metok would be the first of several signs that our pilgrimage would not end as expected. A couple of days later, camping in a sea of rice paddies, a raging thunderstorm reverberated around the valleys causing our tent to quiver like a leaf. The next morning the porters muttered darkly among themselves that our group had upset the protectors – the *suma* who guarded Pemako – although why we couldn't be sure. I found myself thinking that maybe it was because our group wasn't united in a spirit of camaraderie.

Sonam, Ani and I were huddled around the fire drinking morning tea when Ani warned me: 'You have to be careful. When you make the protectors angry you get strange weather. Storms, hail, avalanches. When there's really strong anger, a protector will transform itself into a tiger or a yeti.'

'You believe in yetis?' I took a spoonful of muesli.

'Yes, but they don't look like how I saw them once on a television in Lhasa. They're like tall human beings. I heard one story about the army finding a yeti. It was longer than a truck. The local people who I went on pilgrimage with to the holy mountain, Kundu Dorsempotrang, told me that in the dense forests yetis still roam and when angry will attack humans.'

It was a year after she arrived at Rinchenpung that Ani, together with a dozen pilgrims, mainly Khampas who'd settled in Pemako, embarked on a pilgrimage to the mountain believed to be the location of the heart of the goddess Vajrayogini. It was a perilous journey, inching through thick jungle in torrential rain with no path, only cairns of stones or cuts in trees to guide them. At each river crossing they made bridges from tree trunks, and for ten days Ani's clothes were wet. To test their mettle further, the group had to cross the 'wide and swampy' leech-filled Marshes of Adrathang, spending a night sleeping on plastic laid out on damp branches.

When they arrived at Kundu Dorsempotrang, ringed by lakes and said to be covered with a thousand self-arising images of Buddha, Ani made five inner *kora* – two in one day – and one outer *kora*. (In Tibet the purpose of pilgrimage is to make a *kora* – to walk in a circular fashion around any sacred object, usually a mountain – to increase *wang* or spiritual power.)

'Thirteen outer *koras* lead to the same level as a Bodhisattva [an enlightened being who forgoes nirvana until all others are saved],' she explained. 'For three days I left early in the morning and walked until dark, barely stopping to eat. You can't waste time. I heard there were leopards and tigers but I didn't see any, only one poisonous snake, yellow and white, coiled around a tree.' She blew on her tea. 'It was hard and very dangerous. If you lose the path it may be months before you meet somebody.'

Finishing his breakfast, Sonam collected the rubbish around the camp, and threw it on the fire.

'Aa-oo-uuu, *min, min*. No, no,' cried Ani, as she retrieved the papers. 'You'll make the fire gods angry. You must only burn natural and pure offerings.'

Sonam laughed, swinging his rucksack on his back.

'*Nga tso dro*. We have to go. It's a long walk.'

We spent the next night at Marpung, with huge prayer flags billowing like peace-sails in the wind. The village was a disturbing mixture of tradition and modernity. The children, sent to Chinese schools out of the valleys, wore red lycra and army caps and smoked cigarettes. They offered a bowl of shit to Ian and pelted me with stones. In the home of the village official, dressed in the golden robes of a monk, Hamid was told the mistress of the house was a *dugma* – a poison witch.

'Don't worry,' she said with a shrill laugh. 'Today isn't right for poisoning.'

I was still sceptical about the poison cult stories until I heard the local Marpung doctor ask Ian for medicine, explaining in hushed tones that twenty-eight years before an old woman from the neighbouring village had spiked his *chang*. The following day, when we arrived at that village, the porters pointed out the alleged *dugma* with a wizened face like a walnut, confirming that she was renowned for her deadly brew.

Our porters took the threat of poisoning very seriously, refusing to sleep in certain Monpa villages and warning us not to accept food or drink from strangers. (According to Baker, the wife of Tenzin Norgay, who accompanied Sir Edmund Hillary on the first ascent of Mount Everest in 1953, died 'after allegedly being poisoned by a Pemako witch'.[6])

That night at an idyllic camping spot, affording a view over forested mountains which curved like a woman's reclining body, a villager threatened one of our porters with a gun then charged at him with a sabre. Grabbing a large stick, the porter thumped the man twice. In the darkness a blood-curdling scream rang out as the attacker fell into the bushes. The young porter was left trembling.

When I retired to the tent I couldn't sleep. Since Metok I felt an unsettling undercurrent. Pemako was a melting pot of contradictions: mountains that doubled as wrathful gods, villagers who could poison with a handshake. Today the younger generation were moving away from the valleys with their sprawling military encampment and thriving illegal logging industry. In the middle of the jungle, I saw logs with Chinese writing destined to become dressing tables in Shanghai.

And yet I had seen rainbow after rainbow along the trail and mused that, perhaps, there is some truth in the legends that in Pemako one has no need to fear death, as all beings – insects, dogs, people – are immediately reborn into a 'rainbow body' and go direct to the Buddha lands. For this reason, Ani says it's where she hopes to be reborn. The further I went into the hidden lands, the deeper I seemed to go within myself. Lying in the darkness, hearing the wind moaning gently through the trees, I could see that Ani's ability to be adaptable and spontaneous, to move with the flow and mould with the landscape, gave her both a profound acceptance and a light-hearted approach to life. She seemed at ease fearlessly stepping into the unknown, confident that she would always find her way home. Drifting to sleep, I hoped that I, too, would learn such trust.

CHAPTER 7

Under Arrest

AFTER weeks of meeting no-one except a few barefoot Monpas, the trail widened to become a mule track. Our group was approaching the south-west corner of the valleys and only three more days of arduous trekking lay ahead, before we'd cross the Doshong La pass out of Pemako. I wasn't sure how much longer I could carry on in my flimsy plimsolls, my legs like lead with fatigue. At the end of another long day, Ani and I reached camp. Sonam was waiting for us with a Chinese beer in one hand and a cigarette in the other. He flashed a wide grin, his nose crinkling in delight.

'Welcome,' he toasted me. 'Not far now and we'll be back in Lhasa.'

The guide was dreaming of home comforts and his pretty twenty-four-year-old fiancée.

Taking a sip of his warm beer, I surveyed the scene – a sprawling rubbish tip. Small, black bush pigs and skeletal dogs foraged for food in the piles of detritus: broken beer bottles, empty noodle packets and cigarette butts. Groups of mules were eating from nosebags and a scantily dressed Chinese woman, probably a prostitute, sludged past in high-heeled sandals.

'Where in the hell are we?'

'An army camp. They're bringing in supplies for the winter. Where are the rest of the group?'

'They're coming. For once I'm ahead. I left them snoozing in the shade after lunch—'

I was stopped in mid-flow by an angry torrent of Chinese as a stout, potbellied military officer approached us, three stars glinting prominently on his uniform.

'Who's this foreigner? What are you doing here?' he rattled, his bottom lip quivering. Soldiers in military fatigues surrounded Sonam and me, forcing Ani to step aside, their machine guns hanging loosely in their hands. The officer demanded to see my passport.

'What do I do?' I asked Sonam, my throat dry.

'Hand it over,' he muttered.

The officer flipped through the passport, then slipped it inside his jacket.

'Tell the rest of the foreigners to report on arrival,' he ordered Sonam before rounding on his heels.

Later that afternoon a fierce row broke out between Ian Baker and the Chinese officer who accused our party of walking without the correct permits in a closed military zone. This was a serious crime, tantamount to spying.

Under some trees on the edge of the marshy military encampment, the Sherpas set up the tents. I squatted down by the campfire to attempt to dry my Chinese army plimsolls and was joined by Ani holding her wooden bowl piled with *tsampa* and a tin cup of black salt tea.

'We're unlucky,' sighed Sonam, slouching down next to us. 'Only once a year do the military pass through here to bring supplies – ammunition and guns. That's why the officer is very very angry. He doesn't want foreigners, especially Americans, to see such things.'

'What does that mean?' I said, staring into the glowing embers.

'I don't know. They'll want to see your camera film. Maybe even take the group back to Lhasa for questioning. I think tomorrow when we start the two-day crossing over the Doshong La soldiers will walk with us. The army officer's told his big boss we're coming and once out of Pemako' – Sonam inhaled sharply – 'big problem.'

That night there were leeches everywhere – thin black ones, fat slimy-green ones – even on our sleeping bags. A drunken Chinese soldier tried to force his way into our tent; but we pushed him out with curses and a large stick, and he lurched off into the darkness. Early the next morning, as Sonam had presaged, five Chinese soldiers in military fatigues and transparent plastic ponchos, each carrying an M16 automatic rifle, were waiting, together with an army porter whose grin exposed a mouth of rotting brown teeth. My passport was returned to me but our group was officially under arrest. We would be frog-marched out of the valleys to a military barracks on the other side.

It was a log-slipping, bog-falling day and after putting my shoulder out I gave my rucksack to a porter with a mule. Several hours later I was still trying to catch up with the mule driver and, as Ani had marched on ahead, walked alone through the primeval forest, losing all sense of time and of myself. Just as I had begun to give up on finding Ani, the mule man or my lunch, one of the Sherpas known as Father Pasang, dressed in scarlet trousers, pea-green jumper and a royal-blue beret worn aslant, appeared like an imp from behind a boulder. Enlightened or crazy, I could never tell which, his crinkly face disappeared into a vast smile as he offered me a hunk of bread. Together we climbed up to a wooden army hut in the nook of the mountains.

Inside it was packed with porters and military, steam rising from the wet bodies. Ani sat close to the fire, warming her ruddy cheeks. In a façade of friendliness, Sonam and the soldiers were sharing packet noodles and toasting each other with *bai jiu*. After taking several sips of the foul tasting 'firewater' to thaw my icy limbs, I squeezed down next to Ani to eat my peanut butter sandwiches.

'*Tsering nga mola yin.* Today I'm like an old woman. *Nga ka-le khag song.* I'm very tired.' I grimaced. 'Are you?'

'*Otse.* A bit,' she said. 'My knees hurt.'

'Why?'

'Too much time in cold caves during the winter.'

'C'mon, Drolma, hurry up, we've got to go,' yelled Sonam above the din. 'You have to walk with us this time. The way through the forest isn't well marked.'

I was relieved once again of my rucksack, this time by one of the Chinese soldiers. To ensure I didn't fall behind, Sonam commandeered the army porter to stay on my heels while our party jogged at a brutal pace, ascending several thousand feet in a few hours. Stopping to rest, the guide asked to look at the soldiers' machine guns. Happily they acquiesced, nonchalantly passing the guns around, falling about with laughter when Sonam imitated pulling the trigger. Ani looked on nonplussed.

Upon reaching alpine country, we left the 200-year-old juniper forest to cross misty rain-sodden rock-scapes and at dusk reached another army camp sinking into a bog. One by one the rest of our party arrived for our final night in the valleys. There were basic dormitories and small wooden beds. Ani and I, Sonam and the soldiers all huddled together under thin duvets, trying to warm up, sharing food and drinking tea. The five soldiers whooped and jabbered like a bunch of schoolboys and I sensed Ani was at ease. Without their guns, when not under orders, they were nothing more than fresh-faced young men, barely out of pubescence and a long long way from home.

Early the following day Ani and I set off together. Sonam had already gone on ahead with the soldiers and before he left had warned me to expect trouble once we walked out of the valleys. After crossing the windswept Doshong La pass, where the wreckage of an army helicopter lay scattered near skeletons of mules, we descended down the north side. A heavy sense of foreboding hung over us both. Our pace quickened. Ani's smile had faded; she no longer hummed her mantra.

Suddenly through the trees I caught sight of several soldiers waiting at the base of the forest trail. For three weeks there had been silence – no cars, no aeroplanes. There, expecting us, a dozen guards stood around an army truck. They threatened our party with their guns and fired rounds into the air, the sound ricocheting through the silent forest. Herded like animals, Ani and I clambered into the open lorry, holding on to each other for support. Her face crumpled, my stomach knotted in fear.

As the lorry grunted down the hill I turned back for one last glimpse of the valleys. But the hidden lands of Pemako had already disappeared and, like a curtain, the mist came down.

When we arrived at the barracks in the township of Pe, a Tibetan officer apologised for our rough treatment and offered us tea. I was sent to wait in a soldiers' dormitory. Hanging above three narrow beds were, bizarrely I thought, tan-coloured nylon pop socks with pairs of fluffy slippers beneath. I hadn't imagined Chinese soldiers would wear kitsch mules and slipped on a pair. They were a perfect fit. Moments later, a soldier marched in. When he saw me wearing the slippers, he growled, ordering me outside.

Our group was told to set up camp on the banks of the Tsangpo. Despite the army presence there was an atmosphere of euphoria – at all having survived the journey. The porters were paid and promptly bought beer, while the Westerners took advantage of the hot showers. Ani celebrated by putting on a heavy fleecy coat she had carried throughout the whole pilgrimage (to wear only at the end) and changing her socks. Rather than wear both pairs of new socks I'd given her, she'd worn only one and, giggling, revealed – an advanced case of trench foot – stinking mouldy feet.

Police in jeeps arrived from the town of Bayi. The PSB officer, a wiry Chinese man in his mid-thirties, with sallow features and skin drawn tightly over high cheekbones, was furious when he learned that our group had transgressed our permits. Soldiers were gathering by the river's edge, strident Chinese voices cutting through the evening air.

'What's happening?' I asked Sonam.

'Problems,' he said vaguely. 'Someone's died. They're dealing with the body.'

It transpired that the previous evening two Monpa cousins had become drunk. An altercation ensued when one accused the other of stealing his wife, which resulted in one man being fatally stabbed. The body was now being cut up by the dead man's relatives; then, as I watched, Chinese soldiers rowed out on the tranquil, steely-blue water ringed by imperious mountains to dispose of the corpse.

The arrival of the PSB officer triggered an explosive row between the army and police. The army officers argued that they 'discovered' us and so ought to take control of the case, confiscate all our film and take us to Lhasa. The police disagreed, saying it fell within the jurisdiction of Bayi and we should go there for interrogation. Both were competing for the hefty fines they knew they could extort. Baker and Sardar, for their part, were trying to prevent us being taken to Bayi, several hours away, concerned that we would fail to meet Ken Storm and the Gillenwaters who had crossed out of Pemako by a different route.

The following morning, a light drizzle falling, army officers were hollering at policemen outside the barracks. The PSB won and ordered us into the back of an open truck. We refused, insisting that we should travel in their vehicles. Our cameras were stripped and tossed onto the back seat of their jeeps. Meanwhile a scuffle broke out between Sonam and the porters, who complained that they'd been underpaid.

Turning to us, close to tears, Sonam implored, 'Please, please. Do what the police say. Get in the truck. Otherwise you make big trouble for me.'

Finally, together with some of the porters, all the Sherpas and Ani, we clambered into the truck. Hamid yelled abuse, Ani wept. One of the Sherpas vomited over the side. I crawled to the front and sat next to Ian, who offered me a codeine tablet to take the edge off the bone-rattling ride ahead.

We pulled into the military town of Bayi some hours later, and proceedings began immediately in the police station with the familiar plaque on the gate: 'Section of Alien and Entry-Exit Administration'. Tsering, the third officer in command who spoke reasonable English, told us he was to oversee the interrogation. Wearing a black trilby and slate-coloured suit one size too big, he looked like a fifties detective who'd stepped out of the set of *The Goodfellas*.

Between Ian, Hamid, Waltraut and I were a dozen bags and over 150 rolls of irreplaceable camera film. A Chinese officer and policewoman with thin-pursed lips started to search our belongings. Meanwhile next door Sonam was undergoing rigorous questioning: 'Why did you take these foreigners to the wrong place? Why did you break the permit?' Outside, the porters, Sherpas and Ani stood in the rain as the police rifled through the porters' wicker baskets. Then the police questioned Ani, who sat with her head bowed.

'I was scared,' she would tell me later. 'I have chicken heart.'

As the hours crawled by in the dingy waiting room, I felt as if I were playing a part in a black and white thriller, sinister and surreal in equal measure. We were treated civilly, yet made to feel like criminals. Thanks to an unspoken agreement between us, miraculously none of our films was confiscated (somehow we distracted the officer each time he came close to our stash) and merely handed over a couple of empty rolls. Only my copies of the *Tibet Handbook* and *Magic and Mystery in Tibet* were seized: both considered subversive reading.

When the Chinese policeman rifled through my bag he found my diaries and handed them to Tsering, who began to leaf through them, his eyes glinting. He leaned back and started to read out loud. 'It looks like the Americans are chasing the beautiful porter girls again.' Ian and Hamid looked at me. I blushed. Tsering laughed and, stumbling on a word, leaned across to Hamid to ask: 'What does this mean?'

Without thinking, I leapt at Tsering from the other side of the room and snatched my diary back.

'You can't read that. It's private.'

A hush fell. Tsering's eyebrows arched in surprise; roaring with laughter, he grabbed the journal back and continued reading. In an effort to calm down, I steadied my breath. Tsering eyed me for a moment, then offered me a cigarette.

'I've two types,' he said with a sly wink. 'And ladies like the long, thin type . . . '

With evening approaching and no incriminating evidence found, the police were becoming agitated. Tsering warned us not to make him angry. Then, abruptly, he tried a different tack, calling an end to the day's questioning.

'We continue tomorrow,' he barked. 'Now we go for dinner.'

Our entire party, together with Tsering and his wife, met at a Chinese restaurant close by. Nobody dared mention the subject of our group's arrest.

'America is heaven. I want to go there,' Tsering boomed, seated at the head. Puffing out his chest, he reached for a cigarette and then slowly surveyed the group around the table. For a moment eating stopped, only to resume faster than before. A feast was spread before us, dish after dish of oily Chinese food: exotic mushrooms, pig's trotters, fried tofu and scrawny chicken. The porters sat at the far end; the boys scoffed eagerly, the girls picked shyly. None of them spoke, too awestruck and baffled by the occasion.

'My favourite book,' continued Tsering in slightly American-accented English, 'is *Pride and Prejudice*. My favourite film, *The Godfather*. I want to see how the Americans do it. I want to come to New York.' He sucked hard on a cigarette. 'You can take me to New York?' he half asked, half threatened Baker, who spluttered into his soup.

'Sure you can come to America. Sure we can help you out.'

'I want to change some money,' Tsering went on. 'You change dollars at a good rate?'

'Mmm,' responded Ian hesitantly.

Tsering reclined, smiling, his middle-aged paunch spreading like warm dough over his waistline. His Tibetan wife tittered, pushing her food around the plate with chopsticks. Silence fell. A mist of fatty fumes enveloped the tiny restaurant, condensation running down the walls. Tibetan beggar children peered hungrily through the glass doors. Without warning Tsering rapped the table loudly with a spoon: a signal that the meal was over and the beggars with torn clothes and dirty faces, carrying bags for the slops, swarmed inside. In the sepulchral light the room had an air of a medieval banquet.

Outside we stepped back into the modern Chinese town. Poor imitation pagoda roofs towered over the Bayi skyscape. The Welcome Guesthouse, clad in blue glass, shone outlandishly under a bright street lamp. In a great show of friendliness we all shook hands with Tsering and his wife.

'See you at nine o'clock tomorrow morning at the police station,' he said, diving through the lurid pink curtains of a three-wheeled rickshaw.

My stomach churned with the mixture of greasy food and adrenalin. In the hotel foyer Ani, the porters and the Sherpas went to their cheaper rooms. We went to the 'premium' rooms with fresh rat shit on the pillow. Our passports were confiscated, our group was still under arrest. What had begun as a pilgrimage through a hidden, sacred land, ended with a bitter taste of what Tibetans live with on a daily basis, fifty years after occupation. I knew that whatever happened, we could leave. For Ani, this was home.

CHAPTER 8

Love in Lhasa

GETTING out of Bayi was hugely difficult. The day after the feast with Tsering, the Gillenwater brothers and Ken Storm, found us by coincidence at the Welcome Guesthouse. The entire group then spent another day of interrogation at the police station, catching occasional sight of a harried Sonam, each time a shade more ashen. As the guide had foreseen at the beginning of the trip, his travel agency paid the price: some 6,000 renminbi in fines, followed by a (real) Rolex watch for the head police officer.

Despite hours spent poring over Storm's video footage looking for incriminating evidence to backup their claims that we were spies for the American government, the PSB were disappointed – and rather perplexed – at reams of repetitive footage of dense forest and waterfalls. On their ridge scaling foray in the dense jungles, the three Americans had penetrated the 'five mile gap', and had come remarkably close to the legendary falls. After scrambling to the top of Mount Dorje Bragsen, said to be the wrathful protector who guards the inner gorge, they looked down and through clouds of spray saw a mighty waterfall, which they estimated to be around 100 feet high. Tightly squeezed by the sheer walls of the canyon, recalled Gil

Gillenwater: 'The entire river appeared as though it were being shot out of a giant fire hose.'

Finally, our party was allowed to make our way to the capital. We approached Lhasa from the east, and the Potala Palace was visible from several miles away lording over the city. A majestic gold turreted building thirteen storeys high with a thousand rooms, the central edifice is the colour of oxblood, the rest off-white. With the play of light and shadow it seemed as if it were merely tethered to the slopes of Mount Marpori and could float away like a vast chocolate meringue. Home to generations of Tibetan leaders, the Potala was once the seat of the Tibetan government. It is now a hollow museum, with monks as caretakers, sweeping the corridors and dimly lit chapels, which, for all their sumptuous treasures and jewel-encrusted icons, are gloomy and austere.

Ten minutes' walk from the palace is the Jokhang Temple, the real focus of Tibetan religious aspiration and a magnet for pilgrims. Situated at an altitude of 11,800 feet, the city is encircled by barren mountains with the Kyichu River forming a natural boundary to the south. There are two huge monasteries on the northern and western outskirts – Sera and Drepung respectively – and smaller temples dotted throughout the city. On the streets rural life collided with modernity as pedal rickshaws, a flock of sheep and honking Toyota land cruisers argy-bargied for space. Chinese girls in mini-skirts tottered past wizened pilgrims spinning prayer wheels.

Ani and I found a cheap hotel in the Tibetan quarter close to the Jokhang Temple and parted from the rest of the group. During those tense days in Bayi Ani retreated into herself, looking strained and anxious. In part it was because of the heavy-handed police presence; in part, her concerns that our party would be punished. She dismissed my fears that travelling with foreigners could endanger her. 'Drolma, I'm worried about you,' she insisted. 'They can take nothing from me. They can cause you problems.'

By the time we arrived in the capital, the shared experience of the pilgrimage through Pemako and the arrest had cut through the pleasantries of our friendship, paring us down to essentials that lay beyond language, culture and background. Invisible threads were being spun between us. Only much later would I realise how tight was the weave.

One morning Ani left the hotel early, and returned with a wide smile wearing a wine-red woollen *chuba* – the colour indicated it was her nun's attire – rather than the pink chequered tunic. Her socks, I noted, had also been changed. With my Chinese army plimsolls reeking of over-ripe Parmesan, my one pair of trousers beyond repair, I decided to go native and buy a *chuba*.

'*Nga-tso Barkhor trom la dro, dig gi re-peh? Dhi Boepa rey, Gyami ma-reh.* We'll go to the Barkhor market, OK? It's Tibetan, not Chinese,' she said, ambling down Yutok Lam to the square in front of the Jokhang Temple. Ani steered me through the throngs of colourful nomads, child beggars and awestruck tourists.

Encircling the Jokhang is the cobbled pedestrian street of the Barkhor market, sandwiched between old Tibetan houses with brightly coloured religious symbols painted on the eaves and the walled temple complex. The Barkhor is a microcosm of Tibetan life where religious practice has traditionally been combined with trading. Crammed with stalls, blankets spread out on the ground, there's a surfeit of kitsch trinkets, nails and hammers for sale; prayer flags and shrieking alarm clocks; Chinese tacky toys and 'cheeepie' gold fillings; and in the shadowy recesses, endangered animal skins are strung up – leopard, wild cat and snow-white mink.

The sound of hawkers fills the air: '*Gorma nga, gorma chu.* Five renminbi, ten renminbi.'

'Lookie. Lookie,' cried a strapping Khampa woman, nuggets of turquoise strung through her hair, as she thrust an inexpensive prayer wheel into my hand (made in Nepal, like most of the souvenirs). 'I make you happy price.'

On the left of the temple's thick wooden gates is a paved area where nomads and locals prostrate – a chorus of hands rising and falling to the ground, a whoosh and swoosh of clothes brushing over flagstones worn smooth from centuries of homage. Toddlers barely able to walk awkwardly put their palms together before tumbling forward. I could almost hear the creak of one old woman's knees as she bent down, her bare feet like hooves encrusted with decades of dirt.

'It's good for the whole body,' said Ani as I stared in curiosity. 'It's to the Buddha.'

(When a Tibetan pilgrim prostrates, touching forehead, throat and heart, they repeat a mantra to purify mind, speech and body, while visualising a deity. They believe that this generates merit not only for themselves, but all sentient beings.)

Ani guided me through to the stalls at the back of the Barkhor, where she examined the weight, cut and material of various *chubas* until she found some to her satisfaction. I chose a matt black wrap-around tunic with a pair of black lace-ups to match, two silky blouses (with no buttons, these are cropped with wide three-quarter-length sleeves), one lilac, the other cream, and a plastic lavender brooch to hold the outfit together. From there we cut through a labyrinth of narrow cobbled streets which spiral out from the temple to visit Ani's friend, another nun, called Pema. She lived in an old three-storey Tibetan building above a courtyard with a water pump in the centre, which was surrounded by women washing and gossiping, children playing. The flats had no running water, and communal toilets were downstairs, costing two jiao a time.

Inside Pema's rented home were two sparsely furnished rooms, a bedroom-cum-lounge, a kitchen and another area where she and Pasang, a man in his sixties, ran a small school. Ani and Pema insisted on dressing me in my *chuba*, smoothing out a ruck here, tucking in a bulge there, then deftly tightened the sash around the middle. Murmurs of approval indicated they were happy with the result.

'Wait, wait,' Ani commanded. 'Your hair.'

She foraged in the pouch-like front of her own *chuba* where she kept most of her worldly possessions – a fraying cloth purse, scriptures, her keys – and produced a battered black comb. Ignoring my winces, she coaxed it through the tangles.

When I was finally allowed to see myself in the mirror, I was astonished. It didn't look like me.

'*Drolma nying jepo du. Che-rang Boepa pumo digi re-peh? Inji mar-eh.* Drolma, you're beautiful. You're a Tibetan girl, aren't you? Not English.'

I wasn't sure who I was any more.

I was led into the sitting room, dominated as in every Tibetan household by an altar with statues and butter lamps. On one of the low sofas sat Pasang in his stiff burgundy outer robes. With a maroon hat covering his shaven head and thick square glasses, to all appearances Pasang looked like a monk and would sit cross-legged, reading Buddhist texts bound in burnt-ochre cloth. On the table next to him was a wooden bowl, the size of an open palm, with an ornate silver base for his butter tea and an empty jam jar of wooden quills. He motioned me to sit, and over biscuits and crispy sweet swirls of yak cheese, he pointed to his small transistor radio.

'Princess Diana,' he said. 'I hear she died. Very sorry. Such a good person.'

A few days later in a café, I met Tashi, the guide from the first red lily trip who began with the very same words, exclaiming, 'Your princess, so beautiful. Why she die so young?'

(The death of 'my princess' occurred when I was in the Pemako jungle. I wondered if I was one of the last British people to hear of it and was astounded by the number of Tibetans who expressed their genuine condolences.)

It was towards the end of the plant-hunting expedition, after the conversation with the old monk sitting on the woodpile, that Tashi began to open up to me, talking about his frustrations with life in Tibet and his previous life in India where he'd been sent by his father to be educated. Faced with the stark choice between a costly Chinese education in Tibet, where Chinese is the first language, or a traditional Tibetan education in exile, hundreds of children are sent away, many never to return. (Between 2,500 and 3,000 Tibetans still escape to India each year; over a third are under fourteen years old.)[1] After reccurring bad dreams about his father and on the advice of a lama, Tashi had returned to Lhasa to find his father dying.

Before I left Tibet, Tashi gave me an old bronze *melong* hanging on a red ribbon – a circular disc engraved with the twelve animals of the Tibetan zodiac – with a sour metal smell. Placing it around my neck, he said solemnly, 'This belonged to my father. Keep it close to your heart and say *Om Mani Padme Hung*. It will heal you.'

When I met Tashi again in the Snowlands Restaurant, he smiled brightly and gave my arm a hard squeeze. He was dressed in denim dungarees rolled down to the waist, a tweed jacket straining over broad shoulders, the sleeves of which were pulled up to reveal muscular forearms and teak-coloured skin like satin. Up close the whites of his eyes were tinged with yellow, his smell musky. Between us there were the stirrings of mutual attraction, flirting and playful banter.

Now I was unexpectedly back in Lhasa he offered to take me out and, when time from his tour guiding allowed, to accompany Ani and me sightseeing. Initially I was concerned that Ani would be offended. Not at all, instead she was happy that Tashi could translate when we were all together. Ani's friend Pema wanted her to stay and help with the school, so I changed to another hotel and during the day Ani and I would meet. For all their social shyness Tibetans are remarkably frank about sex. With one eyebrow raised, Ani brought her two index fingers together, giving a light, bawdy laugh.

'Drolma likes Tashi. Tashi likes Drolma. That's good. That's OK.'

Tashi swung open a door to a side of Lhasa I could never have seen with Ani, and for that I was grateful. After the Pemako journey I felt cracked wide open, my internal compass smashed. Somehow I'd lost sight of who I was; being with Ani both reinforced that dislocation and brought out a side of me I don't think I knew existed. With her I was an English girl dressed in a Tibetan *chuba*, displaying a genuine – if slightly forced – devoutness. In an effort to understand this woman so utterly different to myself, who lived in a world so refreshingly alien to mine, I would follow her lead.

I also had a real – and at times profoundly disquieting – sense of belonging. Sometimes I noticed Ani's eyes upon me, resting lightly. I knew that she was taking me all in and could see me just as I am, without masks or shields. When we sat in silence or visited monasteries there was no need to talk. Spending time with Ani was easy, uncomplicated and like being with my oldest friend.

For those three weeks in Lhasa I felt divided between wanting to be only with Ani and drawn to what I was familiar with – beer, cigarettes, dancing and late-night lovemaking – which I found in the wide-open arms of Tashi. At first I could contain this uneasy marriage, but it was not long before it became messy, before the fault-lines between Tashi and me began to show.

The majority of the Tibetans in Lhasa – literally 'place of the gods' – live in an ever-decreasing circle around the Barkhor. The rest of the city is being transformed by modern Chinese architecture into a growing sprawl of monochrome utilitarian apartments, factories and at least a dozen army barracks. In 1991 Deng Xiaoping's 'Spring Tide' movement began, hastening economic reform across China. A year later, Lhasa was formally designated a 'special economic zone' and Tibet 'opened up to the outside world', encouraging Chinese entrepreneurs and casual labourers to migrate west to seek their fortune.[2] Portrayed by the Beijing government as 'civilisers' sent to transform the 'backward' ethnic minorities, these first waves of Chinese cadres and immigrants were temporary residents.

In 1994, with the 'Third Work Forum on Tibet' and the growing market-directed economy, government policy began deliberately to lure Chinese businesses and unskilled workers with higher wages, concessions and benefits, effectively leading to a permanent population transfer to Tibet. As Lhasa and other urban centres became more amenable, even desirable, these industrious Chinese were staying, bringing their families or inter-marrying with Tibetans. From a trickle to a flood, this internal migration – considered the biggest threat to Tibet's future as a race – is leading to Tibetans becoming a minority in the Tibetan Autonomous Region.

In Lhasa alone, out of an urban population of around 200,000 (not including up to 50,000 migratory Chinese workers), Chinese outnumber Tibetans at least two to one. With little attempt to train Tibetans and fluent Chinese the prerequisite for any white-collar or official post, a widening gulf between rich and poor is creating an underclass of alienated and disenfranchised Tibetans (an estimated 80 to 90 per cent of Tibetans are illiterate). As one man summed it up, 'Tibetans have become second-class citizens in our own country.'

Groups of men loitered around the Barkhor, often raven-haired Khampas who passed time playing pool, eyeing up pretty girls, pissing in dark corners. A tea-house culture thrived for the 'No job, still busy' generation who spent hours, days in the 'If Café' discussing how different life would be, 'If I had a good wife . . . If I got rich . . . If the Dalai Lama came home'. This is where I would find Tashi and his friends, who had all returned from India and could find only seasonal work as tourist guides.

Watched like hawks by the authorities, who viewed anyone from India with suspicion – as a potential spy for the Tibetan government-in-exile, 'a splittist' who could fracture the Motherland – they bristled with rebellious bravado and reminded me of hot-headed Italians, sentimental, passionate and somewhat procrastinating. I knew I was something of a trophy to be shown off to Tashi's friends. Nonetheless I enjoyed their contagious, irreverent humour and their idealism, which fuelled my own urgency to live every second, to dream the impossible.

The tea houses, with their stone-flagged floors, wooden benches and blackened walls, were a Lhasa institution full of men in trilbies and dark suits. All day women carried huge teapots of sweet tea and, for a few pence would refill thimble-sized glasses and serve steamed meat *momos* (dumplings) with chilli on the side. The air crackled with laughter and debate.

One afternoon as I sat in a darkened tea house with Tashi and his friends, Tashi casually nodded towards a middle-aged Tibetan smoking a cigarette, whose eyes darted erratically around the room, never resting on one person for more than an instant. Under his breath, he said, 'Be careful what you say, Drolma. Don't speak too loud.' The man was a known police informer.

'Isn't it risky sitting here with me?' I ventured.

'What to do? This is Lhasa.' He gave a slight shrug. 'You must be careful. There are many Tibetans who cannot be trusted. We call it crooked mind.'

'There's that cute girl again, Dorje. She's looking your way,' said Dhondup, changing the subject. All heads turned towards two young Tibetan women who had sat down.

I tried to imagine sitting in a pub with friends back home knowing our conversation could be eavesdropped on, our movements monitored. How it would feel to live with the constant dread that at night the police could search the house without a warrant and, on the flimsiest pretext, drag people away for questioning. If a photo of the Dalai Lama was found, a fine of between 450 and 2,000 renminbi might be levied or the owner imprisoned, the family tainted. I wondered over time what that fear would do to my sanity, my soul and my friendships.

From 1990 onwards the Lhasa authorities had fine-tuned their policies of oppression with a combination of surveillance, neighbourhood committees and policing. Paranoia and fear were actively fomented among the general populace through a widespread, and officially funded, informer network. Throughout the capital there were police stations disguised as town houses, revolving security cameras and a bewildering number of security agencies.

After the Barkhor became the focus of pro-independent protest in the late eighties, the numbers of Barkhor police increased. Every few hundred feet were clusters of Tibetans, drinking green tea and playing cards, whose job was to keep an eye on everyone's movements and report anything suspicious. They could raise the alarm, calling upon re-inforcements from the heavily armed PAP (People's Armed Police) who careered around the city in jeeps beeping their horns loudly. Then there was the PSB who worked overtly and undercover. Intelligence was collated and blacklists drawn up by the State Security Bureau (SSB) who played a considerable, if covert, role in stamping out dissent. Finally, the People's Liberation Army – there are at least 300,000 troops stationed in Tibet – made frequent public displays, especially on sensitive anniversaries or when besuited Beijing dignitatories were on official visits to Lhasa.

Contrary to the popular perception that the perpetrators are always Chinese, I was beginning to realise that the reality was more Byzantine. Without the army of informers and spy monks, corrupt police officers and bent officials – all of whom are Tibetan – China could not con-solidate its power in Tibet. Photojournalist Steve Lehman puts it like this: 'The situation in Tibet is grey; the deeper one investigates the more complex it becomes. The Chinese have repressed the Tibetans, and the Tibetans have repressed each other . . . In order to survive, people make compromises. In Tibet, they call it "having two faces".'[3]

Or, in Tashi's words, 'A smiling face, a black heart.'

Ani was proud to show me her cultural heritage and during our regular outings she gave me a dizzying tour of Tibetan Buddhism. In chapel after chapel, holding her hand palm-up in a gesture of supplication, she would tell me the name of each deity – the compassionate, the wrathful, the wise. If I didn't understand the meaning behind the many-eyed Buddhas with scores of arms, I took inspiration from Ani's reverence. I followed like many uneducated Tibetans in blind faith.

One afternoon we went to Shoton, the Yoghurt Festival, at Drepung monastery on the city's outskirts. Large as a village, alleyways winding between monks' quarters and cavernous temples, the Geluk monastery was once home to 10,000 monks. Today there is a population of around 500. After a scrum of the faithful entered the main Assembly Hall, orchestrated by surly monks who looked like renegade gangsters wielding sticks to stop people getting crushed, Ani and I retired to the kitchens where cauldron-sized saucepans bubbled with *momos*, and monks in overalls carved yak with giant cleavers. A stooping monk offered us bowls of homemade *dri* yoghurt, tart and slimy to taste.

'Are you a *Khandro* [enlightened female teacher]?' he asked Ani, much to her wilting embarrassment. 'You seem like someone special.'

'*Min, min.* No, no,' she said, lowering her gaze. 'I'm only a nun.'

'*Ah ley.*' He nodded, looking her up and down thoughtfully. '*Cherang gom chen chik dra-bo duk.* You look like a great meditator.'

'*Min, min.* I'm not special,' she insisted, a blush rising.

He stared at her quizzically, ladling more creamy yoghurt into her bowl and then said simply, 'Would you like sugar?'

Running through the streets, both wearing *chubas*, invariably attracted attention – Tibetan smiles, Chinese scowls – and I started to feel anxious that being seen with me could cause Ani problems when I left Tibet. I could see that she was utterly selfless and when I repeatedly asked if it was safe, she always gave the same reply: 'Don't worry about me. It's OK. I'm more worried about you in case you get sick.'

Firmly linking arms, she would admonish me if my purse was obvious: '*Kumar dug.* There are thieves. You must be more careful.'

One afternoon we met up with Tashi at Pema's home. She was teaching a class of tiny, cheeky-looking children who sat on cushions on the stone floor, wood blocks on their laps.

'*Dri dang dri.* Write. Write,' Pema instructed.

After Pema had left her nunnery, for reasons I wasn't clear about, she offered to help Pasang with his school for poor Lhasa families. A former teacher at a private school, Pasang was passionate about trying to save the Tibetan language, which he feared faced extinction. Run on a shoestring, with a bucket as a toilet which Pema carried down two flights of stairs to empty, the dozen or so children repeated the Tibetan alphabet parrot-fashion. Pasang stood at the front of the class, painstakingly scratching the elegant swirling Tibetan script on a wooden board with a quill dipped in ink.

As we watched the children Tashi turned to me. 'My young niece and nephew know only Chinese. They even speak it at home to their mother, teasing me for my broken replies. I live with my old mother and look after my younger brother. Since my father died, I have to be like him. I don't like that, how you call. . . ' He stopped, searching for the word.

'Responsibility,' I suggested.

'Maybe.'

'Tashi,' I said, taking him aside. 'I need to talk to you about Ani. I'm worried she'll have problems if she's seen with me. I've heard nuns must be particularly careful, that terrible things can happen if they're sent to jail.'

He quietly translated my concerns to Ani. They shifted uncomfortably, and motioned me upstairs to the roof, where we sat down in a shady corner. 'It's true,' began Ani. 'If nuns are sent to prison they use electric shocks on them – everywhere, even down there.' She pointed towards my crotch.

'The nuns look all right outside,' continued Tashi, shaking his hands violently in front of his stomach. 'Inside they fry like cooked meat. Then when the prisoners get very ill, they're released. Their family takes them home so they don't die in prison.'

'Is this true, honestly?' I said, sickened.

'Yes, Drolma,' Ani whispered. 'This is true.'

'And nothing will happen to you because you're friends with me?'

'No.' She cupped her hand over mine.

'You'll go back to the nunnery when I leave?'

An unexpected shadow crossed her face. I was taken aback.

'I don't know. Last year there was a big problem at the nunnery. The Religious Affairs Bureau came and every day for three months we had to go to meetings twice a day to criticise the Dalai Lama. All the nuns said nothing. It was like a hunger strike except with silence.'

'Were you scared?'

'Yes, at first. Angry also. The officials told us, "Don't think that good karma will make you happy. You have to get a job, have a business, get married, that's what will make you happy."' She frowned. 'They told the local people that, "nuns are like pigs. They do nothing, they're lazy and live off lay people."' She paused for breath, giving Tashi time to translate.

'We were told that we have to sell our house within three years. If not the government will confiscate it. To encourage the nuns to de-robe they offered a special certificate to start a business but we wouldn't give in. At least not in the beginning.' She fell silent.

'In the end we had to denounce His Holiness the Dalai Lama and Buddhism. It was one of the worst emotions I've ever felt.' There was an audible intake of breath and her face contorted. 'It was so sad, so awful, really terrible. I had a pounding in my head and much anger against the Chinese.'

Ani looked down and fiddled with her bracelet. Tashi sat grim-faced.

'I both praised the Chinese and I criticised them. I said there was no liberation at all. I also denounced His Holiness, saying I didn't know who he was. By telling them both ways, they didn't do anything to me,' she continued. 'I sat at the front and was older than all the other nuns who stayed quiet, their heads bowed. I felt desperate to say something because I was tired of the political meetings.'

'What happened?'

'More than a hundred nuns were expelled, kicked out like dogs. I went back to my nomad village where I was given an identity card. I stayed with my brother's family. After one month I desperately wanted to leave; where I grew up wasn't home any more, it isn't a spiritual community.' A resilience rose in her voice.

'I just wanted to be able to go back to the mountain and do my practice without distraction. I tore up my identity card and returned to the nunnery. Then I tried to get registered in the local office, not of the nunnery but of the district. They said no.' She pursed her lips. 'So now I'm not registered anywhere, neither in my village nor at the nunnery. What can I do? I've nowhere else to go.'

'What happens if the authorities come again?'

'The head nun, she cares for us. We get warning if officials or Party people come. We take a few things – *tsampa*, a kettle to make tea – and stay away for one or two days up the mountains until they've gone.' She paused. 'Then I often go on pilgrimage.'

After I had left Tibet I learned that from 1986 onwards, when the TAR regional Communist Party began to address the Tibetans' demands for greater religious freedom, there was a steady increase in the numbers of monks and nuns, and an extensive rebuilding of monasteries, both of which the Chinese viewed as a step backwards in terms of ideology and modernisation of the region.[4]

A decade later a major 'patriotic education' campaign began with the aim of reversing this trend and transforming Tibet into an atheist country. Thousands of monks and nuns like Ani were expelled from their religious institutions across Greater Tibet (including Kham and Amdo) for defying the orders of the Chinese 'work teams' to denounce the Dalai Lama and acknowledge that Tibet is part of China. In order to stem the widespread despair and resistance, in 1998 the Dalai Lama told his compatriots: 'From now on if the Chinese authorities ever force you to denounce me, do that without any hesitation.'[5]

After our rooftop discussion, Ani seemed withdrawn. A couple of days later, when I met a French student learning Tibetan who offered to interpret for us in a tea house, I asked her what was wrong.

'I think I'll have to get a job,' Ani said uneasily.

'Doing what?'

'A housekeeper.' She hesitated. 'As I can't return to the nunnery, I thought of staying in Lhasa. I met this young couple who said they'd employ me to clean and keep their house in order.'

'Are they good people? What's their motivation for hiring you?' I was dubious. I knew it wouldn't be considered good karma by Tibetans to employ a nun to wash the family's underpants.

'I don't know. I don't want the job.' Her face reddened, a discernible sign of the agony incurred when her life's vocation had abruptly shuddered to a halt. 'I used to be a nomad girl, now I'm a nun. I've no work experience. When I see people washing dishes it's painful for me . . .' Her voice trailed off, but then, more resolutely, she said, 'I want to practise religion. That is more peaceful and meritorious work.'

Shouldering his way through the crowds outside the Jokhang, dusk stretching over the golden towers of the temple, Tashi cut a solid, tough-looking figure. He walked with a swagger, his chest puffed out. When we went out in the evenings, he insisted on taking my hand, telling me, 'You're safe with me, Drolma.' In the face of police patrols he only pulled me closer.

Like his friends, Tashi took a lot of risks. His elderly, bent mother feared for her son and his late-night ranting about the future of Tibet, afraid the neighbours would hear and report him to the authorities. Since the death of his father the family were fractured. At times, I think, he felt an outcast in his home town, pining for his easy life back in India: a 'good girlfriend, basketball, no responsibility'.

One night as the full moon rose, I sat with Tashi on the hotel roof. Only in Tibet have I seen the moon shine like the sun, the ice-white beams so bright that they cast a shadow over the land, plunging it into darkness.

'You should give to beggars, Drolma,' he said. 'I noticed today that you didn't. Don't be like other *injis* and ignore them, they need help. Money comes and goes like water. What's in here remains.' He rested his hand on my heart.

I enjoyed tracing the contours of Tashi's sleek, sculpted waist; running my fingers over his arched cheekbones and through his black glossy hair. I liked the way he untied my hair, curling it around my face and how he would tell me: 'I can see into your inner heart.' From both sides there was a hunger for love – and to be loved. I was attracted to his irrepressible vitality and raw sensuality, yet confused at the strength of my emotions for him. I could see he was kind, but there was a meanness in his mocha eyes that scared me, a vale of pain and resentment. I began to notice this kernel of bitterness in other Tibetans, a hunted look, eyes as hard as stone.

Beneath Tashi's cheerful veneer was a sense of powerlessness, fuelled by an ingrained feeling of inferiority – which I was beginning to see as a national trait, a symptom of the Chinese invasion – compounded by a mourning at the bleak future ahead. 'Man crack,' Tashi would say when someone was close to the edge.

In that Lhasa hotel room with the white patterned ceiling, lurid pink duvets and matching His and Her pillowcases I realised my high expectations of Tashi were unrealistic. Who was I kidding, if not myself? A hopeless romantic – as I can also be – this was a boy dressed in the muscled figure of a man, blunt about sex, yet making frequent coarse jokes (which I would come to know as a Tibetan pastime). His body was adorable, his manners in bed deplorable. Afterwards I was left feeling empty inside, my bearings even more skewed.

With my time in Tibet running out and my affair unravelling, I turned to Ani. I was unable to explain in my limited Tibetan what was happening between Tashi and me. Even if I could, I thought it would be wholly inappropriate to broach the subject of sex and men with a nun. I was worried that she would think less of me. After several ugly evenings where Tashi was too drunk to stand, I told him it was enough. He pleaded with me for one more chance. He told me he loved me, that he would wait for me when I left Tibet. I relented. We arranged to go out the following day.

After making a *kora* in the dark around the Jokhang Temple, Tashi and I met up with his friends – Pasang, Dhondup and Dorje. They were tour guides, all dressed eclectically with baseball caps worn backwards: one in a Bon Jovi T-shirt, drainpipe jeans and black leather cowboy boots; another in a shabby blazer, a red Marlboro packet peeping out of the breast pocket. We dipped into JJ's disco opposite the Potala where Chinese single-sex couples waltzed on an empty dance floor.

From there we strolled down narrow streets lined with rows of Chinese-run shacks selling alcohol and cigarettes, and walked by cheap Tibetan restaurants showing violent martial art films where the Chinese protagonist massacres all his opponents. To attract customers the soundtrack is blasted through a loudspeaker outside, filling the back alleys with a cacophony of killing. Back on the main drag, we passed dozens of Chinese hair salons which doubled as brothels – for the price of a perm you can get a fuck – along the banks of the Kyichu River where a new complex of shops and a casino were being constructed next to some luxury apartments.

Finally we reached Make Dreams disco. Outside, Han Chinese food stalls with roasted chestnuts and large woks of sugar-coated peanuts filled the air with treacly fumes. A graffiti-daubed stairwell led into a small nightclub. Tinbox techno and American rap blared, with bizarre lyrics: 'I want to fuck you', 'Don't be silly put a condom on your willy'. Chinese and Tibetans gyrated under flashing neon lights. I was invited up to the state-of-the-art DJ box overlooking the dance floor, replete with neatly made single beds. Beijing entrepreneurs and their babes sat chain-smoking and drinking green tea from jam jars. The girls crooned over the guys who spoke to me in friendly, incomprehensible English.

At the end of the night we bought some supplies – a plastic five-litre carton of *chang* for 10 renminbi and fried potatoes with chilli for 3 renminbi – and retired to the hotel. We drank and drank, friends coming and going throughout the night. The unhappy tourist guides with smiling faces threw aside their masks. Dhondup started acting like a demented teenager, hitting the wall, howling about the end of his relationship. Tashi swung between hysterical laughter and maudlin reminiscences about his life in India. The stories about foreign tourists poured out.

'Do you remember that time in the Potala when the Chinese guide was telling that German group all that Communist bullshit?' said Tashi. 'And the monk punched him on the nose.'

'Yeah, served him right.' Pasang guffawed.

'It's unfair that Chinese guides can get a licence for five years,' Tashi continued. 'We Tibetans cannot; only for one year. Then we have to do an exam.'

'Doesn't matter, we still get kicked out. How many Tibetan guides lost their licence last year?' snarled Pasang.

Dhondup hiccupped loudly, raising his can of Blue Ribbon beer.

'This Chinese beer, it killing Tibet.'

'Yak shit. Tibet killed a long time ago,' retorted Tashi.

'In 1959 Tibet had no guns, it was very easy to kill then,' said Dorje.

'Drolma, do you think we'll get freedom?' asked Dhondup. 'Do you think things will change in 1999? They say the ninth year of every decade is important for Tibet. In 1959 Dalai Lama left. In 1969 big revolt against Chinese. In 1979 I can't remember—'

'Dalai Lama allowed to send his ministers on a visit to Tibet,' Dorje butted in.

'Oh yes.' Dhondup belched. 'In 1989 demonstration in Lhasa.'

'Big revolution that one.' Tashi slapped his leg.

'Sssh, keep your voice down,' snapped Pasang.

'No problem. This hotel OK,' said Dhondup, his voice rising. 'In 1989 His Holiness gets Nobel Peace Prize also.'

'Shurrrup, will you,' growled Pasang.

'So maybe we get lucky in 1999,' Dhondup said, getting unsteadily to his feet. 'Why doesn't the West act? Why doesn't the UN help?'

'Or America?' said Dorje. 'President Clinton he like His Holiness, isn't it?'

A glass smashed. The *chang* spilled. Dhondup rushed outside to vomit.

'What about all the Buddhas, all the protectors?' I asked. 'Where are they when you need them most?'

Slumped against the wall, grinning wickedly, Tashi raised his glass: 'They're drunk like the rest of us.'

◎

The cries of Ani and Pema outside my window awoke me at 6.30 a.m. the following morning. It was still dark. With a pounding *chang* head I dressed, dragged a toothbrush around my furry mouth and rushed downstairs feeling seedy, just in time for Ani and me to catch the first bus to Ganden monastery. The bus was packed with unwashed yak-smeared Tibetans and, to avoid puking, I leaned my head out of the window.

Ani found my hangover amusing and teased, 'Too much *chang* no good for meditation. Better you come to monastery with me than go out with Tashi.'

I agreed. That would be the last night I would spend with Tashi, who had to leave Lhasa to take a tour group to Lake Namtso, bringing our scrambled affair to a natural close.

It took hours to reach Ganden *gompa*. Barely thirty miles east of Lhasa, the bus crawled, snaking up the steep hill from the Kyichu Valley. By the time we arrived my headache had subsided and I was ready for another grand Ani tour. Built in 1409 by the eminent teacher Tsongkhapa, the founder of the Geluk sect from which each Dalai Lama emanates, Ganden was named after the paradise of the Maitreya – the future Buddha. Much of it was razed, stone by stone, during the Cultural Revolution.

After years of painstaking work to restore it, the monks were close to completing their task and as we arrived were painting the final touches to the Assembly Hall in colours of searing brightness. Huge vats of paint littered the courtyard; every fresco, every statue, from the Buddha's pouting scarlet lips to the terrifying cobalt-blue demons, vibrated with newness.

Ani and I went to Tsongkhapa's throne room to receive some sort of blessing from an old monk who struck our head and back with the thirteenth Dalai Lama's shoes and the hat of the fourteenth Dalai Lama. In a cloistered courtyard we watched the Buddhist theatre of monks debating – a swirl of saffron and crimson, punctuated by shouts and hoots of laughter. The monks were arguing in pairs over arcane questions of Buddhist faith: Are you a person? What proof do you have? One stood asking questions, spinning his *mala* like a cowboy with a lasso and clapping his hands to make a point. His opponent sat cross-legged on the floor and if he gave the wrong answer, the standing monk would clap him over the head with his *mala*. At the gong for lunch, the monks tumbled out against the sun-bleached hillside. For such big men they ran with extraordinary lightness.

Ani took me on the pilgrim's circuit around the monastery. A current of joy whipped through us as we walked, ran and skipped along the zigzagging path, putting our fingers in the imprints left by enlightened masters, prostrating where they had, peering into the cave where Tsongkhapa meditated. At Vision Rock we hoped for an enlightened insight; at the charnel ground where they performed sky burials, expectant vultures hovered above.

In mid-afternoon the bus snailed back to Lhasa laden with sixty passengers and, on the roof, a small forest of juniper trees – the following day was a festival and extra juniper was required. We passed through villages in an ocean of golden fields. Women in pink and purple headscarves were using pitchforks to thresh grain and flat circular baskets to winnow the chaff. It was harvest time and donkeys staggered down the road like intoxicated haystacks.

Two days later, with my visa running out, I secured a place in a jeep travelling overland to Nepal. When Ani said goodbye she presented me with her personal *phurbu* – a pointed ritual dagger – and a silky white *khata* for a safe journey. I couldn't stop a loud sob escaping. In a rare moment of sadness, a single tear rolled down her cheek. I had no idea when, or if, I would see Ani again. There was no means of contacting her and even if I had an address, could not write Tibetan.

My lasting impression of Tibet was of sunrays electrifying the clouds that hovered like a tiara around Mount Everest. On the second day of the crossing, in the rose blush of dawn the mountain was lit up like an amethyst jewel of the sky. In front marched a platoon of Chinese soldiers, followed by a train of ragged Tibetan schoolchildren with haystack hair, besmirched faces and holes in their sweaters. They grinned, waving. At that moment the face of Everest was illuminated, before once again the peak slipped behind cloud.

CHAPTER 9

Life in Exile

Around 8,000 Tibetans were living in exile in the village above Dharamasala in India, a place of reversing buses and construction sites, Tibetan jewellery shops and travellers' hotels. Built in tiers up the steep hillside, with the snow-dusted peaks of the Dhauladhar range behind, the focal point was the temple next to where the Dalai Lama lived in a Raj-style bungalow. Encouraged by Ani's reverence for her exiled leader and her commitment to a life of pilgrimage, six months after our journey through Pemako I joined the throngs of pilgrims, Tibetan and Western, who attend the annual March teachings given by the Dalai Lama.

I expected to stay a couple of weeks. Several months later I'd forgone my return aeroplane ticket to London and was renting a cell-like room above the Library of Tibetan Works and Archives in lower McLeod Ganj. *Om Mani Padme Hung* droned from under my window as Tibetans made their daily *koras*. A mynah bird shrilled loudly while I memorised my verbs for the regular Tibetan lessons I was now taking from a tiny twinkle-eyed nun who had spent all her life in exile and lived at home, caring for her ageing mother.

Within a week of arriving in McLeod Ganj I met a fiery Spanish nun in her late fifties, profoundly disillusioned by the persistent inequality she faced as a woman within Tibetan Buddhism. Hearing her personal frustration, an aperture opened to the politicised arena of Western feminist nuns grappling with centuries of tradition. This in turn made me want to learn more about Ani's role within her own society.

It was clear that in Tibet the root of the inferiority of nuns stemmed back to the Buddha himself, who, reluctant to establish a female order, finally consented on condition that nuns took eight extra vows, intended to keep them under the control of the male monastic community. These included a vow that nuns must treat any monk, even a novice, as if he were their senior.

'It seems that the Buddha was torn between his cultural conditioning and the Hindu social system. . . and his conviction that women were as capable as men of attaining enlightenment,' writes Tsultrim Allione in *Women of Wisdom*. By choosing to be a nun, they 'were no longer chattels of their fathers and husbands', yet could never attain equal status as a monk.[1]

A study by Jan Willis reveals that there is not 'a single reference to the earliest ordination of Tibetan nuns'. Prior to 1959, Willis goes on, the estimated population of Tibet was between 4.5 and 6 million, with 18 per cent as monks and 2 per cent as nuns – nine monks for every one nun.[2] Frequently relegated to smaller nunneries, nuns remained uneducated, often performing basic rituals or prayers for the local community, or, worse, working in the kitchens serving the monks. In the words of Nancy Falk, the institutional structure 'offered women admirable opportunities for spiritual and intellectual growth, but not for the institutional and scholarly leadership that such growth should have fitted them to assume'.[3]

Traditionally there were many different groups of nuns in Tibet: those who stayed in the nunnery and studied, others who pursued a life of pilgrimage, while some stayed at home with their family. In spite of the discrimination vis-à-vis the monks, there was some flexibility for nuns to choose their own religious practice to suit their particular needs and aspirations. However, without proper spiritual instruction in the nunneries, they were consistently disadvantaged and so, like Ani, 'many Tibetan women seriously pursuing the spiritual path chose to live the life of hermits or wandering *yoginis*,' continues Tsultrim Allione. 'Women under these circumstances were very free: they formed friendships with other pilgrims and stayed as long as they liked in places they found conducive to meditation, supporting themselves through begging.'[4]

Orgyan Chokyi, a Tibetan Buddhist nun and hermit who lived from 1625 to 1729 in Dolpo, in the Himalayas of western Nepal, writes Kurtis Schaeffer, 'was forbidden to write her life by her lama because of her gender. . . She might be qualified to live the life of a hermitess, but she was not authorised to write the Life of a Hermitess.' There's a consistent theme in Tibetan literature, continues Schaeffer, that women's life stories are 'either entirely or in part owed to the efforts of male disciples or descendants'. Chokyi broke with this by penning her own autobiography. It serves as a fascinating account of a woman from humble origins – like Ani she'd grown up an animal herder – whose dogged determination to leave the constraints of communal life, where she was put to work in the monastic kitchen, brought her the freedom of spirit she craved.[5]

Even though Orgyan Chokyi and Ani have followed different trajectories and live four centuries apart, there are some similarities. Not least the constraints of being a woman in the patriarchal Tibetan Buddhist world. When Ani recalled some of the caves she'd inhabited, she echoed Chokyi's delight with her own rocky retreat. 'What a joyous place,' writes Chokyi. 'Whatever I ponder here, my spiritual experience is elevated . . . signs of joy for this beggar, myself.' She continues, 'Self-serving, self-empowered, I have escaped people. I have attained autonomy.'[6] For both, the cave represents solitude and independence. For both it is where they come a step closer to their highest aspiration: to become a Bodhisattva, devoted to achieving enlightenment for the sake of all beings.

Scouring the Library of Tibetan Works and Archives for more accounts of nuns like Ani who follow a tradition of itinerant female practitioners, I was struck by the paucity of literature on women in Tibet. The number of biographies on Tibetan Buddhist masters runs into the hundreds, while those on female mystics were precious few. The little that has been written does not mean, of course, that such women did not exist, rather that their lives were not considered worth writing about. With no female Dalai Lamas, fewer goddesses and heroines to aspire to, it would seem the nuns in Tibet – uncelebrated, unsung – had to look within for motivation.

Meeting Ani had undoubtedly personalised Tibet for me in ways I had not anticipated when I was there. I began to take the Tibetan cause and its struggle for freedom as if it were my own. Of course, I was not alone. I joined the throngs of other Tibet-heads – hippies and housewives, Hollywood celebrities and human rights activists. Every year the Buddhist beatniks, together with thousands of Tibetans, congregate in the courtyard in front of the Dalai Lama's temple. On the first day of the teachings studying the *Lam Rim* – 'The Stages on the Path to Enlightenment' – the Tibetan leader took his place on a gilt-edged throne. Rocking gently from side to side, Tenzin Gyatso gave the impression of a benign headmaster surveying his flock.

In the crowd were dreadlocks, baldheads and braids. A glamorous and rather dotty blonde French woman dressed in maroon was trying to pass herself off as a monk – she insisted she was some reincarnated master. *Bona fide* lamas listened and dozed, roused periodically by the army of butter tea-pourers – young monks carrying giant battered teapots. I tried to attend the teachings most days, taking my place towards the back among the Westerners, where the English translation of the Dalai Lama's discourse was relayed. Occasionally scuffles broke out as pious *injis* fought for the best view of the Tibetan leader. 'If you don't get out of my place, arsehole,' yelled a wild-eyed Canadian to an American, 'I'll throw you over the fucking rail.'

'Buddhism is a science of mind not a religion. Respect the teachings of Buddha, but use your own logic to understand the transformation of mind,' began the Dalai Lama. 'The Buddhist point of view does not accept a creator or a God. Buddhism is a result of action, the cause of action is the mind, but there is no beginning for this...'

A ripple ran through the crowd when Hollywood actor Richard Gere arrived, wearing dark glasses and black jeans, and tried to slide unobtrusively into his seat.

When I interviewed Gere a week later I was surprised at how seriously he took himself. I asked if Hollywood and films like *Kundun* directed by Martin Scorsese, and *Seven Years in Tibet* starring Brad Pitt had merely turned Buddhism into a fad.

'It's very good for Tibetan Buddhism,' Gere maintained, holding my gaze. 'It's OK if people just follow it for a few years, that's their karmic connection. People who come here are very serious meditators who want to understand the nature of the mind. They're attracted because they hope to find more happiness, to realise their hopes and dreams. People are searching for more answers and Buddha offers that.'

With each passing day, the atmosphere in 'Little Lhasa', as the town was affectionately known, became one of expectant bliss. I often found myself drowning among the reeds of Buddhist doctrine, terrified of falling into one of the many hells – which sounded remarkably Catholic, reminiscent of Dante's *Inferno* – that the Dalai Lama went to great lengths to describe. There was hungry ghost hell, crushing hell and howling hell; black line hell and extremely hot hell. The purpose, he said, on contemplating the hells and the body being blistered, burned and 'boiled alive like frying fish', was 'to cultivate intense practice through fear of suffering'.

While I sat there among the crowd, my mind would drift back to Tibet, wandering with Ani through the giant Assembly Hall at Drepung monastery, bowing underneath the shelves of Buddhist scriptures containing a lineage of teachings and transmission that dated back 2,500 years. I hadn't realised what discipline was required, what diligence to master these texts. The basics, I was told, included the Buddhist saint Nagarjuna's *Mulamadhyamakakarika: The Fundamental Wisdom of the Middle Way* and Shantideva's *The Way of the Bodhisattva.* Both of which were hieroglyphics to me. This was the hard graft that Ani did every day in her early twenties, after she was taught to read and write to a basic level by an old nun. Ani described reading the scriptures as 'like a child attending school, at first difficult, with time and practice easier'. She made it all sound so easy.

Back in the square at the Dalai Lama's teachings, the sun beating down, boredom would set in among the crowd; the Westerners tittered with uneasy laughter at the gruesome hells and the umpteen negative defilements and obscurations if we failed to be a good Buddhist.

'Therefore identify causes and conditions of suffering and the root cause of cyclic existence,' droned the Dalai Lama, then chuckled at the preposterous notion that, 'When I give teachings as a lama sometimes people think of me as a Buddha. I know that I'm not a Buddha. I'm just a simple Buddhist monk.'

Aware of the scrutiny he faced by his 'Western friends interested in female rights', he admitted that, 'Buddhism is a male-dominated teaching and more respect is given to the male *sangha* [community] than female and that the Tibetan word for woman literally means "inferior birth".' But then, quickly, he added, 'This is in terms of strength, not intelligence. In Tantric practice, women practitioners are seen as higher. When we talk of liberation we have to have the help of women.'

❧

A few doors down from my cell-like room, which smelled of mildew and paint, lived a twenty-something Tibetan called Tenzin (his mother couldn't remember the year of his birth). When he learned I'd recently returned from Lhasa, his birthplace, he was eager to hear any news. Dressed in baggy jeans, with long black hair roughly pulled into a ponytail framing a broad strong brow, a *mala* around one wrist and a battered satchel hanging carelessly off a shoulder, Tenzin gave the impression of a happy-go-lucky student. He was always learning something – Japanese vocabulary, Buddhist philosophy – charming the foreigners with his quick wit, his speech marked by a haphazard flow of American and English slang. 'Get us in a pickles' was a typical phrase. A larger-than-life and somewhat unpredictable figure, his raucous, raspy 'Ha-ha-ha' laughter was the sort that would turn heads in the two-street Himalayan town, which, for now, he called home.

When Tenzin wasn't with his girlfriend or helping an old Kushu, a monk whom he treated as a surrogate grandfather (Tenzin's own had been a defining influence in his life), he would tell me about growing up in Lhasa. It sounded a somewhat dysfunctional home life: his mother had four husbands consecutively, at one point abandoning him at around twelve years old for six months over winter when she and his stepfather had to go to China for urgent business. Tenzin became 'almost like a beggar, getting food from the garbage' and sleeping rough around the Barkhor, in the disused *sangs*, cone-shaped altars. This experience, coupled with witnessing the wave of bloody pro-independent demonstrations in Lhasa in 1989, had given him a surliness, and hidden beneath the bonhomie was a smouldering anger.

After 'hearing the riot' he said, 'when the Chinese were beating and shooting Tibetans; people carrying wounded nuns and monks', he felt ashamed. 'I didn't know anything about our history. At school we were only taught about the Great Motherland and Great Liberation. Before the demonstrations I thought that the Chinese soldiers were wonderful. When I saw them killing my own people, I thought they were so ruthless and cruel.' Now in exile, Tenzin was determined to find out the truth of what happened in Tibet and educate others, both Tibetans and Westerners.

One morning, there was a loud knock on my door.

'Drolma. Get up,' ordered Tenzin. 'Hurry. The oracle's going into trance.'

'What?' I said grumpily. 'It's too early. I'll come later.'

'No, you'll miss it. Get up. You have to be there now to join the queues.'

Fifteen minutes later, Tenzin and I were in front of the Nechung monastery, in the middle of a surging crowd of Tibetans clutching *khatas*, all trying to be the first in line to receive a blessed red ribbon.

There are two official Tibetan oracles, Nechung and Gadong, called upon to illuminate earthly matters, acting as a bridge between the tangible world of politics and the invisible realms of spirit. For centuries the Tibetan government has consulted both on affairs of state. In 1959 when the Dalai Lama escaped into exile, it was the former incarnation of the Nechung oracle who divined the day and the route he should take to avoid capture by the Chinese soldiers when fleeing Lhasa.

Every year at Losar and when called upon by the Tibetan government-in-exile, the Abbot of Nechung monastery, who traditionally takes on the role of the medium – *kuten* – goes into trance. For days beforehand he must purify both mind and body, in order, it is said, for the protector deity Dorje Drakden to take possession and lucidly impart his message. The current abbot, Venerable Thupten Ngodup, would describe the experience of possession in one interview as like '"a higher awareness that speaks through me. As it comes it is like an electric current, and after that I feel nothing." Once it is over, Ngodup feels "ill for hours, tired and vomiting" with "great pain" in his arms "where spirit comes".' [7]

On that early morning, the transfiguration from monk to man possessed had happened behind closed doors with only a privileged few – Richard Gere among them – allowed to watch. The *kuten* was then carried by his monk attendants to a throne; on his chest was a mirror, his head rocked backwards and forwards, weighed down by a huge headdress-cum-helmet, and a thin film of perspiration covered his bulging face. As I tried to get close, the *kuten* staggered to his feet, threw a handful of orange barley seeds into the crowd and expelled a piercing scream. Cymbals crashed and thunder rolled in the distance. Tibetans fell upon the barley grains like hungry wolves. When I found Tenzin again a few minutes later, he was holding two ribbons.

'You *injis* are too slow. You have to do it Tibetan way,' he said, handing me the scrap of red cloth. 'Let's try the luck with Gadong oracle, you can get a blessing.'

Gadong is like the number two, the deputy oracle, and his smaller residence was below the grand Nechung monastery. There were fewer people waiting on the grassy lawn as Tenzin and I picked our way to the front of the queue. When the doors opened, with drums beating and long horns trumpeting his arrival, we all rushed forward. The masked Gadong *kuten*, said to be possessed by Shinjachen, a wrathful spirit, sat swaying in trance, the whites of his eyes showing, his open mouth askew, groans tumbling out.

'Now,' said Tenzin.

'What do I do?' I panicked.

'Offer the *khata* and money to the monks. Just don't touch him.'

Edging forwards, I was pushed from behind. Falling at Gadong's feet I brushed his knee with my right arm. As if recoiling from an electric shock, I was thrown backwards, dropping the *khata* and money before the weight of the crowd squeezed me out onto the grass.

I slowly walked away, my arm trembling.

'You OK, Drolma?' asked Tenzin with concern. 'What happened? I saw you falling back.'

'I touched Gadong and now my arm' – I flinched – 'really hurts.'

He looked at me strangely. 'It's a blessing. He's removed karmic obstacles from your body.'

An hour later I had a slight temperature and my entire right arm up to my shoulder was throbbing. I eschewed another day sitting cross-legged at the teachings and started to walk up to the Dhauladhar massif above McLeod Ganj, clutching my notebook and pen. The sun was shining but dark clouds rolling in from the east suggested a storm brewing. I started to feel lighter. It was a relief to take a break from the small town which could be stifling.

At the base of a waterfall I sat on a rock warmed by the sun and started to write reams of strange-sounding poetry about Ani, past lives in

Tibet, the yogi-saint Milarepa. When huge raindrops fell, I retreated to a *chai* stall with a tin roof and continued to write with the rain beating down, trying to flush out this wildness inside, like an electric current that pulsated through my arm. I wrote whatever came through. It was unstoppable. I had no explanation for any of this and after several days of relentless outpouring of words felt exhausted and more confused about my relationship with Ani and Tibet. I was left wondering if what I had experienced in Pemako – how thin the veil between the worlds, the visible and the invisible could be – had unalterably shifted my perception and where this journey would take me next.

Ani had become an invisible presence in my life. When I made an offering of butter lamps at the Dalai Lama's temple I would imagine doing so on her behalf. When I visited the Tibetan Nuns Project and the half-built Dolma Ling nunnery, where nuns stood in lines passing rocks to one another, I recalled how a decade before Ani had done the same to rebuild her own nunnery ransacked during the Cultural Revolution.

On visiting the Gu Chu Sum offices for political prisoners – among them, nuns who had been tortured – I remembered the conversation Ani and I had on the roof of the schoolroom in Lhasa. When I read the account by one imprisoned nun, Gyaltsen Choetso from Gari nunnery, I felt the same icy, sick hollow in the pit of my gut. I recalled the reassuring feeling of Ani's hand cupping mine. Choetso describes how after being stripped naked, 'The guards who did the torturing were women, some Tibetan, some Chinese. They would say, "Tibetan independence is a dream, it will never come. You are disturbing the society with these demonstrations. If you want independence, here, here is your independence!" Then they used electric batons on every part of our body . . . [including] our private parts.'[8]

I learned more about the Kagyu lineage to which Ani was attached. Founded in the tenth century by Tilopa, a Brahmin priest who abandoned monastic life in India, Tilopa was said to be directly empowered by Vajradhara Buddha – Dorje Chang in Tibetan – passing this numinous transmission and empowerment to his disciple, an Indian scholar-mystic called Naropa. In turn Naropa became the master of Marpa who translated the Buddhist teachings into Tibetan, imparting them to a handful of students, among them Tibet's most revered saint, Milarepa.

Milarepa's biography is the stuff of the Grimm brothers, except that Jetsun Milarepa was a man who in the eleventh century is said to have achieved enlightenment in a single lifetime, transforming himself from a powerful sorcerer to an illumined master. On a prediction of the Buddha, Milarepa travelled to Mount Kailash in far western Tibet, and in a cave turned a shade of green from his spartan diet of nettles and *tsampa*. I began to dream of visiting this perfectly symmetrical mountain, Asia's holiest and one of the earth's final frontiers, with Ani at my side.

As I strolled through the narrow streets of McLeod Ganj, engulfed by the smell of open sewers, rotting fruit and Indian incense, I tried to imagine Ani there with me, wondering how she would cope with the heat and *dahl bhat* for every meal. I guessed it was her secret wish – like every Tibetan – to see the Dalai Lama once in her lifetime. Each year approximately 2,500 refugees make the dangerous crossing over the Himalayas, and many find life in exile far from the utopia they had imagined. You could spot a new arrival immediately. They congregated in groups, looking dazed, their cheeks raw from wind and sun exposure, their clothes – often the only set they had brought – ripped and dirty, their skin still smelling of yak. For some, fleeing Tibet would take a few weeks, for others months. Some never made it. Every year the frozen bodies of refugees were found: the death toll has never been counted. The bitter twist is that once the Tibetans have fulfilled their pilgrimage and received a blessing from the Dalai Lama, he encourages them to return.

Many of the second- or third-generation Tibetans born into exile shunned the 'newcomers'. When I asked why, they would make the excuse that they had 'a different mentality' or were 'primitive, backward and violent'. The irony that these were the same words used by the Chinese about Tibetans in Tibet didn't escape me. One Tibetan shopkeeper admitted his confusion: 'My father was a monk. If the occupation had never happened, I wouldn't be alive today.'

There were also deep-seated and legitimate fears that new arrivals could be spies for the Chinese government (indeed the following year, Legchog, Chairman of TAR, would announce that 'splittist activities at home and abroad' were being monitored, indicating that Tibetans in exile, most likely in Dharamasala, were also under scrutiny).[9] In such a small town, gossip thrived and rumours acquired a particular currency. In spite of the tolerance espoused by the Dalai Lama it was easy to get swept up in the tide of anti-Chinese rhetoric, peddled by the locals and the government-in-exile alike.

It dawned on me that inside Tibet, gradually and irrevocably Tibetans are becoming Sini-cised, while in exile they are stateless, widely influenced by Western culture. In Dharamasala I met older Tibetans who still had a suitcase packed, ready to go home when, they told me, 'Tibet becomes free'. For the majority, faith in their leader, considered the patron deity of Tibet – the soul of a broken-hearted nation – gave them hope in a hopeless situation.

One of the few Tibetans willing to criticise the Dalai Lama openly was controversial scholar and playwright Jamyang Norbu, a rangy man with a curling moustache. Over beer and bowls of chips in Hotel Tibet, Norbu would hold court among a small group of young Tibetans all born in exile, urging them not to be apathetic, not to surrender. Norbu blamed the Dalai Lama for 'constantly changing' his views and abandoning the demand for independence in favour of the watered-down demands for self-autonomy. He declared, 'The struggle for Tibet's independence is not just an issue of territory or nationalism but has a more universal and moral dimension. In the final reckoning it's a fight for justice and truth.'

Early one evening in an empty classroom, Jamyang Norbu gave a talk on the history of the Tibetan freedom struggle in which he was personally involved. In 1971, as a young man, Norbu had run away from home to join the last of some 3,000 Tibetan rebels, conducting raids and ambushes on Chinese soldiers from a base in Mustang in Nepal. This secret guerrilla war had begun in the mid-fifties, after the Tibetan government requested help from the US who agreed to train Tibetans and supply arms. At the height of the Cold War, the Americans pursued this policy for as long as it served their purpose of destabilising China. In 1969, abruptly, all CIA support was severed. It was to be a further four years before the Mustang guerrilla base closed, under pressure from the Nepalese and on the request of the Dalai Lama. Rather than surrender, some rebels slit their throats.

'I'm not embarrassed to say I just wanted to shoot a Chinese,' said Norbu. 'To be a good Dharma [Buddhist] practitioner you have to have that edge, the warrior attitude, you have to have the balls to screw it all,' he preached, warming to his theme. The atmosphere in the classroom became electric with bristling testosterone, pride and anger.

'Tibetans are putting on this New Age image – as a peaceful and loving culture – but they must face up to history. A small group of people took on the largest nation in the world and should be proud of that. I don't believe in being militarist but in defending oneself. The only way to keep one's manhood and destiny is to take control of them. Now there's more alcoholism and wife beating in society.' He scrutinised his audience, his brow furrowed. 'It's better to fight than to disintegrate. Violence is not the only way, but it is a way.'

The non-violence espoused by the Dalai Lama had earned him the 1989 Nobel Peace Prize, and yet these days, when a freedom struggle is more synonymous with violence than dialogue, he seemed to find himself in an insoluble predicament. That spring of 1998 was a turbulent time in the exiled Tibetan community. In central New Delhi, six Tibetans staged an 'unto death hunger strike', calling on the United Nations to debate Tibetan independence. When scores of Indian police broke up the protest on the forty-ninth day, a sixty-year-old Tibetan, Thubten Ngodup, doused himself in kerosene and struck a match. The image of a human fireball caught on film shouting, '*Boepa Rangzen!* Free Tibet! Victory for Tibet!' briefly made headlines worldwide.

Two days later the quietly spoken Ngodup died from 90 per cent burns and overnight became a martyr to the cause. In the Dalai Lama's statement he said, 'For many years I have been able to persuade the Tibetan people to eschew violence in our freedom struggle. Today it is clear that a sense of frustration and urgency is building up among many Tibetans... This frustration stems from the fact that the Tibetan people, with their unique cultural heritage, are being gradually wiped out from the face of the earth. This is a tragedy for the whole world.'

A few weeks later, after many months of waiting – and twenty-four hours before my Indian visa was due to expire and I would return to England – I was granted an interview with the Dalai Lama. The high fence and patrolling guards that surround his property give the impression that you are about to enter a fortress rather than the palace of a living Buddha, believed to be the incarnation of Avalokiteshvara, the Bodhisattva of Compassion. Inside the fence the fourteenth Dalai Lama's bungalow was encircled by a garden oasis teeming with birds.

Wearing a magenta *chuba* and carrying a bundle of *thangkhas* (religious paintings) and my *mala* to be blessed, I waited with some apprehension in a room decorated with scores of awards and medals, among them the 1989 Nobel Peace Prize. Aside from the veneration he inspires among Tibetans, who instinctively bow when they hear his name, their eyes often filling with tears, the exiled leader is widely regarded as one of the living moral authorities on the planet.

On meeting the Dalai Lama I was taken aback by his sturdy, muscular appearance. A rosary was draped around one wrist, a chunky watch on the other and when I went to offer him the customary *khata* he waved a hand and was quick to get down to business. I noticed his lips were shaped in a perfect arc, his pearly skin remarkably smooth and unblemished for a sixty-three-year-old. Behind the square spectacles his eyes were bright and his high-pitched voice unmistakable, his speech frequently interspersed with Tibetan phrases and loud, rolling 'Rwwwaaaggghs', meaning 'isn't it' in Tibetan.

Sitting squarely on the sofa, there was a gravity to his manner, a seriousness that I had not expected. I put it down to the recent troubling events. I asked what alternatives he could suggest to those Tibetans increasingly frustrated and losing patience.

'I want to learn actually, I want to know the alternatives. I don't know.' He gave a short laugh, as much from habit as humour. 'I myself am in a dilemma. The government response – the Middle Approach – has failed. . . When I went to see that burned one [Ngodup] I told him, "You must not keep some sort of negative feeling or have any hatred towards Chinese. You should keep positive emotion towards Chinese. Our struggle is not Tibetan victory, Chinese defeat. No, it is mutual benefit, mutual victory."' He paused, his voice softening. 'Later I was very happy when I was told that his mood, his motivation, his attitude over the next few hours [before he died] goes very smoothly.'

When the Dalai Lama floundered for an English word his translator would butt in, and a minder stood close by, glancing down at his watch to ensure I did not go over my allotted forty-five minutes. As he talked, gesticulating wildly, he would jab his finger towards me to make a point. The conversation ranged from compassion – no, Tibetans are not more innately compassionate than the rest of us, 'although Buddhist culture may be and Tibetans from the Land of Snows have a special connection with Avalokiteshvara' – to the karmic reasons behind the Chinese invasion.

'The last few generations of Tibetans made great mistakes,' the Dalai Lama admitted. 'They isolated themselves completely and ignored what was really happening in the outside world. So, due to negligence, today's tragic situation happened.'

'Are you still optimistic about Tibet's future?'

'If you look at what happens in Tibet . . . there are many events which are causing anxiety or frustration. But from the wider perspective there are positive signs. So short-term things are very bad. Time is running out. For long term, China is changing and there's real hope.'

When I came to my question about the value of pilgrimage in modern society, he gave a somewhat startling reply. He agreed that pilgrims can get the blessing from places where those 'of high spiritual motivation' have resided. 'If someone goes as half-tourist, half-pilgrimage, half-picnic and they want to go, very good. You get benefit. But if you ask, is it necessary? then the answer is no.'

To illustrate his point, the Dalai Lama told me a story about a disciple of a Kagyu lama who approached his teacher, to tell him that he intended to go on pilgrimage to Bodh Gaya in India. His lama told him that 'your own heart is Bodhgaya. So better to stay here.' At this the Dalai Lama leaned back and gave a delighted chuckle.

Not certain what to make of his response, I recalled a phrase I had read in Jennifer Westwood's *Sacred Journeys*: that 'pilgrimage leads nowhere and yet in the act of going the old life is left behind and the pilgrim returns renewed.'[10] I resolved to consider this notion that perhaps there comes a time when there is no need to go anywhere: the search begins and ends in one's own heart.

Occasionally the Dalai Lama would stop mid-flow and lean forward, holding my gaze. I had a sense he was looking directly into me. For all his earthy solidity, there was a singular lightness to his manner. He radiated an ineffable warmth, a generosity of spirit that filled the room. With my time drawing to a close, I asked a final question: his personal definition of freedom.

'On March 17th I escaped from Lhasa and the next day I reached southern Tibet. It was only then we could openly criticise the Chinese. Until then, very difficult to express.' He gave a belly-aching laugh. 'That was the first time of appreciation of freedom of speech. So although refugee life, but complete freedom.' He paused, thinking about this. 'Freedom of thought, freedom of expression. That I love.'

I reflected that, by being an itinerant nun inside Tibet, Ani's freedom
to practise her vocation of pilgrimage from place to place, as moved by
her spirit, was circumscribed and although she had freedom of thought,
her freedom of expression – like that of all Tibetans – was severely
curtailed. Yet at least she was able to live inside her own country, the
birthplace of her religion with all its rich symbolism and heritage:
something that her many compatriots living in exile were unable to do,
and mourned.

CHAPTER 10

Lhasa Uprising

LESS than a year later, I was back in Tibet. I arrived in Lhasa a few days before the fortieth anniversary of Tibetan Uprising Day, 10 March 1999 – one of the most significant and politically sensitive dates for years – on a clandestine filming assignment. Once the job was done I hoped to find Ani. (I intentionally kept any of my journalist pursuits separate from my friendship with Ani so as not to implicate her in any way. She's never been aware of that side of my time in Tibet.)

For months I had begun to pine for Ani, to dream of her. I asked myself over and over, was it Ani that I really missed, or what she had come to symbolise in my mind – an independent woman in pursuit of perfection, whose life was devoted unswervingly to enlightenment, 'if not this life, then next life'. I suspected it was both and had returned to find out.

After the months spent in Dharamasala – inspired by the impassioned rhetoric of Jamyang Norbu, the charismatic compassion of the Dalai Lama whose presence had remained with me like an inner glow – I continued working for the Tibetan cause back in England. With the refrain still singing – 'things change every ninth year for Tibet' – I think that year I believed anything was possible.

In Lhasa a cameraman and 'runner' accompanied me. We had only a few days to film general street scenes before the two men would fly to Hong Kong to put a news story together, in time for 10 March. I was to stay behind and bear witness if anything happened on the day of the anniversary. I was both apprehensive and elated to be back in the capital, which since 1997 had grown like a squid, its tentacles spreading across the valley. More shops, more businesses; hordes of smart Chinese businessmen with mobiles and a new fleet of green and white taxis.

On the day after arriving we climbed up behind Sera monastery to take an aerial shot of the city and hoped we could use the vantage point to film, at a safe distance, the walled compound of Drapchi Prison (now known as Tibet Autonomous Region Prison) where an estimated 300 to 350 political prisoners were held. During flag-raising ceremonies on 1 and 4 May the previous year there had been a significant protest and, in the weeks after, inmates were reported to have suffered widespread beatings, some placed in solitary confinement. The following month 'after five weeks of severe abuse, five nuns died together in the storeroom of their cellblock. They were close comrades in their twenties who had all been imprisoned for peaceful protests.'[1]

Security in Lhasa was extremely tight. Under darkness PAP battalions carrying riot shields and batons patrolled; police convoys cruised the streets. Since the beginning of the year there had been a harsh crackdown on anyone suspected of 'attempting to overthrow the state' with a surge of temporary detentions. The Tibet Information Network reported that the TAR State Security Bureau had ordered security personnel to carry out a number of token arrests – at least eighty in the Lhasa area – not necessarily based on any dissent or wrongdoing, as a deterrent to others during the weeks leading up to the anniversary.

Such orders indicated the Kafkaesque nightmare that was being enforced as legitimate policy. Amendments to the Chinese Criminal Code and Criminal Procedure Law had eliminated the category of 'counter-revolutionary crime'. Dissent in Tibet became – as it remains – penalised under the flexible rubric of 'offences against state security'.

Less than two weeks before we arrived in the capital, a report on Tibet TV, intended as a chilling warning, showed Legchog, Chairman of the TAR People's Government, inspecting over 800 police from the Tibet Armed Police Corps during a 'mobilisation meeting'. They demonstrated the use of various weapons – semi-automatic rifles and sub-machine guns, a fleet of anti-riot armoured vehicles – and how police dogs arrested suspects.[2]

And yet in the early mornings the Jokhang Temple still hummed with prayer. The *sangs* of juniper were always stoked, flames licking up the offerings of incense and *tsampa*; smoke rising, soft and silver in the dawn light. Tourists were scarce and around the Barkhor the usual frenzied trading was subdued: in part due to at least four security cameras trained on the crowds.

A decade before, in March 1989, there were armed soldiers on those very same roofs in response to over 10,000 Tibetans taking to the streets in a dramatic wave of pro-independence protest. The demonstrations, spearheaded by monks, were the culmination of eighteen months of sporadic unrest and signalled an end to a period of relative religious freedom. Up to 200 Tibetans were believed killed; several hundred more were arrested, injured or went missing in the indiscriminate shooting and anarchy that followed, leading to fourteen months of martial law.

The events of March 1989 go back thirty years earlier to when Tenzin Gyatso, the Dalai Lama, was personally invited to a theatrical performance on 10 March 1959 at the Chinese army headquarters. Since the annexation of Tibet nine years previously, the Communists had attempted to win over Lhasa's ruling elite with gradual Socialist change. However, with thousands of Tibetan refugees fleeing fierce fighting in the eastern provinces, unrest in the city was growing daily. When a rumour that the Chinese military were planning to abduct the Dalai Lama swept through the cobbled streets, several thousand loyal patriots surrounded the Norbulinka, his summer palace, and held him 'a prisoner of devotion'.

On 17 March, after two mortar shells landed just short of the

Norbulinka, the Dalai Lama and his government, the Kashag, consulted the Nechung oracle who advised him to leave Tibet. Disguised as a soldier, accompanied by a retinue of close advisers, family and bodyguards, the twenty-three-year-old marched out of Lhasa. Just over one month later the Dalai Lama crossed the border into safety in India.

Days after his dramatic escape, vicious hand-to-hand fighting broke out in Lhasa. The major monasteries around the city – Sera, Ganden and Drepung – were shelled and monks shot on sight. By the end of the year, the 1959 Lhasa Uprising and the city's subsequent fall had led to the death of over 10,000 Tibetans. Thousands more were imprisoned or sent to labour camps; 80,000 would follow the Dalai Lama to exile. On 23 March 1959, for the first time, a red flag of the People's Republic of China was raised above the Potala Palace. It has not been lowered since.

Forty years later in 1999, to mark the anniversary, Xinhua, the official Chinese news agency, released a statement giving their version of events. 'The democratic reform in Tibet started in March 1959 after the People's Liberation Army put down an armed rebellion launched by the Tibetan local upper class reactionary clique.' On 1 March, 'The reform put an end to the clerical-aristocratic dictatorship combining political and religious rule that had long plagued Tibet, and rendered freedom to the serfs and slaves that made up 95% of the region's population.'

As the days ticked by to the fortieth anniversary our crew achieved our filming objectives. The cameraman secretly took shots of soldiers on patrol and images of city life. We went to the prison gates of Drapchi and while one of us diverted the attention of the guard, a few shaky images of the prison entrance were grabbed before we all, somehow, melted into the crowd. Two days before the anniversary, my colleagues flew out and on 10 March the footage was broadcast on Asia networks and ITN news.

On the day of their departure, I switched hotels and went for a walk to explore old haunts. I found myself looking for Ani in the crowds. I was tempted to go and find her friend's house, but knew better at such a tense time. Returning towards the hotel I heard someone sing out, Drolma, my Tibetan name.

A young man approached. 'You been to Lhasa before? I think I saw you with Tashi.'

'That's right,' I replied cautiously. 'How is he?'

'No idea.' He shrugged. 'He not come round now he has a new girlfriend. She's a hard one, keeps him home.'

Walking towards a café where the tour guides used to gather two years before, nicknamed 'Broken-hearted restaurant', he pushed aside the heavy Tibetan door hanging.

'Wait here. I show you surprise.'

I ordered a sweet tea, cupping my hands around it to keep warm, when I heard a familiar deep raspy laugh.

'A-ooh Drolma-la, welcome back.'

Striding up to me in a grubby navy blazer was Tenzin from Dharamasala.

'B-but what are you doing here? I thought you were going to Australia—'

He thrust out his hand to shake my own. He looked different: no ponytail, no earring. His hair was cropped and unkempt and he'd put on weight. Sensing my observations, he patted his belly fondly.

'*Nga yakpa. Nga yak sha yang za.* I'm fatter, eating yak meat again.'

'So what happened?' I asked quietly. 'What brought you back after seven years?'

Checking we were alone, he said, 'I got tuberculosis. The Tibetan doctors said the Indian weather no good for me.' He sighed. 'And Ama-la, I missed my mother. I was homesick.'

'She must be happy to see you.' I smiled.

'I'm her only son. She need me.' He raised one eyebrow. 'So on holiday?'

'Sort of, yeah. I want to find Ani again who I travelled with last time I was in Tibet.'

'Are you alone?'

'Yes.'

I decided not to tell Tenzin what I'd been doing in Lhasa. Now on my third trip, I was aware that by associating with a journalist – not officially allowed into Tibet except with permission from the Ministry of Foreign Affairs – theoretically a Tibetan can be accused of 'passing state secrets to the enemy'.[3]

He looked at me for a moment, his eyes narrowed.

'I was hoping to go to the Bumpa Ri today,' I added hastily. 'Do you want to come?'

'Why not. It's a holy place.'

We caught a taxi to the mountain south-east of the city, passing Chinese restaurant after restaurant with cooked chicken feet and pig's trotters hanging in the windows. The new casino by the Kyichu River was close to completion; next to it were mock pagodas with caramel roofs and neon billboards shouting Coca-Cola. On one side of Bumpa Ri was the city's rubbish tip, where grubby-faced Tibetan children picked through the detritus. On the other side prayer flags filled the entire ridge with colour and sound. Lhasa stretched out below, the Potala Palace reigning above. I always marvelled at this remarkable edifice. Its ephemeral nature symbolised something about Tibetans that I could never quite pin down – their embracing smiles combined with an impenetrable guardedness. The longer I spent with them, the complexity of their lives unfolded like the Potala Palace itself with 1,000 rooms.

As Tenzin and I walked he told me in fragments about his dangerous journey back to Tibet once he crossed the border from Nepal. With no identity card he was quickly picked up by the police, interrogated and thrown into a bare, freezing concrete cell with no blanket.

'After three months I found out one of the Tibetan guards went to the same school as me, so he had some sympathy. He called my stepfather who came to pick up me [sic],' said Tenzin. 'My stepfather paid 7,000 renminbi for my release. Nobody knew I was in prison. I could have stayed for two or three years because I came to Tibet illegally.'

He squatted down. 'There's much change in Tibet in seven years. These days, you have money you do anything. People don't know how to spend money so they drink or gamble or go with prostitutes for 150 renminbi a go.' Bending down out of the wind, he lit a cigarette. 'Women also like to play mah-jong; they don't care for their kids. They don't spend money on television or fridges, just on the table.'

Listening to him, I was reminded of that kernel of bitterness, that heavy defeatism I had come to know in Tashi. An image came to mind of a cage, and inside a bird with clipped wings.

'Drolma, many social problems, more than before. This part of Tibet in great danger of becoming Chinese within a few years. Today if someone protests, they're alienated by their friends and family.' He glowered. 'Lay people are too frightened to do anything.'

'Do you think Tibetans have given up the freedom struggle?'

'I think people still want independence.' He threw his hands in the air. 'But you have to survive. All my friends only think of money and don't act for independence.' He stubbed out the cigarette. 'I still love my people and my country.'

That evening Tenzin came over to my hotel. I was keen to pursue our conversation about the change in Tibet since he'd left. After hesitating, he agreed that we could talk in the room and I could record the conversation.

'For a Tibetan it's becoming impossible to get a Tibetan education and even a Chinese education is only possible if the parents can afford it,' he began. 'In the rural areas children remain uneducated and help in the fields, look after sheep, collect yak shit. As we're Tibetan isn't it right that we should know how to speak and write our own language? It carries the teachings that Lord Buddha brought to Tibet and in our culture we say words are precious. If you even lose one word, it isn't good—'

All of a sudden he stopped, motioning me to be quiet. His face clouded over.

'I lost my point. Let's talk about something else.'

I flipped the tape, put on some music and lit a stick of incense.

A few moments later there was a knock at the door and before I could respond, four PSB walked into the room, surrounding us, snapping questions at Tenzin. What was he doing? What was I doing? Who was I? One cast a glance over my scribbled notes, another picked up the tape recorder. A Chinese female officer sat down, scrutinising both of us. Tenzin casually responded to their questions. He was my tour guide, he said. 'We were planning a trip out of Lhasa.' They asked for his identity card and his details were taken.

I showed them my Chinese visa and permit, trying my best to appear indifferent. My palms were sweaty. The fear was so strong, I could taste a bitterness in the back of my throat. I can't remember what other questions, which came from all directions, were fired at me.

At one point the Chinese policewoman said, pointing to the incense, 'Very nice smell.'

'Yes, it's from India,' I replied, without thinking.

After about ten minutes, they nodded politely and left.

The silence between Tenzin and me was thick, icy. He glared at me, and at my trembling hands.

'Why you say you knew me from India?' he snarled. 'Why you tell like that?'

'I didn't. I said, "The incense was from India,"' I protested.

'You did not,' he retorted. 'I was really shocked when you said that you know me from India. That's why they check my identity card.'

I shook my head. 'Honestly, Tenzin—'

'You only just made it, Drolma. The PSB are very clever, they see fear. You looked scared,' he hissed. 'Worst thing to do.'

'I'm sorry,' I said, my voice now shaking. 'I tried my best to look like normal.'

He looked profoundly disappointed in me and motioned that I check that the door was secure. Outside the corridor was empty.

'If you come to Tibet and do these things you have to be better ready for the worst case,' he said. 'Where's your courage?'

I bowed my head, biting my lip.

'Look, I don't mean to be angry but you have to be—' He broke off, exasperated. 'You have to seem like tourist. I'm helping you because I know you do good work for Tibet. You are a window to the outside.' His voice dropped to a menacing whisper. 'They've no right to check the tape, but they check if they think you're lying and you look like you're lying.' He pulled out a cigarette and after a long drag, went on. 'If they'd checked the tape then you'll get kicked out, but I'll go to prison. In one week you go back home to your country. I live here.'

'You'll be OK won't you?' I stopped, tears smarting. 'I mean they got your details and—'

He gave a tiny shrug. 'I think no problem. But no more talking in the hotel room. That my fault also. We must be more careful.'

We sat in the room for at least an hour chain-smoking and then left the guesthouse separately. Only then did I find out that the PSB were registering every foreigner in Lhasa. If Tenzin had not had a premonition moments before the police walked in, I shuddered to think what could have happened. Although Tenzin had agreed to talk to me and we remained friends, several years later he would tell me that after the incident he lost '80 pcr cent trust for me'. Today we still disagree on what I actually said to the policewoman.

It took months for me to shake off the insidious blend of angst and guilt I felt at placing Tenzin's life in danger, particularly as I knew the risks and, like a stuck record, the sensation of fear would replay itself over and over. I lost faith in myself – for a while anyway – in my ability to hold my ground. Any illusions I still clung to about Tibet also fell away. No longer could I see it through Shangri-la spectacles, pretending that it was some enchanted pilgrim's playground where exotic flowers bloomed.

After that evening I got 'the fear'– an emotion of devastating power that can destroy lives, wreck families and tear up the moral fabric of society – a weapon as destructive as batons. Coupled with this, I felt an immense respect for all those Tibetans – and for people all over the world who live in oppressive regimes – who can survive living with such fear, in such darkness, and do so with dignity, grace and without com-promising themselves.

Later that night Tenzin and I met some of his friends for dinner at a Chinese restaurant. Three drunken Chinese policemen arrived, guffawing loudly and belching. When they noticed a young Tibetan woman sitting with her boyfriend, the police started making offensive comments and lobbing food missiles. The boyfriend did nothing. After the earlier events, it felt as if we were subsiding into the first layer of hell: the floor greasy with spittle and chicken wings; the crescendos of drunken male laughter; the sensation of one's own destiny spiralling out of control.

The conversation withered at our table. When the young Tibetan snapped, making a move towards the policemen, they coolly put their hands on their guns, threatening him with arrest, a few years in jail. His shoulders slumped and, with an emasculated stare, he sat back down. More threats, more abuse, before the cops paid up and left.

'Fuck, I can't carry on living here, I'm too frightened,' said the young man, his hands trembling as he tried to light a cigarette. His girlfriend remained mute. 'What can you do? You can't fight back. If the police decide to throw me in jail they can.'

As we walked back to my hotel, we passed a furore of raised voices and fisticuffs; women were shouting, pleading for calm.

'Drunk,' said Tenzin. 'Why Tibetans start fighting? They're family. All the ignorance things are happening in Tibet. Desire, there's so much desire. People can't think about peace because there's too much anger in their heart.'

On the morning of 10 March I woke while it was still dark and crept down to the Jokhang, already busy with Tibetans making offerings to commemorate the anniversary through worship. I had an impression of entering into a web, a tapestry of devotion, sewn together over centuries of repetitive action and ritual. These days it was particularly the women who ensured the butter lamps were alight, the *sangs* stacked with juniper and the fire of Buddhism stoked. Such commitment was in itself a silent protest, a passive form of resistance to the growing incursion of modern culture and to secular Chinese rule – an unspoken re-enforcement of national identity.

Outside the police stations there was a flurry of activity, vans coming and going and, just like a decade before, security personnel had binoculars trained on the crowds from the Barkhor rooftops.

I went to have a tea in one of the cafés overlooking the square in front of the temple. At 10.20 a.m. three white vans and one police Land cruiser roared past. Inside Alsatian dogs were barking on the front seats; at the back sat police in full riot gear. The crowd, visibly agitated, pulled apart to let them through. The vans were heading for the back of the Barkhor where two young monks, both of whom had been expelled from their monastery, were shouting pro-independence slogans. They reportedly raised their fists into the air and began shouting 'Free Tibet', 'Tibet is not part of China'. One of the monks was caught immediately, the other chased before being brought down, beaten with batons and fists, and bundled into a police van. I heard later that during interrogation one of the monks had allegedly said, 'You can beat us as much as you like, but we'll never give up.'

I reported the protest and over the following months, once I'd left Tibet, monitored the grim trajectory of the two monks from Taklung monastery outside Lhasa. Sixteen-year-old Phuntsok Legmon and Namdrol, twenty-five, were sentenced on 9 July 1999 to three and four years' imprisonment respectively. Accused of 'plotting or acting to split the country or undermine national unity' and 'incitement and propaganda', the two young men were believed to be held in Drapchi Prison.

By eleven o'clock it was business as usual and the rest of the fortieth anniversary passed peacefully.

CHAPTER 11

The Sky Burial Cave

A FEW days later, Tenzin and I were on the road to Ani's nunnery to the west of the capital. The further Lhasa was left behind, the happier I started to feel. As we approached a lake, a flock of Siberian cranes swooped down. These elegant birds, with spindly orange legs, a black head, white body and inky tail feathers, are associated with the Dalai Lama and since I had never seen one before, I took the sighting as a sign, perhaps, that I would find Ani again.

Of course, I'd heard nothing from Ani. I had no idea of her whereabouts. When the road left the lake, snaking up the valley, I wondered whether she had decided to take up a job as a housekeeper or if she had persevered with her vocation. Knowing her commitment, I assumed she would have soldiered on, whatever obstacles the government had placed before her. Perhaps she was on pilgrimage, or the nunnery had been closed down like the twelfth-century Rhakor *gompa*, which was abandoned after a hundred armed soldiers forced most of the eighty-odd nuns to leave. These days anything was possible.

In the months leading up to the fortieth anniversary there was a continued onslaught of cultural and religious restrictions. On 8 January the authorities launched a three-year propaganda campaign aimed at promoting atheism. The purported goal was to promote economic development and prosperity in the region: the subtext was to weaken loyalty to the Dalai Lama. The official anti-Dalai Lama rhetoric was becoming increasingly hard line, attacking both his political stance, and personal and religious integrity. Tenzin Gyatso has variously been described by Beijing as a traitor, a child-eating cannibal and, most commonly, a 'splittist' bent on separating Tibet from the clutches of the Motherland.

The potholed road to the nunnery passed an astonishing frozen fifty-foot waterfall, then petered out at the end of a valley. Behind, castles of grey rock pierced the evening sky. There were no trees, only small nut-brown bushes and sparse grass. The nunnery, a collection of rough stone houses around a squat temple, was marked by the inevitable tapestry of faded prayer flags.

My heart was pounding as I walked down the path with Tenzin. I had anticipated this moment for many months. Ani had become an inspiration in my life, one I couldn't ignore but didn't necessarily understand. Everywhere seemed to be deserted. But in the office-cum-shop stood a short fat nun, her face buried in a balaclava against the biting wind.

'*Ani L. du geh?* Is Ani L. here?' Tenzin asked.

'*Mindu. Mindu.* No, no,' she cried.

My heart sank.

'*Kawar du-geh?* Where is she?'

She looked at us warily. 'Are you friends of hers?'

'*Re, nga Drolma yin.* My name is Drolma,' I said. 'We met in Pemako.'

'*Ah-leh*, all right.' Jerking her head behind her, she whispered, 'She's on retreat in a cave high up.'

'Can we go and find her tomorrow?' Tenzin asked.

She thought for a moment. 'Take two nuns to show you the path and leave at sunrise. The way is very hard. It will take you all day.'

Tenzin and I were shown to a basic dormitory. One bed was already made up. On top, neatly laid out, were an olive-green military coat with a brown faux fur collar and a matching Cossack-style military hat with earflaps. Too tired to register the significance, I collapsed into bed.

At first light, together with two young nuns, Tenzin and I set off along a path to the west of the nunnery towards a huddle of fortress-like houses and a small temple, where the spiritual head of the nunnery lived in a small hermitage. Two giant ravens sitting on the roof cawed noisily as we approached.

'Those are the protector-deities of the nunnery,' explained Tenzin. 'Warning of our arrival.'

Inside, a dozen nuns lived in desperately poor conditions. The highly revered head, a short woman with greying hair and a dimpled face who was usually on permanent retreat, auspiciously agreed to grant us a brief audience. After blessing the *khata* I offered, she placed it around my neck and then pointedly stared down at my shoes. I hadn't planned on trekking in Tibet and had only brought one pair: luminous orange pumps from Camden market in London.

'*Dee yagpo mindu.* Those are no good.' She waggled her finger. 'The path is very hard. One fall in these parts and you die.' Turning to the nuns accompanying us, she ordered, 'Better the girl waits below the cave and you go and fetch Ani-la.'

Our party set off again, buoyed by the blessing. In my rucksack were flat bread rolls, candles and some dried yak meat for Ani. Not acclimatised, I took the climb steadily, but fell down twice on one of the narrow ridges. By the top of the pass, over 13,000 feet, a glacial wind blowing from snowy peaks, I was struggling, my nose bleeding from exertion. Tenzin looked nervous. In an attempt to forget my physical discomfort, I focused on Ani. I tried to recall the details of her face, her slightly hooded chestnut-brown eyes, her cranberry complexion and high fruity laugh.

When we reached a sky burial site, where clothes were scattered, a human spinal cord tossed to one side, Tenzin visibly shuddered, and warned me not to go close.

'You wait here,' said the younger nun. 'We'll go and find Ani-la.'

I watched the two women climb up and up, until they disappeared into the crags of the limestone massif. I paced around, Tenzin dozed. No trees here, no plants, only eagles wheeling in a vast empty sky. I could not imagine surviving in such desolation. The silence was hypnotic, the air crystalline; there was a strange magical atmosphere, as if the air were filled with unseen spirits. Behind the charnel ground, an unusual shaft of white light shone down. Minutes ticked by, an hour passed. I lay down and must have drifted off. When I jolted awake I saw three figures coming down the mountain. They looked like miniatures, wine-red beacons against a background of ice, snow and rock. Ani was at the back and, from what I could see, was wearing a hat. I started climbing up towards them.

'*Drolma-la, Drolma-la. Tashi delek*,' echoed a familiar singsong voice down the mountain.

'*Ani-la, Ani-la. Che-rang debo yin beh?* How are you?' I echoed.

'*Debo, debo.* I'm well. *Che-rang?* And you?'

For a few minutes we stood awkwardly, shyly. Ani threw her head back, pealing with laughter, then bent her forehead towards mine in the customary Tibetan greeting. We stood for a moment, our brows touching and, inside, I felt an unexpected joy. She did not seem surprised to see me. (Several years later, she would tell me that my visit brought her much happiness. She was 'only sad' that I had to climb the mountain to find her.)

'*Acchuuu*,' she said, taking my hand. 'You're cold.' Turning to Tenzin, she clicked her tongue. 'This *inji* girl does not wear enough clothes.'

Ani was barrel-shaped, dressed in two thick, scuffed sheepskin *chubas* and on her head a matching dark red woollen hat, which gave her the appearance of wearing a crown. It was slightly peaked with two flaps at the front folded back into a U-position, and wisps of black hair sticking out at the edges. Recalling how her straw hat in Pemako would always hover a few inches above her head to accommodate the spiral of dreadlocks, I wondered if she'd cut them off. When I asked her, she explained that she no longer had her 'meditation hair' and that now it was in the Kagyu tradition of 'a top-knot with hair hanging loose'.

Ani seemed to shine from within, as if there were a fire in her belly. A heavy, clear plastic *mala* hung around her neck; on her fingers were the rings she was in the habit of fiddling with. We sat down on the ground, Tenzin offering her the bread and yak meat, which she took appreciatively. It felt surreal to see her again, especially in such bleak surroundings. I was sorry not to have been able to climb up to her cave, which according to mythic tradition is where Guru Rinpoche spent time.

With Tenzin translating, Ani explained, 'The cave is big like a large car. In one part there's a shrine and a statue of Guru Rinpoche. I sleep in the other corner.'

'How do you keep warm?'

'There's very little wood so I only have a fire in the morning and in the afternoon, when I make tea, scraping a little snow for water. After one o'clock there's no sun. My knees are painful sometimes from the cold, but I use meditation to send away the pain.' (After three months it would be the arthritis in her knees, which she had previously treated with the medieval-sounding practice of cauterisation – 'burning the infected area with a red-hot iron' – that would force Ani to leave the cave.)

'How do you use meditation?' I was intrigued.

'I meditate on the Tibetan syllable "Ah" and imagine a circle of light around it – like the light coming into the cave. When I do that in a strong way, I don't feel pain in my body.'

She had been in the cave for twenty days, following the same routine with four periods of meditation a day and one meagre meal of *tsampa*. Her only company, except for eagles and vultures, were blue sheep.

'Are you lonely?' I asked.

'No. I'm really happy to be alone; it's been my inner feeling for a long time. It's very peaceful, quiet – a good place to meditate because there're no distractions.' Her hands automatically folded into a prayer position. 'It's where Guru Rinpoche himself meditated. He spent several years in the cave with his consort Yeshe Tsogyal. I'll receive special blessing from him because he was there. I can imagine him close by.'

'Why do you always pray to Guru Rinpoche?'

'I don't know exactly except that it's very deep in my heart,' she replied simply. 'I've had dreams of Guru Rinpoche and get encouraged if I feel he's behind me.' She paused to think about this. 'Guru Rinpoche was not a normal person. He was born magic, from a lotus flower, not from a woman's womb. He has limitless wisdom and isn't bound like most ordinary lamas.'

At that place, near the shreds of human beings, a few bones, a scattering of frozen clothes, where nothing else could live, Ani thrived. Without any comfort, without anybody, she was able to let her mind expand into the vast space, into the limitless limpid horizon and, as she did so, I observed, seemed to expand with it. It was fitting that rather than look for teachings from an earthly lama, who she saw only once a year, Ani sought out through direct experience the wisdom of Tibet's yogi-saint, Guru Rinpoche, said to be immortal with a rainbow body of light.

'Have you ever felt Yeshe Tsogyal's presence?' I asked.

'No.' She shook her head. 'But the stories I hear about Yeshe Tsogyal inspire me. She was like a mother to all the world, to all sentient beings. I heard that when she was born, she was already in the prostration pose and repeating the mantra of Tara.'

'So she was a goddess?'

'No, a woman like you or me; and how she suffered to achieve her goal – to become enlightened. She didn't eat for a year, so she could experience hungry ghost hell. She did *tumo* [the yogic practice of inner heat] for a year to experience the cold hell.'

'Is that really what you do to keep warm Ani-la?'

She stuck her pink tongue out in a show of embarrassment, and roared her rich and deliciously contagious laugh.

'I'm not a *yogi* like that. *Yogis* are people like Jetsun Milarepa who can fly, who can shape-shift, who've mastered the Tantric practices. In Tibetan a *yogi – drub tob –* must hold the image of the deity in their mind all the time.'

'Isn't that what you do?'

'I try,' she conceded. 'But I'm just a wandering beggar, crazy to go anywhere. I never care about anything. I don't stay in society.'

'So you never took the job as a housekeeper?'

She shook her head, saying with an imperceptible sigh, 'Still problems at the nunnery. Here the Chinese don't trouble me, it's too far to walk. I've been told to leave several times, but this is home.'

Over the previous year she had gone alone to Kongpo and made a *kora* of Bon Ri, the sacred Bon Mountain, stopping in caves associated with Guru Rinpoche to meditate and recite scriptures. For one month she was fortunate to stay for free with a Khampa lady, where she repeated twelve times 100,000 mantras, before setting out again to visit more power places.

Tenzin, who'd stayed quiet, except for interpreting between Ani and me, made a point of looking at his watch. The two other nuns were also getting restless. I realised that we would have to go; hours of walking back to the nunnery lay ahead. My time with Ani had been all too brief. I offered her some money.

With a flick of her hand, she said defiantly, 'I'm like Milarepa. I beg for alms. I want for nothing.'

Picking up the bag of provisions we had brought, Ani smiled as we started making our way down the hill. When I turned to wave she had already gone, striding briskly towards her high, rocky home. Several years later, when she knew me better, she would tell me that the focus of that year, including her time next to the sky burial site, was to follow a highly advanced spiritual practice called *chod*, devised by the great twelfth-century *yogini* Machig Labdron.

Chod – literally 'cutting through' – is said to be a powerful way to sever emotions such as hatred, desire and ignorance to reconnect the practitioner to their own true nature. It also limits one's attachment to the physical body and the inherent fear of dying, so on the point of death the adept is able to set their mind or consciousness free. Traditionally *chod* practitioners meditate near cremation grounds to arouse this innate fear.

'*Chod* is the short path to Enlightenment,' writes Philip Rawson, 'a vivid enactment of self-sacrifice.' It involves visualising one's body and brain 'being totally dismembered, smashed, crushed and shredded to bloody pulp' before calling upon the spirits or hungry ghosts to devour it. This re-enacts 'the total compassionate self-sacrifice the Buddha had done in the previous incarnation when he fed his own body to the injured tigress nursing her cubs'.[1]

Ani would tell me later that she does the *chod* meditation alone, day and night, somewhere remote. 'Some people consider it a frightening practice especially when meditating at a sky burial site. But I don't find it difficult. It just depends on one's own mind and one's own concentration.'

In that desolate place, Ani and I were together for barely three hours. As I slid down the snowy slopes, my spirit was soaring. I reflected that Ani had grown in stature and lost some of her youthful girlishness from Pemako. Fierce and determined, she looked in her element. On the long walk back, I grasped that it was this fearlessness, this strength of her inner motivation and commitment to remain true to her own heart that I wanted to emulate. Her life unfolded like a silk thread, spirit took her, called her, and nothing, not even the authorities, would stop her. I hoped it would inspire me to carve out my own path – not necessarily Buddhist, to remain true to what I believed, in spite of all the distractions of the resolutely materialist world in which I lived.

When we arrived back at the nunnery, the shadows were stretching over the temple roof, the honeyed sound of women's voices rising in the evening air. Sitting outside the dormitory was our driver. During the day, he told us, half a dozen cars of police and government officials had come to check on the nuns. They intend to halve the numbers, yet again.

In the dormitory, the same khaki-green coat lay on the bed. Its owner, the Tibetan Religious Affairs Officer whose job was to monitor the daily activities of all the nuns, and report anything suspicious, was still on duty.

CHAPTER 12

To the Nunnery

MY own life had begun to echo, at some level, and in ways I couldn't always explain, the pilgrimage that Ani is making of her own life. Since first reading about Mount Kailash in my cell-like room in Dharamasala, I had resolved to go there with Ani, my *cho-drok* – Tibetan pilgrim friend. The fleeting reunion with Ani the year before, in early 1999, among the burnished limestone escarpments, eagles soaring above, had only left me wanting to know more about this 'wandering beggar, crazy to go anywhere'.

The following summer, in July 2000, I returned to Tibet via China. I had joined David Burlinson again – the hardened Tibet traveller whose company had arranged the red lily trip three years before – and we drove, together with Pascoe, a broad-shouldered, quick-witted Englishman, and Geleg, a diminutive Tibetan monk, from Beijing to Lhasa. An odyssey at high speed, covering 6,000 miles in twenty-five days, it was a rare opportunity to travel overland across China, through the eastern Tibetan provinces of Kham and Amdo (Sichuan and Qinghai respectively to the Chinese), and a chance to see first-hand the breadth and diversity of this vast continent.

As we sped towards the town of Golmud, passing through the barren

Tsaidam Desert on the northern reaches of the Tibetan plateau, we came across a group of prostrating pilgrims. They appeared out of nowhere like shadows on the shimmering road. A family of four, shepherds from Labrang in far east Amdo, they had sold their flock to make the pilgrimage to Lhasa over 900 miles to the west. The youngest boy, around ten years old, pulled a small wooden cart with the family's meagre possessions. Each member wore thick wooden gloves and protective aprons; their faces bleached white from dust.

We had seen other prostraters on the road, but there was something arresting about this group: the look of love on the mother's face as she pulled her two boys close as trucks sped past in a cloud of fine grit. Awkwardly offering a donation, we were all silenced with emotion. I gave them four beads from my sandalwood *mala*, blessed by the Dalai Lama when I'd interviewed him two years previously, and which, now that I was back in Tibet, I was giving to pilgrims along the way.

The mother's hands trembled, tears streaking down her grimy face when she took the four wooden beads like nuggets of gold.

'It should be you who get to see him,' I said, my voice breaking. 'Not me.'

'Thank you, it's a blessing. It's auspicious for our pilgrimage.'

Barely a word was spoken in the car for the next few hours. In my mind's eye I could see only the caterpillar-like motion of the family inching towards Lhasa. It would take at least another year through the arctic winter and, arguably, nowhere else in the world would such a spectacle not raise an eyebrow. To all appearances prostration is a violent assault on the body, akin to self-flagellation. And it is, in one way. When I see Tibetans do it on the open road, I'm awed, yet simultaneously ask myself, 'Are they mad?' It is considered the most meritorious way to travel – an ultimate act of submission that erodes pride and brings the pilgrim's body in touch with every mile of the sacred road along the sacred journey. It is also said to purify the body by removing psychic knots – known as *mdud* – in the subtle channels, thus removing past negative karma and allowing the 'subtle winds' to pass through smoothly. If the channels are clear, meditation is better.

My own pilgrimage was luxurious compared to that family's, I thought, as I stared out of the car window into the gathering dusk. I had left England from Glastonbury and shortly before departing, a friend, Nicki, gave me a cloth bag of tiny multicoloured crystals: 'love-seeds to scatter in my wake'. I had left a few there, some more at the Great Wall of China and among the Terracotta Army in Xian; I sprinkled some in divinatory lakes in Kham and on the windswept passes in Amdo; and as I did so, I pictured a line of love and friendship, connecting my life with Ani. My dream was that, with her, Mount Kailash would be the final full stop.

I was inspired by Ani's sixty-odd journeys throughout Tibet and the way that she could travel simply with a knapsack and a stick, knowing she would survive the rigours of the road. In turn I began to pare my own life down – not always very effectively – and accumulate less. I tried to listen more closely to my inner guidance, to be alert to my intuitive promptings. As a way to make sense of what Ani had committed herself to – and as a new compass for my own – I began reading about the power of pilgrimage, which for all its medieval resonance is undergoing a remarkable renaissance in the West.

Tibetans have been pilgrims for over a thousand years, walking with devotion across their land, strengthening the link between people and place. I realised that whichever tradition you choose, whatever words you use to describe the journey, ultimately all paths lead to the same destination: an encounter with the divine, a deepening of faith in the sanctity of all life. I was particularly touched by one definition: 'A true pilgrim, working with love, moves the earth energy through the landscape. . . helping to vivify the Earth and create patterns of light.'[1]

The Japanese Haiku master Matsuo Basho spent the final decade of his life on pilgrimage. No longer was it the goal that was 'important as much as the wandering itself and the deep motivation for attaining an interior state, an ecstasy'. Every experience –

Fleas, lice,
A horse pissing
By my bed

– is part of the path, 'a metaphor for a spiritually lived life'.[2]

On pilgrimage the 'old' personality can die a mystical death, bringing the pilgrim closer to liberation. For Tibetans their entire life may be viewed through this aperture – as a journey from 'ignorance to enlightenment, from self-centeredness and materialistic preoccupations to a deep sense of the relativity and interconnectedness of all life . . . The goal of pilgrimage is less to reach a particular destination than to transcend through inspired travel the attachments and habits of inattention that restrict awareness of a larger reality.'[3]

☙

After the hard travelling and two bouts of sickness on the way to Lhasa, I barely left my hotel room for two days once we reached the capital. When I emerged it was to go to the Jokhang Temple. I was surprised to see hordes of Chinese tourists – three summers before they were a rarity. Two sassy women who worked for Saatchi and Saatchi in Shanghai told me, as they purchased a prayer wheel each, that they'd come to Tibet because it was 'exotic'.

A tour group of middle-aged Chinese, all in matching slacks with ludicrously large cameras, jostled for the best shot of some Amdo pilgrims who fled with high-pitched mirth. I found myself wondering if Tibetan culture was now being appropriated for tourism, in danger, like some of the other so-called 'minority areas' of China we'd passed through – such as Lijiang in Yunnan, home to the Naxi tribe – of becoming a Disney-style tourist destination: cute, colourful and chic, for the burgeoning Chinese middle class.

It did not lake long to track down Tenzin who I spotted in a purple Hard Rock sweatshirt. He looked harder; his back hunched. Under his broad brow, framed by wavy black hair, his face was thinner. Over the year we had kept in erratic contact and I knew he had become friends with Tashi, my ex-lover, through tour guiding. Tenzin and I went to the roof terrace of a favourite café overlooking the Barkhor. Sitting down, I asked, 'Have you heard anything from Ani?'

'I saw her one time in Lhasa.'

'How was she?'

'She's well. I think she's at her nunnery. The political situation is still difficult for her.' He took a sip of Coke. 'She's good for you, Drolma. After you climbed to the top of the mountain last year and saw Ani, you were a much nicer person. I don't think you understand. You received many blessings from her. It shows in your body. I can see it at the time.'

'Really? I don't know what I received from her. Except that those few hours we spent together stayed with me. I'm hoping we can go to Kailash on pilgrimage.'

'I'll write a letter for you and help you organise transport.' His eyes drilled into mine. 'Drolma, very few nuns wear a hat like Ani, it's the hat of a *yogini*. Very few can meditate in that cave. If they don't have the power, they'll lose their mind.' He hesitated. 'I think Ani and you have a strong relationship in the past and present. She gave you her *phurbu*, didn't she? A very secret and nice thing.'

'And a ring.' I held out my finger.

'You must learn Tibetan better. I think she really wants to talk to you without any translator.'

'I'm trying,' I whinged. 'I keep starting and then I stop. It's not easy.'

Tenzin was restless. His knee jiggled, his eyes flickered around. After the incident in the hotel room the year before, we were still on uneven ground. When I had departed from Tibet, he gave me an antique statue of Tara, 'for good fortune', he wrote. 'I am Tibetan. It's so difficult to do my responsibility, but I always do inside of my heart.'

It struck me that, as a foreigner, I symbolised both trouble and the potential of hope – a lifeline to the outside world. Since Tenzin and I first met, two years before, there was a familiarity coupled with a certain ambivalence. It was a quality I had observed in other Tibetans – a fortress mentality – epitomised by their houses, their monasteries, even their land surrounded by mountains which for centuries had kept intruders at bay. Smiles are there from the first meeting; nonetheless it may take many years to fathom the depths, to understand what moat of sorrow – perhaps – keeps them separate and apart.

It appeared the space and luminosity of the landscape, and the Buddha's teachings had given Tibetans a cradle of compassion in their hearts. But I was learning that, as in Europe after the First World War, every Tibetan family knows someone who has suffered in the occupation. If Lhasa appeared concrete, psychologically its foundations were fragile.

Tenzin shifted under my gaze.

'Last year I always talk peaceful way with people. Now some days I just want to fight.' He pulled open his bag to reveal a big shiny knife. He thought for a moment. 'You don't know about Tashi, do you?'

I shook my head.

'Things got bizarre, Drolma. Tashi getting drunk all the time, drinking that cough medicine to get high. Problems with his travel agency, problems with his girlfriend. Too many problems. . .' His voice petered out, and then, sharply, he said, 'He left Lhasa a couple of months ago and went to Shigatse to be with his old mum who was ill. She was taken to hospital there and one time it all went too far. Tashi got angry with a Chinese doctor. He fight, the doctor lose an eye.'

'What—' I gasped.

'The doctor's in hospital with head injuries. Tashi's still there, inside prison for three years. No chance to come out.'

I felt a pang of nausea. Those fissures that I had seen in him three years before had become canyons of despair. I recalled his words when someone was close to the edge. 'Man crack,' he would say. Listening to Tenzin I feared he was heading down the same slippery path.

'A few weeks back a friend went to see Tashi inside.' Tenzin pulled out a cigarette from behind his ear. 'He has a very beaten-up face. He passed on a message. *Kyi-po tang.* Enjoy yourself. That's all.'

Tenzin took me to his new lodgings. We walked in separately to avoid attracting attention from the neighbours. The doorframe was still splintered and buckled where Tashi had taken an axe to it in a drunken fury one night. On the floor were empty bottles of brandy, on the bookshelf, *The Celestine Prophecies, Jonathan Livingston Seagull* and *Atisha's Lamp for the Path to Enlightenment.*

Tenzin slumped down on the bed.

'Such bizarre things happening on Dalai's birthday. People weren't allowed to make offerings, to burn incense.' His voice dropped in despair. 'I can't be free, I can't be independent. I can't express what I want, I can't do what I want to do.' He paused and said heavily, 'If you do, sure they come and find you.'

I knew that only weeks before there had been a heavy crackdown on 6 July, the Dalai Lama's birthday. The tanks of the People's Liberation Army paraded the streets. Families, schoolchildren and individuals, especially Tibetan members of the Communist Party, were prohibited from visiting temples or burning incense at home. Video cameras were set up to film anyone who defied the ban and officials conducted house-to-house searches, looking for photographs of the Dalai Lama. I glanced out of Tenzin's window. A new security camera was fixed on a lamppost outside. I found myself going a bit numb, recognising that sensation of sliding into a hall of mirrors – where nothing is as it seems – the feeling I had begun to associate with Lhasa.

I was keen to leave and get on the road to Mount Kailash. With a letter in my pocket explaining, 'that it's our karma from positive actions in previous lives to travel to Mount Kailash together', written by Tenzin with poetic flourish, and a large bag of fresh vegetables and some bread, I set off two days later for Ani's nunnery.

As I approached the collection of low buildings, my stomach tightened when I remembered Tenzin's parting words: 'Don't be obvious, stay low.' I knew the Religious Affairs Officer in the khaki-green coat might still be at the nunnery watching for anything irregular.

Fortunately Ani was at home and a young novice was hailed to show me where she lived, above the main temple. The small flat-roofed houses were like steps climbing up the rocky valley side. Each whitewashed cottage had rust colour painted under the eaves, the lintel and doors. On reaching Ani's, I let my breathing settle before climbing up the steps into her walled back yard. To my dismay, the door was locked.

'*Ani mindu*. Ani isn't here,' I cried out.

'*Du, du*. She's here. She'll be back later,' said a nun in her late sixties, who emerged from a next-door house. After about an hour, Ani appeared clutching some muddy potatoes, wearing her thick claret-red *chuba* and matching pointy cloth hat; around her waist was a peacock-blue apron.

'*Lo, Drolma-la, tashi delek. Yar pheb, yar pheb*. Welcome, welcome,' she said warmly, without a glimmer of surprise, her voice tinkling like a bell in the clear sharp air.

She motioned me inside and, stooping, I walked through the narrow hobbit-hole doorway. After my eyes had adjusted to the gloom, I found myself standing in a six-foot-square area, which served as her kitchen. In one corner, a circle of charred stones for the stove, a few blackened pots and a peat-brown butter-tea churner. Above on a stone shelf, cut into the rock, was a huge pile of dried yak pats and stacked wood. Metal ladles, a water jug and a battered kettle hung from a massive beam running down the centre.

A dirty curtain divided the 'kitchen' from the bedroom-cum-living area, barely the size of an average bathroom. On either side were two benches, which doubled as beds, yak-hair rugs in a neat pile and a couple of grubby pillows. There was an orange cupboard, a huge trunk made of yak skin coarsely sewn together and, the focus of the room, a shrine fashioned from a small cabinet, decorated with pictures of various lamas. I recognised Guru Rinpoche and Machig Labdron, the famous twelfth-century Tantric *yogini* and *chod* practitioner, and the late Dudjom Rinpoche, supreme head of the Nyingma order. Everything was covered in a film of soot, including the tiny window (they are kept small to keep out the cold in winter, consequently the sun's rays barely penetrate).

Ani fussed around. 'Drolma-la, *shu, shu*. Sit down. *Ngey ja so gi yin.* I'll make tea.'

The house was soon filled with bitter, pungent smoke from burning yak dung. I tried to get comfortable on her hard bed, drawing my coat close to me, and looked around Ani's little home, built some fifteen years before with the help of her parents, who'd quarried local stone and felled trees for the sturdy beams. It was one of the first hermitages to be built, close to a spring and high up from the main nunnery, which suggested that even then Ani was committed to a solitary life. There was no electricity and the toilet was a hole in the ground or a quiet spot among the bushes.

I wondered how she could do prostrations in such a small space – there were barely a couple of feet between the bench-beds. When first ordained, she had begun, as is customary for novice monks and nuns, with the Preliminary Practices known as *bum-shi* – literally 400,000 – which start with 100,000 prostrations. Every day for over a month Ani did 3,000 prostrations on a yak skin on the floor. Her hands bled, she lost all track of time.

'It was difficult,' she had told me. 'During the day I felt normal but at night, when I stood up after my last prostration, I was dizzy, as if my skin was no longer attached to my body.' To follow were 100,000 repetitions of the Vajrasattva mantra – Dorje Sempa in Tibetan – the equivalent number of Mandala Offerings and, lastly, 100,000 invocations of her lineage, known as Guru Yoga.

I tried to imagine spending periods of isolated retreat in here, without suffering claustrophobia or hypothermia. I knew that after the Preliminaries, at the age of twenty-five, Ani's guru, P. Rinpoche, instructed her to spend three months shut in her house doing an advanced purification practice on the chakras known as Chiksay Kundrol, which requires the renunciate to remain in complete darkness. Before beginning, a vow is taken that the practitioner will see nobody; if not, Ani explained, 'you can get crazy'. With the slit window of her house covered, and a special piece of pointed wood outside the door to indicate that others should not disturb her, Ani would begin every day at 3 a.m., meditating in a wooden box, for four periods a day, taking breaks for *tsampa* and tea, finishing at midnight. Only under cover of darkness could she go out to dispose of her toilet waste and fetch water.

'At first it was very difficult. I got very hungry during the meditation. My body became weak,' she had said. 'By the end, I felt very comfortable and light. Then I found it difficult to be around other people, even their smell gave me a headache.'

Next door I could hear the sucking, swishing sound of Ani churning the butter tea and she came in holding two chipped china cups. I produced the vegetables and other gifts I'd brought: socks, a green fleece jacket and a cherry-red sunhat from Beijing. I also had a bundle of precious objects: photos of the seventeenth Karmapa, holy medicine and, from my own *mala*, some wooden beads blessed by the Dalai Lama. These she took eagerly, carefully stringing one onto her rosary; the rest she put aside to give to other nuns.

'I can't have photos of His Holiness. If the Chinese find them,' she said, smacking the air with her hand, 'they slap us. They rip up the pictures.'

I handed her the letter written by Tenzin. Her eyes straining in the dim light, she traced her finger over the words and as she read out loud, a smile crept across her face. When she reached the words 'Kang Rinpoche' – Mount Kailash and literally 'Precious Jewel of Snows' – she patted my knee then leapt up in a state of great excitement.

'*Che-rang dro toob gi dug-geh*? – Can you come?' I asked, in faltering Tibetan.

'Yes, yes. Of course,' she replied, her eyes shining.

Smoothing her hands down her apron, as if we were going to leave immediately, she began to pack a few possessions into a small cloth bag: her knife with the yak-bone handle, an extra *chuba*, the cherry-red sunhat.

'We'll need some of this food you brought,' she said, pointing to the sugar and powdered milk. 'Plenty of *tsampa* and butter.' She dragged out a large leather sack from under a shelf, used a ladle to heap *tsampa* into another bag, and unwrapped an unappetising hairy yak skin to reveal her stash of *dri* butter. It was potent-smelling, thankfully not rancid.

'*Shimbo du*,' she insisted. 'My relatives gave it to me; it's from my nomad village. They're good to me. When I'm at the nunnery they give me money.'

She certainly looked healthy. Her features lacked the defiant resilience from the year before when we had met at the wintry sky burial site, which was perhaps a reflection of the season: it was mid-summer, the bushes were olive green, the streams rushing.

'Do you miss your house when you're not here?'

'No,' she said, tearing off a bit of dry yak meat, dunking it like a biscuit in her butter tea. 'But I'm always happy to be home because then I don't have to beg.'

'How are things at the nunnery?'

'The officials come back next month, so I have to leave,' she said in a flat tone of resignation. 'They're not here in summer, too many tourists.'

'Even repression is seasonal,' I replied in English.

She looked confused.

I sighed, frustrated. '*Dhe kaley marey*. Don't worry, I don't know how to translate that.'

We talk in a version of Tibetan charades, using my phrase book, flamboyant gestures and lots of eye contact. I sigh noisily again at my inadequate Tibetan. Tenzin was right: I must improve. The silence grows between us, and with it a wordless dialogue begins. I can't quite put my finger on it – except I know it as a feeling of coming home – and all the questions that I want to ask dissolve into the kindness pouring from Ani's eyes. When she stares at me, I find myself looking away, self-conscious and shy.

Two timeless days passed with continual rounds of butter tea, hot potatoes and vegetables dripping with butter. We went for walks and made a small *kora* of the nunnery. We took a bus to visit a nearby monastery and on the way back stopped at some hot springs, popular among nomads and local people, with an enclosed bathing area for women.

Ani started to undress. First she took off her red peaked hat. Her ebony mane was worn in two plaits, which she pinned around her head, giving her the appearance of a pretty Bavarian maiden. Slipping out of her *chuba*, she revealed milky white skin: only her face and hands were suntanned. The other Tibetan women in the pool strained to look at me – surely the first time they had seen a naked Westerner – and, having undressed with fumbling fingers, I made a clumsy splash into the water, gasping at the heat.

Ani called me over, took the soap, and lathered my back; then, she rubbed a handful of small pebbles in neat circles across my shoulders for a gentle massage and exfoliation Tibetan-style. Soothed by the hot water, the frothing bubbles and the low murmur of women around me, I let my mind drift. I realised how much I appreciated Ani's tactile nature. It would perhaps seem odd, I thought, to hold an English friend's hand, but here such affection was normal. I liked to think her example encouraged me to be more warm and open to others. After I had scrubbed Ani's back, we relaxed, staring up at the sky, clouds scudding above, then slowly, cautiously, we got out. I sat for a few minutes, my head spinning, letting the cool air wrap around me.

Back at the cottage, Ani insisted I sleep on her bed. Curled up in my sleeping bag, I heard her change the water bowls on the altar, a ritual she performs morning and night, then she lit a stick of incense and twirled it three times to the Buddha. Before she lay down, Ani made three quick prostrations on her bed. I recalled how, three years before, on that first night in Bhakha monastery on the edge of the Pemako valleys, she had done the same. Back then I could not have imagined how the search for the red lily would not only lead to a new flowering of consciousness, but also be the start of such an unusual and enduring friendship.

Ani's daily routine at home begins before daybreak with recitation of prayers. After face washing, tea and *tsampa*, she settles down to read scriptures by candlelight, until the sun illuminates the room sufficiently. Every month she tries to memorise and understand one of her thirty Buddhist texts; some complex teachings take longer. Nuns who are permanently in the nunnery spend the majority of their time memorising scriptures (and are fined by their teacher if they're too slow; in the past it 'would have been the stick'.) Ani's focus, however, remains on meditation and the day is broken up into periods of contemplation, breaks for food and time to chat with other nuns.

She will chose a different deity to meditate on according to religious festivals, and her own inclination. Green Tara is for generating compassion; Vajrasattva (Dorje Sempa) removes obstacles; White Tara is for longevity and Guru Rinpoche, a good rebirth. She also has her own *yidam* – personal meditational deity – given by her guru. It is the union of Hayagriva and Vajravarahi Chintamani (in Tibetan Tamdrin and Dorje Phagmo or Tawa Yab Yum for short), known as 'The Wish-fulfilling Jewel, Horse-necked One' and 'Vajra Sow'. This was the principal meditational deity of the famous nineteenth-century eastern Tibetan lama Shabkar, also an itinerant hermit.

Shabkar Tsogdruk Rangdrol, who lived between 1781 and 1851, has been described by his translator as 'a humane and emotional man of sentiments not always attributed to hermits'. He was born among the Nyingma *yogis* of the Rekong region in Amdo, who were famous for their hair, often six feet long, which they wore coiled on top of their heads, and who would gather in their thousands to engage in meditation and rituals. 'They were much admired and sometimes feared for their magical powers.'[4] (Until I mentioned it, oddly Ani did not know that she shared the same – and uncommon – *yidam* as Shabkar.)

A *yidam* is the equivalent of an archetype that the practitioner can identify with during the meditation process. Deities are like subtle manifestations of the mind and as there are angry or calm people, so there are wrathful or compassionate deities. An aggressive person may need a wrathful deity in order to transmute anger into wisdom. Over time and with dedication, it is believed that the practitioner will acquire the enlightened aspects of the deity, which merely represent their own enlightened powers. Some adepts can become 'so fully identified' with a deity that 'they radiate empowerment to others and into the surrounding environment.'[5]

The next step from the *yidam* practice is to meditate directly on the nature of mind. This is moving from *Kye Rim* or Arising Stage to the advanced *Dzog Rim* or Stage of Perfection, which Ani does. Not only more complex, it is, she says, 'secret' and special vows are taken in the presence of her lama not to reveal anything she experiences, not even to other nuns. She would tell me later, 'If nuns are good in scripture they don't talk about it as that could lead to pride and jealousy.' She also said that she's 'never heard an argument in the whole time at my nunnery. If people are jealous, they won't show it. They keep it in their heart.'

As Ani is no longer officially part of the nunnery – since she was cast out during the 'patriotic education campaigns' – she's not obliged to participate in any of the month-long ceremonies of twenty-four-hour prayer held at the nunnery, although she does help with the communal cleaning. Some of the nuns, mostly uneducated village women, become ordained because they think they can receive a good education. The majority are there 'because of positive motivation and the desire to follow the spiritual path, not because it's an easier life. They aren't afraid of hard work in the fields and don't take up the robes to avoid that.' Beneath the head of the nunnery, appointed through a collective vote by all the nuns, there are six nun leaders who guide the nuns on what to practise.

Once a year Ani will go to her lama for teachings but does not like to 'spend time at the monastery in the company of monks, as people may talk behind my back'. After Ani has received instruction, she chooses where to practise, pursuing the tradition of the wandering hermit to make it her own.

CHAPTER 13

Journey to the Sacred Mountain

I KNEW arranging a journey to Kailash would not be straightforward: obstacles are part of the pilgrim's progress. A magnet for *yogis* and explorers, Western scholars and seekers for centuries, the mountain is held sacred by four religions: Buddhism, Bon, Hinduism and Jainism. Pilgrims have travelled immense distances to this 'navel of the world' in the hope of purifying their sins and attaining enlightenment. Historically, Tibetans fiercely guarded it, so much so that if a foreigner were found in the vicinity, the local headman would face execution on orders from Lhasa.

The mountain's enigmatic nature is, of course, part of its magnetism. It is 55 million years old and is mentioned in records dating from the Bronze Age of Mesopotamia. 'The stranger,' writes Sven Hedin, 'approaches Kang Rimpoche (Kailash) with a feeling of awe. It is incomparably the most famous mountain in the world [and] the holiest throne of the gods of the great Asiatic religions.'[1]

Once back in Lhasa days went by as I tried to organise our pilgrimage and find other Westerners to share costs. I found my initial enthusiasm wavering and when nothing progressed, began to feel as if I were in a vortex. Hemmed in by mountains, isolated from the rest of the world,

Lhasa can feel dangerously oppressive. I made excuses why we shouldn't go: the worst floods in twenty years had caused the southern route to disappear; the cost; the red tape.

I had not anticipated the labyrinthine process to procure the necessary documents, not for me, but for Ani. The mountain's position, close to the Nepalese border, on a route taken by Tibetans escaping across the Himalayas into exile, means that a Tibetan requires an internal permit to travel there. As an 'unauthorised' nun, Ani had no identity papers. Without them, no permit.

A Japanese scholar in search of pre-Buddhist pyramids offered me a lift, only to decline when he heard I was travelling with a Tibetan nun. A crazed young German woman insisted we all hitch together (illegal for Westerners). In Tashi 1 Restaurant I found an entire table filled with would-be Kailash pilgrims. After it took forty-five minutes to split the bill, I decided Ani and I would go it alone.

Knowing it would be safer for her to travel as a lay woman, Ani went to the Barkhor market one morning and bought herself a deep plum *chuba*, for some reason one size too big. Back at the hotel, she said she was going to try it on and show me, but first she wanted to take advantage of the hot showers – a novelty that she savoured. Afterwards Ani sat on the balcony, methodically combing her hair, eking out the tangles with her crusty black comb, the same one she had in Pemako.

I recalled her saying that as a young girl she always loved to brush her hair, and would tell her friends 'how to dress nicely, keep their face clean and look pretty'. Back then she was 'slimmer, more rosy-cheeked, with a reputation as a joker, always singing – her mind going everywhere'. I was glad she had retained this playful streak and still harboured that grain of vanity. Once satisfied with her appearance, Ani showed off her new outfit, donning the red sunhat and green fleece jacket.

'Aw-ooo, Drolma,' she complained. 'This *chuba* is too big. I don't like it.'

'*Nying jepo du.* You look beautiful,' I assured her, unable to keep my face straight.

'You're not being honest. It's too big for me.' She giggled, imitating how two people could fit inside and, sashaying across the hotel room, sang out, 'Not one Ani, two Ani.' Gripped by the image of Ani in double, we both dissolved into helpless laughter.

The next day she took me to see her old friends Pema and Pasang, who ran the tiny school. When I met Pema in 1997 she was a nun. Three years later the couple had a son. Embarrassed to talk about it, Ani would only impress on me that they were 'very good, very kind people', which I could see from their dedication in running the school. (It's inevitable bad karma if a monk or nun breaks their vows, with one Buddhist text stating, 'The nun who goes astray is despised in this life and falls to hell in the next.'[2] However the current circumstances in Tibet mean it isn't uncommon.)

Ani chose to spend the afternoon with Pema, so I made a visit to the Jokhang Temple, where for over a millennia pilgrims have journeyed, imbuing every brick, every lick of paint with a particular and palpable resonance. When a Tibetan approaches the Jokhang they will not enter directly. First they encircle the city on the outer pilgrimage circuit, make up to three *koras* around the Barkhor market and only then are ready to enter the temple. As I walked into the inner courtyard, I was over-whelmed by the familiar sweet oily smell of burning *dri* from hundreds of flickering butter lamps. Within the thick walls of the complex a circuit of prayer wheels weaves among the red solid wooden pillars. Letting my hand drift over the letters of *Om Mani Padme Hung* engraved on the battered wheels, I appreciated the stillness that comes with ritual.

Built by the seventh-century King Songtsen Gampo, acknowledged as Lhasa's founder, the original building has been extended over the centuries and now stands three storeys high with a maze-like interior of dark blood-red shrine rooms; in the inner sanctum, protected by a heavy metal chain, is the bejewelled and gleaming Jowo Buddha. The original statue was destroyed during the Cultural Revolution when the Red Army used the Jokhang for grain storage and as a pigsty.

I paused to look at a faded fresco, and a young monk sidled up.

'Hello. First time Jokhang?'

'No,' I said cautiously.

'You look likes Tibetan. Are you Buddhist?'

'Well, sort of,' I said, clutching my *mala*.

'You want guide?'

Before I could reply the monk pointed towards the image in front. 'That Manjushri, Wisdom Buddha,' he said. 'Watch eyes when you go past.'

Walking behind him, I was startled at how the eyes seemed to follow me. The monk waited, an expectant grin sweeping his face. He spoke in clipped textbook English, frowning intensely as he tried to arrange the words in the right order.

'Good, no? Buddha eye all-seeing. He follow you. I'm keeper of Guru Rinpoche shrine, you come, you see.'

I found myself being led up the stairs by the young monk, whose oval face and slightly pointed ears gave him an elfin look. His name was Lobsang, he told me, flinging his saffron robes over his shoulder, and he had many '*inji* friend, from place world over'. He was learning English at night school with thirty other students, twenty of whom were monks and nuns. 'They want to learn English, so they can tell *injis* true Tibetan history,' he said with evident pride.

Lobsang invited me for tea upstairs. We climbed more unsteady steps onto the rooftop above the temple and through a warren of passageways into his spacious room. Light streamed through a window onto a low sofa covered with a thick crimson carpet. There was a blackboard on which English words were carefully written, a small table with wooden cups of half-drunk, congealed butter tea, and, along the length of one wall, a vast glittering shrine. At the back were two small bedrooms, each with a single bed, where he and another monk slept.

'Comfortable make,' he said, pointing to the sofa. 'I'll get tea.'

'Are you sure it's safe for me to be here?' I asked.

'It's OK. *Injis* come before.'

Surveying his quarters compared to Ani's impoverished hermitage encapsulated the economic gulf between monasteries and nunneries – historically monasteries have always been better endowed, particularly a leading institution like this – and the second-rate status of nuns in Tibetan society. A loud, piercing ringtone broke my thoughts. It was Lobsang's mobile phone which he deftly flicked open to answer a call.

Lobsang was ordained at the age of seventeen because he 'wanted to have good clothes and play, and not be a farmer'. Now, he said, he was committed to 'be a monk all the life'. One of eleven children, with an identical twenty-nine-year-old twin, also a monk in India, Lobsang told me that although they've been apart for eight years they still have the same dreams. His elder brother, who worked in a nearby restaurant, tried to discourage Lobsang from becoming friends with Westerners. 'He's always telling me to be careful,' he said, reaching for his wooden bowl of butter tea. 'Whenever a tourist asks me political questions I answer truthfully. In Tibet that dangerous.'

I arranged to meet Lobsang again with Ani in a small teashop opposite the Jokhang, where the monks would be found after temple hours. He arrived in jeans, a beige corduroy shirt and leather baseball cap.

'Better I not wear monk clothes if I'm with a foreigner,' he explained, slipping into his seat without drawing any attention to himself. 'If any problem, police always take monks first.'

When it transpired that Ani knew – and trusted – his older brother, I tentatively asked if he would help us make her identity card. Tenzin had agreed to do what he could to arrange Ani's internal travel permit, if we supplied him with some photo ID.

'Yes, that's no problem,' said Lobsang. 'It just takes some time. Once you have the card it's the first step towards leaving Tibet. Better you do it proper way, legal way.' Glancing to see that no one was listening, he said in hushed tones, 'If you want to escape then wait till winter when more Tibetans coming back and forwards. Right now impossible, too tight—'

'I don't think she wants to escape, Lobsang,' I interrupted. 'It's just that we need some sort of identity card for Mount Kailash.'

He looked at me and then in Tibetan asked Ani. Fear darted across her face.

'I'm scared to go. I want, but I don't want –' She crossed her wrists over, as if bound. 'I've heard of so many dangerous escapes, people falling into rivers, lost in the snow or even worse, caught by the Chinese police. Big problem for nun if they capture me.' She caught herself and said sadly, 'Even if I go, I would have nothing to offer His Holiness the Dalai Lama. I would depend on him for everything.'

Lobsang and I exchanged glances.

'If you could go, would you? If you could do it legally?' I asked softly, with Lobsang translating.

She fiddled with her ring, her gaze lowered.

'It's not my fortune, it's not my karma to go.'

In early October, with five signatures and four stamps from various government offices on Ani's internal permit, we left Lhasa at breaking light. Tenzin had found a driver, Pemba, who asked no questions, agreeing to take only Ani and me without the mandatory Tibetan tour guide and costly Alien Travel Permit, which I required but could not afford. Pemba assured me that he knew the route and I could walk around any military checkpoints where permits were checked. I told him Ani was my cook.

Within a day, bumping along China's grandly named National Highway 219, the countryside became arid and the road pitted by monsoonal downpours. The ride became a rollercoaster over mountain passes, each one ascending a few hundred feet higher, the petrol cans at the back of the car leaping dangerously high – all our fuel had to be brought with us as there are no petrol stations in western Tibet. The four-wheel-drive Land cruiser was an old model, with no air-conditioning or radio. Every few hours it ground to a halt and after Pemba poked around under the bonnet, we would set off again. A small, wiry man, given to excitable outbursts of lyrical song, he had a clipped moustache and a steely glint in his eye, suggesting a dogged streak.

According to Ani's new identity card she was a thirty-five-year-old lay woman. I thought that wearing her new plum *chuba* would bring a novel freedom. She could tie her hair in a blue ribbon, rather than the nun's statutory red hair band. She could dance, she could travel incognito without worrying about the police. Several years afterwards, Ani would tell me a very different story. She said that the difficulty in obtaining her documents brought home to her 'the lack of human rights in Tibet. The People's Republic of China is always saying that Tibet is open to the world community. In fact it's only open for the tourist. There isn't any freedom for the Tibetan people. We can't go out, we can't come in, we can't move in our own country. We're restricted like a beautiful bird in a cage.'

Our route to Mount Kailash took us through the central U-Tsang region, via the city of Shigatse and the one-street towns further west of Lhatse and Saga. 'Civilisation' – a few mountain-brick houses – was rapidly left behind. Ahead the road stretched to infinity under an immense sapphire sky. We drove parallel to the silky green Tsangpo River, which has its source at Mount Kailash together with three others – the Indus, Sutlej and Karnali (which becomes the Ganges). Pemba, playing bongos on the wheel of the car, would serenade the Tsangpo as if it were his lover. Ani sat at the back murmuring mantras under her breath; since our departure, a wide, beatific smile had been etched on her face. This would be her second journey to the mountain. On the first she travelled with pilgrims in the back of a truck, her lips dry and bleeding, her face burned. 'By day the sun was like the heat of a kettle, at night so cold tears would freeze.'

Over the next few days we forded rivers that coursed with melting snow, saw herds of *kiang* – wild ass – and deer streaming across the rugged, treeless land. Hares leapt high, and brown eagles with fluffy 'trousers' spiralled into the thermals. In the late afternoon the plains became awash with a golden buttery light before night crept up suddenly to reveal the Milky Way, vast and endless.

I had no problem at the military checkpoints. One time when we were stopped, a young Chinese soldier accepted my passport (read upside down) as proof of a permit. Some nights we stayed in rudimentary guesthouses with grim open-pit toilets, the three of us sharing a dormitory. I worried that Ani would mind sleeping in the same room as Pemba: she said she was used to much worse. They were soon chattering like old friends and when he found out about her false identity card, he scoffed, 'I knew it. I could tell you weren't a real cook.'

In jest, Pemba renamed Ani *ma-chen nyonpa* – 'crazy cook'. I found myself wondering if her apparent wildness – the hair, the outbursts of rip-roaring laughter – was the result of spending extended periods alone in caves. There was no hint of insanity, far from it. Her exaggerated comic gestures were suggestive of a long and respected Buddhist tradition known as 'crazy wisdom'. Described by the Kagyu lama Chögyam Trungpa, one of the first to propagate Tibetan Buddhism widely in the West, crazy wisdom is 'an innocent state of mind that has the quality of early morning – fresh, sparkling, and completely awake'.[3] In the words of Steve Goodman, 'It refers to someone who seems to be intoxicated with an un-bounded, luminous, loving energy. What we call crazy is only crazy from the viewpoint of ego, custom, habit. The craziness is actually higher frequency enjoyment.'[4]

Yak-hair tents studded the sparse grasslands, and when we stopped to make Tibetan butter tea stunted nomad children would gather round, their reddish hair betraying the signs of malnutrition endemic across Tibet. Ani would fetch bread to hand out before going in search of dried yak dung for the fire.

'Ding-gid-ee, ding-gid-ee. Pasaaaaghh So-ha La,' sang Pemba, hitting his knee with gusto, as he put a match to the pancake-sized yak pats.

'*Za ge? Sha?* Eat meat?' said Ani to a nomad girl with bells around her ankles who snatched it hungrily, then watched Ani make butter tea in her wooden churner. Crouching on her haunches, Ani plunged the stick up and down with the rhythm of habit, swirled it clockwise and poured it into our metal cups – we had one each, brought especially for the journey.

'Ha-ha-hah,' said Pemba delightedly, blowing on his tea. 'Thank you, *ma-chen nyonpa!*'

By day four we were driving through desert, the Himalayas cascading to our left. Next to sculpted sand dunes we stopped for a break. My mouth dry as sandpaper, I was happy to be out of the bone-rattling car. Pemba and Ani scampered to the top of the dunes, Ani waving like a thousand-armed Chenresig. I followed, yowling like a banshee at the sheer space and desolate beauty.

'We're all like children,' hooted Pemba before cartwheeling back down.

In such a breathtaking landscape, it was time for a vile pot noodle. Surveying the food supplies – *tsampa*, porridge, bread, some weird Chinese biscuits and a few bags of apples – I sighed: being a vegetarian is never easy in Tibet. After lunch Ani and Pemba began to bury the plastic noodle pots. I insisted we take them with us.

'They'll grow into a pot noodle tree,' teased Pemba.

'No. We can't leave them in such a beautiful place. Ani, you understand.'

But she didn't. Throwing rubbish away – except when on a fire that could anger the elemental spirits – was not considered contrary to any Buddhist precept. Against my better judgement, I left the pots behind – to join the others, plastic bags and mountains of empty beer bottles, now littering Tibet.

With my Tibetan improving, we all managed to communicate. I taught Ani some English words that she found knotty to pronounce, crazy becoming 'kwazeee', driver turned to 'dwivvar'. Pemba alternated between venting his anger against the Chinese and recounting entertaining stories of his journeys. I told him I hoped to write a book about Tibet one day. This caused a violent, unexpected reaction. Thrusting his fist in the air he bellowed, '*Boepa Rangzen!* Free Tibet!'

CHAPTER 14

Following in the Footsteps of a Mystic

FIVE days and over 600 miles later we reached the gateway of Mount Kailash marked by prayer flags, a palette of primary colours against a chalky blue sky. The pyramidal peak, 22,028 feet high, was half hidden by golden-fleece clouds. Pemba did a little jig. Ani's eyes half closed in prayer. I cheered.

'We've arrived, we've arrived,' I cried.

'Vivv awwived, vivvv awwived,' Ani repeated, turning to Pemba. 'Drolma *nying jepo du. Inji pumo.* She's very beautiful. She's from England.'

At the foot of the mountain lay Lake Manasarovar, shimmering an unearthly blue and venerated by Hindus as the lake of the gods; close by is Rakshas Tal – the lake of demons. On the snowy south face of the mountain is a fierce striation known as the Stairway to Heaven. Legend has it that this was caused by the Bon shaman, Naro Bonchung, who tumbled off the peak after losing a battle with the Buddhist *yogi* Milarepa, said to be the first and only person – Kailash is considered too holy to be climbed – to reach the summit. (Milarepa is said to have flown.)

We arrived at dusk at Chiu monastery on a knoll above Lake Manasarovar, which stretched out like a sheet of pewter in the evening light. A smiling monk with a ruby nose ushered us into the adjoining guesthouse and all together we ate rice and cabbage: a feast after days of *tsampa* and pot noodle.

The next morning, a Hindu *sadhu* (holy man) with a black beard, wearing a skimpy saffron cotton lungi, ochre scarf and flip-flops, politely introduced himself as Arun. Settling down on rug-covered sofas in the communal dining area, I asked him what he did.

'I am a seeker of truth,' he replied in perfectly enunciated English. 'I am a seeker of the unknown.'

On hearing these words, I shivered. They brought to mind that phrase of three years before – 'surrender to the unknown' – that I'd read in my Brixton flat. Since then there had been frequent moments when I seemed to be navigating unchartered waters. Frequently I asked myself why I kept returning to Tibet, why I had this hankering for answers. Meeting Arun suggested that I was on course. Over cups of sweet tea he told me about his life-long pilgrimage and four previous visits to Kailash.

'In my younger days I visited London and travelled to sixteen countries in Europe with an inter-rail pass,' he said. 'Then I renounced my family and home to devote my life to exploring what lies beyond the mind, in the realm of spirit. I now have a larger family – the world.'

He turned to look at me, tears welling. 'There's no other truth but that which lies within our heart,' he rhapsodised. 'Truth is not what is, but the understanding of what *is* opens the door to truth. In fact we need not climb any mountain or circumambulate any lake, but turn inwards. Truth is not some far distant place, it is in the knowing of oneself.'

He echoed the Dalai Lama's words – that of itself pilgrimage is unnecessary – and that what is truly important on a sacred journey is inner contemplation. Still, I reasoned, for most of us – including scores of mystics and wandering *yogis* drawn to Kailash – an outer journey is necessary for an inner transformation to occur. The Tibetan word for pilgrimage, *neykhor*, means 'to circle around a sacred place' and, writes Peter Gold, 'As one circumambulates [or makes a *kora*] of a sacred mountain one links up with its psychospiritual energy and enters its ideal universe through the powers of the imagination.'[1] This walking meditation stills the mind, allowing pilgrims to be touched by the spirit of the place and find their own quiet centre within.

At dawn the follow morning our party set off for the sacred mountain. Overnight the car radiator had frozen and within a few miles the top overheated, while the bottom remained icy. On reaching a tea house, Pemba bustled around trying to fix the car. Outside on the dirt, a sheep had just been slaughtered, its intestines, bile and shit strewn everywhere, making me feel a touch queasy. To my horror, Pemba decided to light a fire underneath the bonnet to thaw it out, assuring me that it was 'the Tibetan way'. Impatient to get going, I paced around. Miraculously the radiator defrosted without blowing up and Pemba drove cross-country at high speed, rattling over rough ground. Frightened *kiang* bounded and a fox tore in front, running as if we were about to chase and to skin it for a winter hat. With the rising sun, the landscape transformed into lilac and lavender, soft coppers and deep browns.

One *kora* of Kailash is said to purify the sins of this lifetime, 108 to secure a ticket to nirvana. Some Tibetans make the thirty-two-mile *kora* around the mountain in a single day. Most Westerners take three. A strenuous trail that crosses an 18,600-foot pass, the Drolma La, then descends to a river valley, it begins and ends at the town of Darchen at the foot of the mountain. The town was known for its notoriously vigilant PSB, so Pemba advised that as I had no travel permit, he would drop Ani and me to the west of the trail and stay behind with the car in Darchen, playing mah-jong with other Tibetan drivers.

Ani and I looked a motley pair, I thought. I had opted for a grey woollen scarf to stop my ears freezing over, fashioned around my head like Lawrence of Arabia, and a bright orange puffa jacket; a video camera was flung over one shoulder. Ani wore her plum *chuba*, a psychedelic pink sweatshirt and nun's saffron gold blouse, the cherry-red sunhat perched on her head. Walking through thick scrub – we were dropped a couple of miles before the trail began – Ani's woollen long johns soon became peppered with barbed ears of corn, which would take days to extract with painstaking care.

Finally we reached the start of the *kora*, Tarboche, the large prayer-flag pole. Every May during the Saga Dawa festival that marks the start of the pilgrimage season, the prayer flag is raised. Close by were ruins of thirteen stone *stupas*, which, together with four out of eight monasteries around the mountain, were demolished during the Cultural Revolution.

It was a perfect, mostly cloudless day. With the play of light and shadow, the face of Kailash was constantly transformed from a giant breast to a pyramid to a cathedral of rock and ice. For both Buddhists and Hindus it is regarded as the *axis mundi* connecting the earth with the universe, corresponding to Mount Meru, the physical and metaphysical centre of the world. In the words of the Dalai Lama, such a power place 'seems somehow blessed or charged as if there is some kind of electricity around it. Pilgrims come to feel these mysterious vibrations and to try and see some of the same visions the devout master saw.'[2]

I felt the dutiful pilgrim with my bundle of photocopied sheets from various guidebooks explaining the mythology of the mountain – the significance of each rock, the story behind each miracle. I wanted to be open to the mysterious power of this storied landscape, which in the tradition of sacred geography is envisioned as the abode of Demchok, Buddha of Great Bliss. More than that, I hoped to experience the *kora* through Ani's eyes, to touch the master's footprints in rocks as she did, to fall into the depth of silence as she fell.

I quickly realised it wouldn't be that simple. Starting at over 14,000 feet, I soon tired from my heavy load and regretted piling my rucksack with such useless rubbish; I was somewhat envious that Ani could travel so lightly. It seemed an apt metaphor for my life: still weighed down by unnecessary clutter, physical and mental, and needless worries. While Ani kept a steady rhythm, muttering *Om Mani Padme Hung* – its vibration is said to mirror that of the universe and by repeating it the practitioner comes into harmony with the heartbeat of life – I attempted to focus on the mountain and ignore the pain seeping through my shoulders.

We took a detour to a tiny monastery perched on a crag several hundred feet above us, where an old monk, his right eye lost in a map of wrinkles, invited us into a soot-covered kitchen and insisted we drink tea and eat *tsampa*, while he read scriptures out aloud to us. With blackened feet, nails curling like claws, he resembled a ragged crow. Another monk with long hair and an ethereal manner opened the inner temple. Inside lies the famous Choku statue, a white marble Buddha with a faint smile, believed to possess many magical gifts including that of speech. There was also the conch of the eminent Indian *yogi* Naropa and his huge cauldron filled with *dri* butter; to lay eyes upon it is said to bring liberation from the cycle of rebirth.

Looking down from Choku *gompa*, the Lha Chu – 'divine river', said to carry the empowerment of the mountain – had become a slither of blue and the pilgrims in the valley below looked like stick people. After a sheer path down, Ani and I continued our *kora* on the left bank of the river. The west face of Kailash, dripping with overhanging snow then disappeared from view. A curious hush enveloped the whole area, only broken by fierce, guttural cries from the sky burial site on the cliffs above. In the sky vultures wheeled and wild dogs gathered to feast on a fresh corpse: two old men had died making the *kora*, considered highly auspicious for their future rebirth.

I began to relax, to appreciate the feeling of the earth beneath my feet, my body falling into rhythm. I reached over to give Ani's hand a firm squeeze. A surfeit of gratitude spread through me at being alive in such an extraordinary place. I was filled by an overwhelming tenderness for this woman at my side. Her childlike enchantment awoke a chord of joy within me. Striding along together, frequently laughing at nothing in particular, our hearts seemed to communicate.

All of a sudden, Ani cried out, 'The north face!' Spontaneously, without missing a beat, we both fell to our knees as if we had been pushed from behind: together our heads bowed to the earth. It was an authentic and strange gesture of surrender, which took me completely by surprise. Above loomed the north face of Kailash, a palace of jet-black rock, so sheer that the snow barely clung to its side. Its ghoulish eyes gave an impression of doors, a portal perhaps into another world – the way out of the endless cycle of birth and death into bliss.

In the late afternoon, after a boulder-to-boulder crossing over a fast-flowing river, Ani jumping like an agile goat ahead, goading me on when my balance wavered, we wearily scrambled towards the welcoming lights of Drirapuk monastery. By good fortune, Ani knew an old monk there who invited us to spend the night, rather than continue on to the pilgrims' concrete rest house. Inside the dim, smoky kitchen a gaggle of pilgrims were slurping *thukpa*. After a tour of the small Kagyu *gompa* built around a retreat cave where the *yogi* Gotsangpa had meditated, Tsewang, the jolly Khampa Rinpoche, invited us into his simple meditation room with a spectacular view directly onto the north face. Next to a large wooden cot where he slept was a cushion piled with rugs for his meditation.

'Sit down.' He smiled, packed away his scriptures and presented each of us with a blessed red ribbon. In turn we offered him a white *khata*, some of the herbs I had brought blessed by the seventeenth Karmapa – his guru – and some precious sandalwood beads from my *mala*, which I'd been handing out to pilgrims en route. In spite of a rash of teenage acne, there was something oddly transparent about the thirty-one-year-old Rinpoche, with a finely chiselled face and long tapered fingers.

'Where are you from?' he asked, studying me closely.

'England,' I said in Tibetan, shifting uncomfortably.

'You like Tibet? Not too cold?'

'No. My health is good, mostly.'

Reaching over to clasp my wrist and read my pulse, he said, 'I'm a doctor.' He closed his eyes and smiled. 'Yes, good health and a big heart.'

'And what about you?' he asked Ani.

'I'm a nun,' she replied coyly.

'A nun . . .' He looked perplexed.

'Yes,' she said hastily, smoothing out her *chuba*. 'It was easier to travel dressed like this. Fewer problems.'

He nodded in sympathy.

Settling comfortably in his wooden seat, the Rinpoche began to show us photos of past and present Kagyu lamas. When he came to a picture of the Karmapa, he sighed heavily, describing the emptiness he felt since the fifteen-year-old had made his dramatic escape across the Himalayas to freedom earlier that year. 'Again the sun in Tibet has been obscured by clouds.'

I noticed, particularly in front of Tibetan lamas or older monks, or, in her words, someone 'of a higher standing', Ani would become nervy. I suspected this was a reflection of the uneasy position of nuns in Tibet. But sitting with the jolly Rinpoche, Ani's shyness evaporated.

Staring at him curiously, she asked, 'Why do you have such pimples?'

It was his turn to become bashful and he muttered something about the cold weather.

Seemingly unaware of his embarrassment, she persisted. 'But so many spots. You don't have medicine for them?'

I changed the subject and asked if he stayed at the monastery throughout the winter.

'Yes. There are two monks, a cook and myself. Snow falls to waist height, and I stay there.' He pointed to his meditation box. 'I'm happy then.'

Outside a crescent new moon rose and the north face gleamed silvery white. Inside, butter lamps flickered, and the sweet woody aroma of incense threaded through the room. I was transported back in time as the Rinpoche regaled us with tales, his elegant hands painting pictures in the air, pulling strands of stories together like a lyrical tapestry, about the *yogis* who had once lived at Mount Kailash. He described Milarepa's transformation from black magician to enlightened mystic and his supernatural feats in the contest with the Bon master, Naro Bonchung, evidence of which are visible along the *kora*. He talked about Demchok, the deity of supreme bliss, whom Tibetans believe resides at the mountain, and who is 'pale as the moon like [the Hindu god] Shiva and wears a tiger-skin around his waist as an emblem of power'.

Listening to the Rinpoche as he brought to life the characters on this epic canvas of Buddhism, Ani sat entranced, her face animated. She mirrored the lama's wonder, uttering bird-like one-letter syllables of encouragement. I could see for her there was no suspension of disbelief. This was her reality, founded on a potent mixture of the magical, divinatory and mythical. My worldview was grounded on the rocks of empiricism and logic and I thought that this linear view of cause and effect tended to exclude, rather than embrace, life's mystery.

The lama instructed me in some mantras, noting the words in neat Tibetan handwriting. He then turned to Ani. 'You have deep compassion,' he said gently. 'Sometimes your mind gets troubled and upset. You should try to become more calm.' Ani nodded, her eyes bright. And then, abruptly, the audience was over. The young Rinpoche politely said he must continue with his evening practice, and offered us the shrine room opposite for the night. At one end was an empty throne, and a candle flickered in the chill breeze. Bedding down, I was lulled to sleep by the hypnotic hum of the Rinpoche's prayers.

During the night snow had fallen and we awoke to a dazzling wonderland, with even the north face covered by a dusting of snow. A funnel of dawn light illuminated Dronglung – Wild Yak – Valley, scattering rose-coloured rays across the peaks. At sunup, the Rinpoche waved us goodbye like dear friends, and, climbing towards Drolma La, Ani and I joined three other pilgrims – two young, taciturn farmers in bobble hats and an old toothless man with a leathery face, mostly hidden by large square sunglasses.

The seventy-nine-year-old *po-la* – old man – wearing red tracksuit bottoms, flimsy plimsolls and a straw hat, holy cords strung around his neck, told us he'd done the *kora* 500 times. This should mean by Tibetan lore that he was enlightened. I glanced at him for any potential signs of this and, sensing my gaze, he turned to ask: '*Kyi-po dug-geh?* Are you happy?'

I was, sort of. Except for waves of dizziness and needing to stop every few paces to catch my breath. Ani walked ahead, and every so often patiently waited for me, often turning nervously to check my face for signs of altitude sickness. We were over 16,000 feet and ascending fast. Without prompting, one of the young farmers offered to carry my rucksack. Gratefully I handed it over.

The higher we climbed, the more there was to see, touch and feel. The *kora* can be viewed as symbolically enacting one's own death before being reborn at the Drolma La – Pass of Tara, the Saviouress, or 'she who ferries across'. Tibetan pilgrims traditionally leave a piece of clothing, a tooth or a strand of hair as a renunciation of their old life. As we passed the area scattered with frosted pieces of clothing I attempted, without much success, to grasp the impermanence of life.

Further on, the *po-la* came into his own as our guide and watched, smacking his pink gums together in approval, as we all wriggled through the sinner's tunnel, a narrow passage about fifteen feet long, through which pilgrims must go on their bellies. Tibetans believe that only the virtuous can get through: even fat sinners should be able to make it while the slimmest will get stuck. After all our group had crawled through, he said, 'You all have good hearts.'

When we reached a stack of three giant boulders, each bearing pronounced circular indents, the *po-la* said Milarepa and Naro Bonchung had left them after their contest to see who would rule the mountain. While Ani took off her hat in reverence, bowing down to receive a blessing, I was suddenly overcome by a wave of scepticism. In spite of my best efforts to believe, I still doubted – the footprints in the rocks said to be left by lamas as if they'd put their sole through Plasticene, the self-arising images of Buddhas. I was in a sublime landscape; inside I was suffering a crisis of faith. Aren't miracles simply a way to hoodwink believers? Icons and ritual: don't they bind people into a dogmatic religion, encouraging blind faith rather than an individual relationship with the divine? And even entrusting oneself to a lama, surely, wasn't that disempowering, placing oneself in the hands of somebody else?

Faced with an onslaught of negative judgements, scorn and disbelief – for my fellow pilgrims and Ani, that she was able to believe and that I couldn't – I stormed off, stumbling along the trail alone. I soon felt somewhat foolish. But my own demons were armoured for battle, and still the questions kept coming. Who am I? What happens when I die? What is the purpose of it all?

I forced myself to stop, to step back and witness my thoughts, rather than corkscrew into them. With that, some of the negativity fell away. I was left vulnerable and exposed, wishing I could explain my erratic behaviour to Ani. I knew that a pilgrimage forces old stuck patterns and unexpressed fears, latent emotions and tendencies to rise to the surface. I knew I had to face them firmly, squarely – and do so alone.

By the time we reached Drolma La, the highest point of the *kora,* over 18,000 feet and where legend attests that the pilgrim crosses from one dimension to another, to be redeemed by the goddess of compassion, my head pounded from the lack of oxygen. My mind was wiped clean. A light flurry of snowflakes fell. '*Lha Gyalo! Lha Gyalo!* – Victory to the gods!' – shouted the Tibetan pilgrims to proclaim their arrival. Too busy trying to breathe – everybody was gasping in the thin air – my angry outburst dissipated and, pausing, I looked around.

Covering the pass were thousands of prayer flags heavy with ice, spiralling from a large boulder. The high altitude caused everything to pulsate, while the snow muffled all sound. I was standing in an ancient, otherworldly moonscape of colour and sparkling light. All around were pilgrims. One Tibetan man had a tiny baby in a swaddle of blankets strapped to his back; a group of nomads with thick plaits and ragged clothes, whooping with glee, were stringing up prayer flags.

The entire experience felt hundreds of years old, of a forgotten, distant era when there was little to do but pray and devote one's life to a higher purpose. I reached into my pouch and scattered the last love seeds. In my pocket I felt the photo of Tara, my talisman from three years before. Now standing on top of her pass, with Ani at my side, I couldn't help wondering if there wasn't a mysterious connection between them.

(Later I would learn that when Ani meditates on Green Tara – Drolma in Tibetan – she visualises shining a green light on all sentient beings, in all realms. Ani then imagines taking every being into her own heart and into her own body. As she does so, she focuses on the image of Green Tara in her mind's eye and at the end of the meditation, Ani explained, 'I go into the heart of the goddess.')

My moments of quiet contemplation were broken by excited shouts. Ani had mentioned to one of the pilgrims that I had a *mala* blessed by the Dalai Lama. Within moments I was surrounded by a horde of warrior-looking Khampas, each with a knife in a silver scabbard on their hip.

'*Kuchi, kuchi*,' they cried, hands clasped together, thumbs up. 'Please, please. Give me a bead for my wife, my child. Please, just one more.' After exhausting all of my 108 beads – handing over half a dozen to the *po-la* – we were off again, beginning the descent from the pass on an ankle-twisting path of jagged moraine, which overlooked a circular pool of silvery jade, known as the '*dakini* bathing pool'. Following Ani's footprints in the snow, my eyes smarting from a touch of snow blindness, I quickened my pace under the Axe of Karma – an ominous-looking rock hanging from a cliff as if about to strike.

After a brief lunch, sharing bread and butter, salty tea and biscuits, with our fellow pilgrims, the path levelled to a gentle river plain. For the next few hours Kailash was hidden. I didn't see any Westerners all day, only bands of Tibetan pilgrims swinging prayers wheels, in outlandish hats and ruffled-up *chubas*, who would not have looked out of place at a medieval pageant.

At teatime we arrived at the 'Miracle Cave' of Milarepa, nestling into reddish cliffs. Inside were clear imprints in the roof where the *yogi* is said to have pushed it up with his head and shoulders. Determined to leave my sceptic's hat at the door, I joined the queue for a blessing and lit a candle in the darkened grotto. The monk in charge was a *nakpa* – Tantric *yogi* – with dreadlocks coiled around his head, with whom Ani fell into lively conversation.

The *po-la* insisted we continue on and complete the *kora* in two days (the harder the pilgrimage, the more merit accrued in the believer's karmic bank balance). I was sorry to leave as I'd hoped to spend a night at the 'Miracle Cave'. Unable to explain and my fellow pilgrims insistent that we all finish together, I chased after them. A barefoot Indian *sadhu* limped past, rags between his toes, grimacing with each step.

Towards the end of the *kora* we passed a woman in a lilac blouse and grey *chuba*, trainers on her hands for protection, prostrating around the mountain. Any of my minor achievements and aches paled into insignificance. Ani explained her husband would give her food and make a shelter at night during the fortnight it would take to complete one *kora*. Her husband sat patiently further along the path, smoking a cigarette. It was hard not to be moved by such faith, or by the *mani* walls, each rock intricately carved with prayers, which littered the landscape. I could appreciate why the Bonpos believe Mount Kailash is a giant crystal, reflecting and transforming light, and why the Tibetans say it is the seventh – and highest – chakra of the world.

With each step, I tried to release my doubts, envisaging Kailash as a symbol of consciousness, an unchanging reality that lies beneath the maelstrom of one's emotions, thoughts and desires. In its raw power, its shape – a pyramid with four distinct sides – it seemed to mirror the diamond of enlightenment which Buddhists believe lies within one's heart. In an inexplicable way everything about the mountain only confirmed that we are spirit and the rest – the body, the personality – are the garments we've chosen to incarnate in this time round, and which we discard at death.

I reflected that for over two decades Ani's life purpose was devoted to polishing her own diamond, to fathoming the depths of her own heart. She had something of a swan's flight of purpose and vision, a quality of rose petals, a scent of fresh oranges; the good things of life wrapped up in a person who has no idea that she possesses so much. And for precisely that reason is only the more delightful to be around.

Towards the end of the trail, Ani nestled her arms and elbows in four deep indents in a rock, motioning me to follow suit. They are said to be the last marks of a Khampa woman whose baby drowned at the start of the pilgrimage. In penance the grieving mother made thirteen *koras* of the mountain and on her last, left her physical body to become a *dakini*.

'*Toe, toe!* Look, look,' said the *po-la*, jabbing his stick to the heavens. There among the clouds were splashed the vibrant colours of the rainbow. I joked with Ani that it was a message from the *dakinis* and she seized my hand, and we ran along the path. Finally at dusk we arrived in Darchen where we bade goodbye to our friends who were going to spend the night in a rest house. On the outskirts of the township I saw the familiar sight of our white Toyota. Pemba was waiting for us with hot sweet milk and steamed dough balls.

Although physically exhausted, I was content. Ani glowed, 'happy and satisfied'. I sensed that the shared experience of the pilgrimage would stay with me. There was an underground stream of understanding between us where words did not – could not – reach. But only later would I come to know its significance. The intensity of the journey – a time to contemplate one's whole motivation for living – meant I needed to take a pause to absorb what I'd learned and, with my visa running out, I felt ready to return back to the world. Our pilgrimage, for now at least, was complete.

As the sun set, the peak of Kailash was transmuted to gold. Ancient and noble, it stood apart from the other mountains, like a king surrounded by his ministers. What has this mountain witnessed, I wonder, in its 50 million years? In comparison the life of a human seemed pitifully short. The town of Darchen, at the foot of the mountain, has brothels and gambling dens. Kailash remains, untouched and unclimbed, a place where the human spirit can stretch without limit.

CHAPTER 15

Drifting like a Cloud Wanderer

SEVEN months had passed since the end of the Kailash pilgrimage and
I was ready for the next stage of my journey. I had brought a new
video camera for a documentary on Tibet I was preparing and timed my
visit to Lhasa for the annual Saga Dawa festival – to celebrate the
Buddha's birth, death and enlightenment – when pilgrims descend on
the capital for a vibrant month of prayer, alms-giving and ceremony. I
tracked down Ani's whereabouts through the monk Lobsang with whom
I'd kept in touch. Periodically he would send group emails to his posse
of *inji* friends.

'Hi! My dear how are you nowadays [*sic*]?' he would write. 'I really
miss you so please if you have time you can send to me about how you. I
am at the Jokhang Temple just fine.' Soon after arriving in Lhasa, in May
2001, I found Lobsang on duty in one of the shrine rooms. He looked
nervous, his features drawn, and before he would talk to me his eyes
darted furtively around to check no-one was listening. Later he pointed
out a Jokhang 'spy monk', whispering, 'Life's very difficult now. We're
given money from the Chinese government but we're not happy. I think
I'm not a good monk. I don't do practice like the Ani-la.' His older
brother who worked nearby in a restaurant barely acknowledged me.

Together with Pema, Ani's friend who ran the small school, Lobsang and another friend of mine, Jane, who spoke fluent Tibetan, I made a day trip to see Ani. Despite a concerted effort to improve my Tibetan, living in Kathmandu for several months and attending regular language classes, I still spoke broken Tibenglish.

Ani was staying temporarily in a cave above Shugseb *gompa*, some fifty miles south of the capital in Chushul County. I was intrigued to see what her 'home' would look like inside. Some caves, built close to a monastery for limited periods of retreat, were known as meditation-cottages; *ritod* or remote caves were always perched high in the lee of the mountain, overlooking a lake or stream. From the anecdotes that pepper the writings of Alexandra David-Neel, the first European woman to set foot in Lhasa in 1924 and who spent time living among hermits, there were even caves built like a 'small fort', spacious and well appointed with servant's quarters. 'After ten or twenty years, or even a longer time, in the wilderness', these hermits 'are far from being insane', she writes. 'There is nothing really remarkable about this . . . their days are occupied by methodical exercises in spiritual training.'[1]

Since the twelfth-century Shugseb nunnery has been a Nyingma retreat centre, associated with the famous female adept and *chod* practitioner, Machig Labdron. Situated on the side of Mount Gangri Thokar or 'white-skull mountain', this ridge is identified in the tradition of Tantric sacred literature with Vajrayogini – the Tantric goddess of Pemako and that of Ani's personal *yidam* (meditational deity). The caves scattered along the ridge symbolise Vajrayogini's chakras or energy centres and have been consecrated by renunciates throughout history, among them the great fourteenth-century Nyingma master Longchen Rabjampa, who practised the highly advanced Dzogchen meditation.

To mark the annual Saga Dawa festival the Shugseb nuns were performing a special ceremony dedicated to Tara. When we arrived, strains of sweet mellifluent chanting floated on the breeze. From the ornate temple it was another hour-long climb to the cluster of caves above, nestled into the sandy hillside. Some had neat wooden doors;

others were roughly protected by a heavy piece of cloth. All afforded an expansive view over the latticework of barley fields, a sinuous river meandering through. Ani's cave was locked but after we called her name a familiar figure bounded towards us, her unruly jet-black hair streaming behind.

After a brief embrace, we sat down for butter tea and presented her with our gifts, among them a Miss Kitty vanity set – with a comb and hairbrush – which she examined with delight.

Pouring the tea into tiny cups, shared among us, Ani turned to me and, with Jane translating, she said, 'I knew you were coming. I dreamed of you three times. Once in America, another time with me filming in modern Chinese buildings and then recently in Lhasa.'

I beamed inwardly.

'I was up in a cave helping an old lama,' she continued. 'He's teaching me a practice called *trulkhor*. The rest of the time I'm on *ngyun ney* – fasting and meditating.'

It sounded a typically gruelling regime with only one meal a day and three hours' sleep a night. I noticed heavy bags under her eyes and, like the cherry-red sunhat from the trip to Kailash the year before, her natural glow seemed somewhat faded. Her *chuba* was filthy, covered with soot and grease, her lace-up shoes worn through.

'I hope we're not disturbing you,' said Jane, concerned.

'Don't worry,' Ani replied. 'I'm happy to see all of you.'

Her fifty-nine-year-old teacher was a fat, bear-like lama with a sanguine complexion and shaved head who had been instructed by 'a great miracle-working *yogi*' from Kham in *trulkhor*, 'a sort of Kagyu spiritual exercise for good health by controlling air'. (The thirty-eight *trulkhors* – 'magical wheel' in Tibetan – are a Tantric practice originating from the Six Yogas of Naropa. They are vigorous, active yoga-style exercises graded from gentle to advanced, used together with breath control. By generating inner heat, the *trulkhors* reinvigorate the body's subtle pathways, enhancing the connection between mind and body.)

'The lama used to know how to do it well,' Ani said, rolling her eyes.

'He knows how to do the special breathing but he can't jump. I'm learning with another monk and when the lama gets tired and his breathing is rapid, he looks very funny.' She pealed with laughter, impersonating his bloated wide-eyed face. 'When we laugh, he gets very angry.'

'So can he jump?' I asked.

'No. I don't know if it's because his body is too heavy or because he's drunk too much *chang* but he can't jump at all. I don't think the teaching is very good. I've been trying to jump but haven't succeeded.'

'He drinks *chang*?'

'Yes.' She pulled a long face, her mouth puckering. 'I'm scared of that lama. Sometimes he comes knocking on the door at night making rude jokes. I get frightened and go to another cave or into the nunnery.'

'Ani, that's no good,' I said, feeling protective over her. I want to know more. Has this happened often? Do many lamas drink *chang*?

She gave a tiny shrug, without elaborating further. She stood up and pushed open the door to the cave, ushering me in. Inside was an area roughly ten by six feet, just high enough for a small person to stand up. It smelled musty, of damp earth and wood smoke, the misshapen walls exuding a glacial chill. In one corner was a flat stone ledge for her bed. On top, a piece of plastic, a thin carpet and a multicoloured Chinese blanket; by the entrance, a blackened kettle, a *tsampa* bowl, one candle and a plastic pot with tea leaves. Some black plastic bin liners were stuck to one wall to prevent leaks. Womb-like it was not. Any romantic notion that I had about the life of a hermit seeking out the natural hobbit-holes and cosy grottoes was roundly banished as I tried to imagine surviving for months in temperatures below freezing.

'Ani-la,' I exclaimed. 'You've nothing warm. Not even a mattress.'

Mustering a brave smile, she admitted that for the first few months it was very cold. 'Now I'm OK, the weather is better. I wear two *chubas*, two blouses. I enjoy being here.' She paused. 'I'm happiest alone, I'm happiest meditating.'

In an attempt to bring my world to her, I'd brought some photos of

Australia – the azure sea at Byron Bay – which I had recently visited. It dawned on me that Ani never asked about my background – a cultural trait of Tibetans who tend not to pry or enquire beyond social pleasantries: a reflection maybe of their insular past and inward-looking nature.

Curiously, when information is offered, I've found Tibetans are riveted and love to gossip. Their reserved nature is epitomised in their tea-drinking ritual. As a guest it's polite to decline tea three times before accepting, and then only with much nodding of the head and a chorus of 'No, no. Not for me. You're too kind.' Anxious to please, Ani admitted that as part of her religious practice, she 'doesn't like to offend anyone'.

Staring at the photo, she looked perplexed by the sea. 'Ossit-rail-ee-ah. Ossit-rail-ee-ah.'

'You have to go on an aeroplane to get there; it takes twenty-four hours from Tibet.'

Her face fell vacant.

Jane explained, 'On a horse, it would take a year.'

'Ah leh.' Ani's eyes widened. 'It's very far.'

After a couple of hours we descended to the nunnery. She thanked me again for the 'exciting and wonderful' trip to Mount Kailash and all the trouble in securing her travel permit. Her mouth wiggling from side to side like a horse chewing hay, she repeated the English words I'd taught her the year before.

'Dog. Dwivvverrr. Sun. Moooooon.' And then, perfectly imitating me, she clapped her hands together: 'Okaaay!' Lessss go!'

'Werrry goood.' Pema giggled.

Turning to her friend, Ani reeled off the costs for the Kailash journey – the guesthouses, driver, food – much to my embarrassment. I've always been surprised that for someone who has no money, or perhaps because of that, Ani can be a worrywart about how much I spend. She refused anything from me.

'I can beg,' she said. 'You've come on an aeroplane which is very expensive. You need it.'

As she was on retreat she could not come to Lhasa with us and I promised to return to see her again before I left Tibet. During the drive back, it occurred to me that however brief, each time I saw Ani it was always rich. Unlike most people who are defined by what they do, how they dress, what car they drive or how much money they earn, none of that makes Ani who she is. She has no commitments, no dependants, no possessions. No plans, no earthly goals. Nevertheless she exuded a robust solidity, as if sustained wholly from within. By what, I was not sure. I had the impression that in her solitude she found a deeper mystery, one that I had not yet touched, and perhaps might never do so.

I recalled John Crook's description of *yogis* he had met in Ladakh, which came close to pinning down this elusive quality that Ani possessed. 'The most striking feature of the *yogins* was equanimity. They seemed to reside within an aura of inner peace and total certainty . . . All of them possessed a species of assured happiness rooted in an absence of ordinary attachment as the world knows it: land, wealth, marriage.' In the words of the Japanese Zen monk tradition, Crook continues, these *yogis* 'had become cloud wanderers . . . who drift from monastery to monastery with no premeditated plans'.[2]

The image of Ani as a cloud wanderer captured my imagination and as we entered the city at nightfall, I remembered Ani telling me that when she was a child, herding yak, she would look up at the sky and see every passing cloud as a Buddha, bestowing blessings on all who passed beneath.

Back in Lhasa, I met up with Tenzin briefly before he left the city to take a tour group to Mount Kailash. We joined the throngs of pilgrims to walk around the Potala. This time he was strict about speaking openly with me. His girlfriend, a policewoman, had warned him that many of the PSB informers were women dressed in *chubas* who mingled among the crowd, eavesdropping on conversations. If any

Tibetans were heard speaking unpatriotically, he said, 'They would be taken easily and fast.'

Tenzin had shaken off some of the morose apathy of the previous year. His hair had grown back long and thick, and, with it, his unruly rebelliousness. His head-turning laugh, a 'ha-ha hee-hee', punctuated his speech. Tenzin said he was determined to get a Chinese passport – no easy matter, requiring reams of paperwork and substantial bribes – to leave Tibet legally.

'Life's so rough here, man. No chance to earn good money. Already this year more tour guides from India get kicked out from their job. Three hundred more guides coming from China. There's no security.'

After spinning battered prayer wheels that lined the alleyways running parallel to the Potala, Tenzin and I cut behind the palace to the lake and visited the tiny Lukhang Temple. Once used by generations of Dalai Lamas for contemplation, it's a favourite haunt, quiet, hallowed and rarely visited by tourists.

'Many more Chinese visitors coming to Tibet,' he said. 'Even though they don't like the yak butter smell—' he stopped, and I expected a tirade to follow.

'Ya' know, sister Drolma-la, I sometimes like them more than Tibetans these days. So often Tibetans don't care for anyone except themselves. Look at all those beggars from Shigatse.' He pointed to a line of ragged women, snot-smeared babies to their breasts, hands raised to the heavens pleading for a donation. 'They come to Lhasa to make money. Tibetans are still very regional, Drolma. They're only loyal to where they're from.' He shook his head. 'There's no national loyalty.'

Tenzin and I found a secluded spot behind the temple and while we tossed bread to the fish and ducks, he updated me on contemporary Tibetan life.

'There are more checkpoints on the road to Kailash,' he began, lobbing a crust into the water. 'You were lucky to make it last year without problem. This year would be impossible. The Golmud to Lhasa railway is definitely coming.' (Crossing the vast, high Changtang plateau, one of the most forbidding places on earth, the Qinghai–Tibet railway, 670 miles along, will be the world's highest.)

Tenzin stretched out his legs.

'Good news about Tashi. He'll be freed in the next two weeks. His brother-in-law's a policeman and through his *guanxi* helped him get an early release.'

'That's great. How is he?'

'Fine,' he said shortly, implying it was a stupid question. 'In the prison he was working as a cook. I heard that inside was like a big mafia, lots of fighting. Every time new prisoner come in, Tashi have to beat him – just like he was beaten up. It's bullshit, man.' He stared into the lake. 'My country's gone to the dogs since red flag over Tibet. Everything is illegal, but anything's possible.'

Lhasa looked like a construction site. New sewage pipes were being laid and the road widened between the Barkhor and the Potala Palace. A PSB building, several storeys high, was being built, a smattering of new security cameras in place. Gusts of wind carrying fetid dust whistled down the streets: no doubt contributing to my racking cough. While I watched from my hotel window, a yellow bulldozer swung within a hair's-breadth of decapitating an old woman. Chinese men in hard hats were hollering at crowds of shoppers to stand back. Nobody took the slightest notice, least of all the children playing in their new sewage-laced mud pit.

After a few days sick with flu and nights haunted by vivid nightmares – Tibetan female torturers, police break-ins – I arranged a final outing to see Ani together with Sonam, the cheerful curly-haired guide from the Pemako trip. We had barely seen one another since then and when I met him, he told me that shortly after Ian Baker's final journey to Pemako, sponsored by the National Geographic Society, the region had been shut to foreigners.

(In November 1998 Baker and Ken Storm made headlines worldwide when they reached and photographed the lost 'Falls of Shangri-la', which they measured at 108 feet and named the 'Hidden Falls of Dorje Phagmo'. National Geographic would later name Baker as one of its six 'Explorers for the Millennium'. His claim to be the first to discover the falls was challenged by other Americans, among them Gil Gillenwater, and vigorously by the Chinese who had led an expedition into the valleys around the same time. In January 2000 the *China Daily* published an article – 'Chinese Explorers get to the falls first' – reporting that in 1987 an army helicopter had been the first to photograph the waterfall. According to some Chinese news reports, there was suggestion of flooding the entire region for a massive hydroelectric power project at the great bend of the Tsangpo – submerging a literal paradise on earth.)[3]

These days Sonam preferred desk jobs to taking clients out: 'That's boring, I've been all over Tibet.' He laughed. 'Now I'm trying to go to America.'

We hired a car to go to Chushul County and the Shugseb nunnery. Inside the courtyard the nuns' chanting was softer, worn down from days of ceremony. Carrying groceries and my foam camping mattress to leave with Ani, we climbed up to see her and had a picnic outside her cave. Sonam was shocked at her basic living conditions: 'It's like going back to the eighteenth century.' When he teased her for being 'a fashion nun', pointing out the bracelets and rings carved with Buddhist symbols, Ani threw her head back and gave a loud, resounding laugh.

'Other monks and nuns have problems from the police but I don't because I look like an *agi* – a lay woman,' she said. (I later discovered that as a Tantric practitioner it's customary to wear, like Ani does, a ring engraved with a bell on the left hand, symbolising the feminine and on the right hand, a ring with a *vajra,* for the masculine, to represent 'the integration of the external and internal energies of the masculine and feminine'.)[4]

I had a score of questions I wanted to ask Ani and settled for a handful. Sonam offered to translate. Why does she go on pilgrimage? It makes her happy. Where next? She shrugged. Would she stay in the city? Emphatically no. 'I don't like the smells. I get confused and lose my way,' she said. 'There's too much to see and look at in Lhasa. It's not like it used to be.'

Ani had first visited the capital at the age of twenty-one, in 1982, when the political situation eased and Tibetans could begin, cautiously, to practise religion again. Back then it was very small, with few buildings and 'no chance to get lost'. At night there were no street lights and people milked their *dri* (female yak) in front of the Jokhang. She went there on pilgrimage, she began, turning the beads of her *mala*. 'For the first time we were allowed to visit our sacred temples after the end of the Cultural Revolution. I remember being very excited.'

'Were there many Chinese?'

'Not so many, only two or three Beijing jeeps. Mainly officials dressed in blue Mao suits with patches on the knees and soldiers smoking cigarettes. In the morning, the army would shout slogans and jog anti-clockwise on the *lingkhor* [outer pilgrimage route] around Lhasa. The Tibetans would go clockwise, dressed in their best woollen costumes,' she recalled, smiling. 'It was our tradition at that time to wear our new clothes when visiting monasteries. Many of the pilgrims came from the villages with horses and carts. As there was no lodging, they stayed in large white tents on the edge of the city.' She paused, and then said, 'I never heard or saw thieves or beggars. Not like now.'

I knew that Ani's grandparents had suffered during the sixties but the details of her childhood were still hazy and I was hoping she would tell me more. It was a safe place to talk and knowing she was comfortable with Sonam, I broached the subject. Yes, of course, she said.

Like every family Ani's parents had to destroy their Buddhist icons, scriptures and altar during the Cultural Revolution, living under a shroud of fear. As a child, every day there were revolutionary meetings led by zealous Tibetan Red Guards and, later, Chinese officials. It was a time, she recalled, when 'to stand up was wrong, to sit down was wrong. People never knew what they would be punished for next, everyone was very scared to speak out loud – even the sound of one's voice could incite trouble.' During the meetings they had to denounce the old government, religion and praise Communism. The popular Buddhist prayer – *Om Mani Padme Hung* – was replaced by *Mao Tse-tung wan sui*.

As rich nomads who owned land and animals – over a hundred yak, goat and sheep – Ani's grandparents were among many of those singled out. Their land was confiscated and the animals were taken by the government and dispersed among poorer families. Her mother, Lhamo, was forced to watch as her parents were paraded, mocked and humiliated in public *thamzing* – speak bitterness meetings – before being taken away and tortured.

Ani said she was very young and doesn't remember – or want to remember – the details of what happened. A 1967 report, quoted by the Tibetan historian Tsering Shakya, from one rural district gives a clear indication about one typical campaign against 'the poverty stricken peasants and labouring people who had been branded as demons and monsters. [Apart from] beating with fists, kicking, hair-plucking and ear twisting, other terrifying forms of punishment and torture were also used. These included. . . the wearing of handcuffs and fetters, scorching the body and head with fire, feeding human excreta . . . The forms of torture are really too numerous to mention one by one.'[5]

On their release Ani's grandparents were sent to do manual work and paid a meagre wage to atone for their 'crimes' as wealthy nomads. The family were allowed to keep their yak-hair tent, two small plots of land and some animals. For decades afterwards they were tarred as 'black' – capitalist. At the village school Ani attended for two or three months a year, the teacher would humiliate her: 'You are black brain, you should be white brain. You mustn't listen to your grandparents but be a good Communist.' She paused, fidgeting with her cloth hat.

'Back then we lived in such fear and uncertainty. There were no human rights, no justice. The authorities were very powerful and we never knew when they could make us a scapegoat, when they could imprison us for no reason or give us a death sentence.'

When describing these events Ani betrayed no hint of rancour or blame. 'It was traumatic, it still brings much pain,' she admitted. 'Not just for me, for all Tibetans, especially those who've had no lama, for them that pain never goes. The time when Tibet was deprived of Buddhism is like a body without a heart, it leaves a deep emptiness inside.' She looked down, and then said, 'But the Tibetans didn't give up hope, we always believe that the sun would shine, that the dark clouds would go away.'

'When you were younger,' I asked, 'were you ever angry towards the Chinese for what they did to your parents and grandparents?'

'My lama told me, "no compassion, no enlightenment". You have to look at your enemy as your teacher, as a method of developing compassion. So without the enemy, also no compassion. When I've felt angry about what happened or if I think bad thoughts, I ask for forgiveness. I invoke the Buddha.'

As we walked down the hill, our hands clasped, our step effortlessly falling into rhythm, I knew it would be years before I returned to Tibet. On explaining that to Ani, our feet dragged. Tears trickled down her face and poured down mine. I turned back to look at her on the crest of the hill and thought it remarkable that in such a repressive regime bent on eliminating the ideals that Ani lived by, she continued to radiate an inner freedom. She embodied something of those words attributed to Nelson Mandela: 'As we let our own light shine, we unconsciously give other people permission to do the same. As we're liberated from our own fear, our presence automatically liberates others.'[6] Going alone down the mountain, I felt her gaze follow me and in my mind heard her voice like wind chimes in the breeze, whispering prayers for my onward journey and my own liberation.

CHAPTER 16

A Vanishing Culture

As I had foreseen my life did follow a new course. I moved back and forth between the northern and southern hemispheres before setting up a base in Australia. After I had spent four years focusing on Tibet, it ceased to be centre stage in my life, becoming more of a background hum. Well, almost. In a prominent place in my kitchen I had a photo of Ani and me holding hands at the gateway to Mount Kailash. On occasion I would pick it up and polish the glass, drinking in every detail of that memorable scene.

Behind us are cairns laid by pilgrims and billowing prayer flags. My face is awash with ecstasy, my arm outstretched like a ballerina. Ani looks more serious, her mouth upturned in an enigmatic smile, clutching the cherry-red sunhat and her plastic *mala*. I had not realised how we are identical in height, nor had I noticed the similarity of our faces – both with full cheeks, laughter lines around the mouth, a pronounced chin. Her nose is more tapered, mine blunt; her hair is black, mine brunette. Nevertheless, friends would often remark that we could be sisters.

Since our journey to Mount Kailash the resilient self-containment and faith that seemed so central to Ani had persuaded me, in small ways, to trust more in the abundance of life and surrender to the unknown. My spiritual life opened in its own quiet, mysterious way. There were whispers of grace and miracles all around me if I took the time to look – a thrush singing at dawn, a butterfly landing on my windowsill, a shaft of sunlight illuminating my lover's sleeping face – if I stepped out of myself and my routine to notice. I liked to think I could be an itinerant pilgrim of the spirit, with a few more trappings of modern comfort than Ani. I was no match for her physical toughness nor her iron constitution to cope with *tsampa* three times a day.

Over time I started to miss her more. I would daydream about throwing a few things in my rucksack and tramping, wild and free, through the back ways of Tibet. All roads led to the winding track up to the rust-coloured door of Ani's hermitage. The occasional twinge and swift-footed fantasy became a dull ache. By 2004, on the first day of Losar, Tibetan New Year, I made a commitment to myself that I would go back and find her. I was living in Byron Bay at the time and was friends with a talented and wise Tibetan artist, Karma Phuntsok, who lived with his wife in the bush of northern New South Wales. When I called to wish him *tashi delek* for Losar and told him I wanted to return to Tibet, he supported me.

'You should go back. You have a special karma with Ani, I can see it in your photos. You look alike. She's more important to you than other relationships and you should learn from her. Maybe you were near to each other in a former life, maybe you were even a nun in Tibet.'

Over the months my resolve wavered like a weather vane – finances, work commitments, family – all became excuses not to go. And then, I went to see a film, *The Yogis of Tibet*. This unique documentary interviews a score of *yogis* in exile from the Drigung-Kagyu lineage and, for arguably the first time, they talk with candour about some of their secret practices 'to preserve for posterity their vanishing culture'. Seeing the film made me realise that there was a final lap of my own pilgrimage to go, and because Ani had always been involved in the previous stages, it was almost unthinkable that she shouldn't be there for this one too.

The narrator of the film, in an American voice as thick as treacle, describes how, 'The complete cultural environment that produced the mind masters of the past no longer exists. Without the unbroken lineage of teacher teaching disciple, without the vast stretches of time, without the isolated retreat free from earthly distractions or the support from the Tibetan community, the tradition of the *yogis* is nearing extinction.'

One *yogi* is filmed performing an advanced *trulkhor* exercise – the sort Ani had been trying to learn from the drunken, lascivious lama. In the film the *yogi* is shown soaring several feet high and in mid-air folds his legs into the lotus position, then uncrosses them on landing. Only one *yogini* was interviewed, Konchok Khadro. The others were monks, some bald, some with long wispy hair tied in a top-knot and one particularly striking eighty-five-year-old, Drubwang Konchok Norbu Rinpoche, who was shown with a splendid turret of taupe dreadlocks, a tiny bird in the centre of his palm. After he spent twelve years in retreat, Konchok Norbu Rinpoche was preparing to die. The Dalai Lama intervened, asking him to live a little longer. Konchok Norbu Rinpoche agreed to live until he was a hundred years old to help people and give teachings.

Long after I left the cinema, the phrase that these *yogis* were 'the last of a generation' remained singed in my memory. I had not grasped the extent to which the tradition of the *yogis* was dying out, both in Tibet and in exile, nor that women like Ani were so rare.

In September 2004 I arranged to lead a small group back to Kailash with a travel agency whose manager, Dorje, knew of Ani and who promised to warn her in advance so that she could accompany us on the journey. I was also in touch with Tenzin and the monk Lobsang, who both agreed to pass on messages to Ani's nunnery. With the departure date looming and no word from Ani, I found myself trying telepathy to let her know of my impending arrival.

Through all this, a thought started to haunt me that ours was an unrequited friendship. In Tibetan 'Ani' is actually a generic term for nun. I have always known her simply as Ani, rather than by her spiritual name (which she asked me, after much deliberation, not to disclose to protect her identity) and over the years Ani, in my mind, had become whatever I imagined her to be – my teacher, my soul mate, spirit sister, *cho-drok* or pilgrim friend – my heroine no less. As the weeks passed and I heard nothing from Ani, I would say to my friends, what if it's all in my mind? What if it's just chance that in some of the photos we look alike? What if she doesn't really think about me at all, and my friendship with her is with a friend I have created in my imagination?

From the outset the trip back in 2004 was a litany of challenges. Days before leaving we were re-routed via Chengdu after a Maoist uprising in Nepal. I was leading a group of one – Jurgen, a German who hoped to celebrate his sixtieth birthday at Mount Kailash and accompanying us was Jane, my friend and interpreter.

Once in Lhasa, Jane called the nunnery only to be told that Ani was in Tsari, in southern Tibet, on pilgrimage. We still made a visit to her nunnery. I left her a bag with money, clothes and toiletries, and a note to say how long I would be in Tibet. I was told that she could be back in a few weeks and throughout my second journey to Mount Kailash I hoped we would meet again in Lhasa, even for a few hours.

After barely three days on the road, Jurgen had to return to the capital with altitude sickness. Jane and I continued in a truck and did one *kora* around the mountain. It was wonderful to be back there, physically much tougher than I had remembered. With Ani, we finished the *kora* in two days; without her at my side, I struggled to finish it in three. I realised how much support – seen and unseen – she had given me, and without it I felt adrift.

Back in Lhasa I called the nunnery again. When I heard the short answer, '*Ani mindu*, Ani isn't here,' I felt devastated, the sort of grief I know when leaving my mother on the other side of the world – someone who is of my heart, of myself. Lurking in the back of my mind the doubts remained: that ours was a one-way friendship, that I had fabricated any 'special' connection. A whiny voice inside my head was jubilant. 'See, it's all in your mind. Fancy yourself telepathic, heh? Well, that'll show you.'

⌒

Three years away from Lhasa and the old haunts no longer had the power to send me into raptures. I realised that it was no longer Tibet that I wanted to see, but Ani. I sought out Tenzin only to learn that he had left Tibet after obtaining a Chinese passport: current whereabouts unknown. An acquaintance updated me about Tashi, whose life, happily, seemed back on course. He had settled down somewhere in eastern Tibet, and his wife was expecting their first baby. My friends' lives were moving, like Lhasa, in an unpredictable, inexorable way.

The city was ever expanding, the Golmud–Lhasa railway nearing completion. I went to the Jokhang to find the old gates were locked. To enter, there was a fee of seventy renminbi. In the teashop opposite, where Lobsang and I would meet when he was off duty from the Jokhang, I found his older brother sitting, alone. From the forlorn look on his face, I instantly knew something terrible had happened. Two weeks before, Lobsang had fled to India. I only gathered the bare bones of what had occurred; the rest I learned later from Lobsang who was seeking asylum in the West.

It transpired that a letter he'd written to a foreign friend had been returned and opened by the Jokhang security officers. Another monk, also a member of the security administration, warned Lobsang and his best friend that they would be arrested. Faced with the unenviable choice that confronts thousands of Tibetans – prison or exile – he 'left Tibet full of tears in his eyes' and after a perilous three-month crossing over the highest mountains in the world, reached Nepal.

⌒

With over a week in the capital before my flight out, and little interest in visiting the sites, all of which I'd been to numerous times, I decided to research the city's thriving sex industry for a newspaper article I was preparing. I'd heard reports that HIV/Aids was becoming a major threat, with an epidemic already gaining ground in neighbouring Yunnan, Xinjiang and Nepal. It was a side of Lhasa so different to the one I had discovered through Ani and I was taken aback at the increase in Tibetan prostitutes who, driven by economic hardship and widespread illiteracy in rural regions, were flocking to the city for work.

In Lhasa the unregulated red-light districts covered entire neighbourhoods. Such scant official surveillance and a rapid turnover, caused by the floating migrants from inland China, meant I could find no accurate figures on the number of sex workers, Tibetan or Chinese. But I did find a Tibetan willing to take the risk of accompanying me on several 'night tours'. On the first evening we began at Adam's (after Adam and Eve), a high-class nightclub in the neon-lit Chinese district of Thieves Island. Golden statues of naked woman stood either side of the door. Inside was a warren of karaoke rooms, bars and private booths splintering off a dance floor. As I arrived so did a 'girl', called by a 'mummy' – often ex-prostitutes – who manage the sex workers.

'At Adam's there are at least twenty mummies with thirty girls each who are on call,' my interpreter said. 'It costs 100 renminbi to sit and talk, around 400 renminbi for "more" and up to 1,000 for the night in a room off the premises. The mummy takes a large cut.'

Such clubs are where one businessman I spoke to took officials from the military or police to improve his *guanxi*. 'I hate it,' said the middle-aged Tibetan. 'I'm a family man, but I've no choice if I'm to continue doing my job. The officials expect to go to a banquet and then a high-class brothel. There are also banquet halls where girls are included in the price of the meal.'

'Do you go with the prostitutes yourself?' I asked.

'No. Sometimes I have to take one otherwise the officials will look down on me. I just talk and make jokes with them. The Tibetan officials prefer the Chinese girls because they're clean and professional. Tibetan girls are shy, always drinking, saying nothing.'

After visiting a couple of nightclubs I explored several streets lined with bars, many shuttered to avoid frequent police raids. Bored-looking Han Chinese women, knitting and playing mah-jong, filled scores of hairdressers-cum- brothels. Split along ethnic lines, Chinese worked one side of the road, Tibetans the other. There were sex shops selling giant dildos, fake breasts, fancy condoms and potions to improve sex drive. Outside, Han Chinese sex workers touted for business, drunk young Tibetan men loitered. According to one report, 'Tibetan customers, mostly married men, have a mixed perception of Tibetan prostitutes', preferring 'Chinese because "they're more wild" and will "do more".'[1]

A twenty-six-year-old married sex worker from Sichuan explained to the translator and me that she used to earn 300 renminbi a month in a factory back home. In Lhasa she can double her wage, making up to 800 renminbi on a good day. 'I'll earn money here and then go home,' she said pragmatically. 'I always use a condom and won't sleep with a man unless he has one, even if he offers me double.'

The Tibetans I met in the pink-lit low-class brothels, the windows blacked out with newspaper, were less professional, giggling and fawning over each other in embarrassment. In one bar, a mummy, visibly nervous when police sirens wailed outside, offered us drinks upstairs. A large poster of Chairman Mao surrounded by flowers hung above a single bed. A shy seventeen-year-old had arrived only days before, having run away from home. Her eighteen-year-old friend insisted, like some other Tibetan girls I spoke to, that she was a hostess, only drinking beer with the clients. ['They do sleep with men but are too shy to admit it,' the interpreter said later.]

Not all the Tibetans were so coy. In the brothel-bar next door, I met a savvy twenty-one-year-old from eastern Tibet called Drolma, dressed in shiny black trousers and a flaming crimson coat, rouge on her doll-like cheeks. Her world consisted of a tiny room, divided from three others by a paper-thin partition, with a single bed and a shiny portable stereo. Brought up a nomad on the grasslands of Kham, she attended an impoverished school for barely three years – 'no chairs, no blackboard' – and, like a moth, had been attracted to the lights of Lhasa.

She said she charged 200 renminbi for the night and, when the interpreter left the room, opened her bag proudly to show me four condoms, which she 'mostly used' to avoid pregnancy. She'd heard about HIV/Aids, but had no idea what it was.

'Sexually transmitted diseases are rife,' a Tibetan health worker told me, on condition of anonymity. 'Tibetan girls especially have no idea. One sixteen-year-old from eastern Tibet was told she could get work in a Lhasa restaurant and ended up in a brothel. She had genital warts all inside her vagina. The doctor told her not to sleep with anyone. Three days later she slept with a student.'

Hearing the stories of these vulnerable women brought home the plight of the younger generation of Tibetans, who no longer want the relentless drudgery of rural life but lack the skills to survive in the city. Magnetised by the trappings of modern consumerist Lhasa – clothes, make-up and mobile phones – their bodies become their only currency. Some of the village girls I met hoped to go home, one day. For now they were caught, their wings burned. Shortly before leaving Lhasa I heard that Tibetan prostitutes had been noticed plying their trade around the traditional pilgrimage circuit of the Barkhor. I found myself wondering if the 'forbidden city' was at risk of losing its spiritual heart.

CHAPTER 17

Found Ani

MY hopes for the final stage of my own pilgrimage thwarted, I still hoped to return to Tibet once more to see Ani. When I heard that she'd become keeper of a monastery in Tsari and, with heavy winter snows, was expected to stay there indefinitely, I had no idea when that would be. And then in late 2004, when I had returned to Australia, I received an unexpected email.

'Found Ani!' wrote Dorje. 'Good news! I met Ani this morning in Lhasa. I made a following appointment for you. Losar happens on 9 Feb next year. I asked her to be in Lhasa and then you can go with her to do some sightseeing together.'

This time, I knew I would not be disappointed.

The aeroplane from Chengdu was crammed with Tibetans returning home for Losar. There was an air of expectancy, of excitement. Below stretched an ocean of splintering snow peaks and black knife-edge ridges. Walking into the shiny new domestic terminal, I immediately felt the familiar breathlessness and a light throbbing in my temples. Outside I waited nervously for Dorje. Since I received his 'Found Ani!' email, we had been in regular contact and he'd offered to meet me at the airport.

A long forty-five minutes later, a car pulled up and out tumbled Ani. 'Awoooh, Drolma,' she cried.

For a moment, we stood facing each other until she tenderly pulled my forehead towards hers in the traditional Tibetan greeting. I stroked her cheek with the back of my hand. She seemed smaller than I remembered four years before. With her hair tied in a ponytail and her thick padded wine-red *chuba*, she reminded me of a compact, diminutive Russian doll.

Ani took time to scrutinise me – wrists, face, hands – boring intensely into my eyes.

'You look better than the last time.'

'Which bit?' I asked.

'All over.'

Settling into the back seat of the car, she put on her peaked cloth crown. As he pulled away, Dorje explained, 'She didn't want to wear her hat in case of problems from the police at the airport.'

'She's still nervous of the police?' I asked, reaching out to squeeze her hand.

Dorje told me that it was by chance he'd met Ani in the Barkhor the previous November. She was on her way back home from the pilgrimage in Tsari. 'She looked thin and sick,' he said. 'I hope it's OK but I gave her 800 renminbi from you to buy food and clothes.'

'Of course,' I replied. 'Thank you.'

When he stopped the car to make a phone call, Ani leaned forward and said how sorry she was that the previous year I'd come all the way to Tibet and not seen her, before chiding me: 'Now you come when the weather is cold.' And then, reverting to type, she chortled, 'We're talking with eyes. Your ring, the ring you gave me.' She pointed. 'Look, I still have it.'

It was the rainbow moonstone ring I'd given her five years before on the Kailash pilgrimage.

'From Drolma,' she added quietly, as if to herself.

I noticed her hands had aged; the palms were becoming creased like antique parchment, the knuckles swollen. She pulled at the moonstone ring. It would not budge, firmly stuck on her third finger. A lick of sadness shot through me. She would be forty-four by now, not old for a Westerner, but deep into late middle age for a Tibetan. From her other hand, she slipped off a battered brass ring. In the centre was the Tibetan word for *phurbu* – ritual dagger – engraved in a love heart and curling my fingers around it, she said, 'For you.'

The ring was too big so I hung it on my silver chain. She nodded in approval.

I turned to look out of the car window at the silky tresses of the Tsangpo, the harsh beauty of slate-grey mountains etched against a limpid cerulean sky. I had imagined this moment many times over. Now I was here and, blissfully, there was nothing to say.

Unusually the Tibetan and Chinese New Year in 2005 fell on the same day and all night deafening fireworks exploded, rattling windowpanes and filling the air with acrid smoke. Ani and I were sharing a hotel room and as I lay awake I heard her snoring faintly, her face burrowed in the sleeve of her *chuba*. 'I love to sleep,' she told me. 'It's one of my weaknesses. Even if I'm hungry I'll sleep.'

Traditionally Losar lasts for fifteen days and, like our Christmas, is a whirlwind of drinking and eating with relatives and friends. On the first day Ani and I joined the crowds of Lhasa citizens dressed in their best garb – the men with hats of fox fur and women in exquisitely embroidered apricot, olive and lavender silk *chubas* – strolling around the Barkhor. The air was thick with juniper smoke. A line of worshippers laden with offerings snaked around the Jokhang Temple. Among them were scores of nomads, who escape the harsh winters in eastern Tibet to spend several weeks in Lhasa every Losar.

The rest of the city was deserted, every restaurant closed. There were few Westerners. The Chinese had also gone home to celebrate, back to the familiarity of paper dragons, swaying red lanterns and feasts with a thousand dishes. Ani took me to see her friend Pema who'd moved from her old decrepit flat into a larger apartment with a monastic interior – substantial wooden pillars and thick walls painted ruby red.

On first appearances their living room looked the same, with sofas doubling as beds, except now a new fridge purred in one corner, a wide-screen television and DVD player in another. Pema had also expanded to become a solid buxom woman; her son had grown and was fooling around with a toy gun he'd received for Losar. Old Pasang looked the same, sitting in his corner, maroon robes wrapped around him, sniffing snuff and supping butter tea from his carved wooden bowl.

When I arrived, everyone spoke at once. Pema wanted to show off their new classroom where they now taught Tibetan, Chinese and some English to almost a hundred pupils. Pasang offered me tea and *kapse* – fried batter dusted with icing sugar, a Losar speciality. Ani bustled around, telling me to relax and insisted I watch a DVD of traditional dancing from Amdo. Images of undulating grasslands and sheep like fluffy clouds reeled across the screen, followed by Tibetan dancers in leopard-skin *chubas*, their red sashes billowing.

Ani sat like a child transfixed, lost to the television, her mouth slightly agape. Every so often she would get up and wave her arms from side to side, imitating the performers. It was clearly a favourite. Turning to me, she said, 'I want to go to Amdo this year on pilgrimage.'

'Are you going alone?'

'Yes. I don't have anyone to go with,' she replied, an unguarded moment of sadness crossing her face. Then she disappeared out of the room and on her return, presented me with a deer antler.

'Your present. I got it from my nomad relatives in the mountains.'

Fawn-grey and lightly ridged, it was about a foot long and weighty like bone. Running my fingers over the three spikes, smooth on one side and rough on the other, I was assailed by the pungent aroma of wood smoke and earth, mountains and melancholy.

'Thank you. Thank you.' I smiled, touched.

'The deer is a sacred animal,' she said. 'They have deep compassion.'

(This belief dates back to the Buddha's life. Legend attests that in Sarnath, close to Varanasi in India, a group of deer overheard the Buddha's first sermon given in the Deer Park.)

Back at the hotel Ani leafed through the photos I'd brought of us on previous journeys. In 1997 in front of the Potala after our pilgrimage through Pemako: she with her dreadlocks piled under the battered straw hat, me looking about fifteen years old in round spectacles, dressed in a black *chuba*. Two years later among burnished rocks at the sky burial site; under a chalky-blue sky at the gateway to Mount Kailash; inside her icy cave at Shugseb. She then carefully picked through the toiletry bag I'd brought her – filled with soaps and shampoo, a pair of socks, toothpaste – and began the ritual of combing her hair.

'You should brush yours, Drolma. It's messy.'

'This is the fashion,' I replied.

She scanned the photos again.

'Your hair used to be longer, it looked better then.'

She began to undress, peeling layers off one by one. Hidden under her rather staid *chuba* she revealed an entire wardrobe – no, more than that – each item displaying another aspect of her. There was a sturdy, practical woollen skirt; a gold-saffron silky blouse denoting her nun's status. Around her neck hung a heavy bundle of blessed red cords and various other sacred talismans from her abundant pilgrimages and teachings. Instead of lace-up shoes she'd reverted to the traditional knee-high Tibetan monk boots, made from coarse red wool with soles of beaten yak leather. And most improbable of all was her flowery underskirt in shocking yellow, orange and green, a hippie chic number – and a nod to Ani's exuberant teenage self.

'Where's that from?' I hooted.

'Chinesey,' she squealed in delight, flapping it from side to side.

She laid her worldly possessions by the pillow – keys, tattered cloth purse and *melong* (Tibetan astrological disc) – and her undergarments on top of the bed sheets then took a shower. Plonking herself down on the bed afterwards, she sighed. 'Now I'm happy.'

She refused to sleep under the covers, telling me, 'It's very hot in here, I'm used to much colder.' I, meanwhile, wore most of my clothes, snuggled into a four-season sleeping bag, with an extra duvet on top and a woolly hat.

Once I acclimatised to the altitude we planned to go for a short road-trip outside Lhasa with 'Uncle Norbu' whom I knew from five years previously. Since he wasn't due to arrive for some days, as he was celebrating Losar with his family, another friend, Phuntsok, offered to interpret for us. An affable, haphazardly dressed man, with a thatch of black hair, Phuntsok mooched into the hotel early one morning clutching a jam jar of tepid green tea. He had met Ani many years before on her first trip with Ian Baker and I asked him if she'd changed much over the decade.

'Back then she was more calm and serene and looked much younger, like a young girl. Now she laughs and talks more. I guess she's used to being with foreigners too. On that trip I remember she was very generous, always helping everybody, even though we told her that she didn't have to.' He took a gulp of his tea.

'I remember one time when we were camping and I was sleeping outside on the sand. It rained and my sleeping bag became full of water, so I crept under the shelter. All the places were taken. Ani said, "Why don't you lie next to me?" And she covered both of us with a blanket.'

'Isn't that unusual for a nun?' I asked.

'I felt embarrassed and shy about doing this, but she didn't seem to mind. We talked for about an hour in the darkness, laughing and telling stories, until finally we fell asleep.' He paused, thinking this over.

'You know, Drolma, she isn't like ordinary women. Whereas most people are closed, she has a more open heart. She had no shame about holding my hand when it was cold, or reaching out to help me when I needed support. One time I met a *Khandro* [enlightened female teacher] believed to be an incarnation of Yeshe Tsogyal. She had the same elevated mental qualities – very tactile, not shy, with this higher presence around her – just like Ani.'

When Ani joined us she asked Phuntsok for news about Sonam, the guide from the Pemako expedition (they knew each other through their work) and his wife.

'Sonam's in America now,' said Phuntsok. 'He divorced his wife about two years ago.'

'Oowwagh,' she gasped. 'Is it so easy to get together and then to leave each other? It's like a game.'

Phuntsok and I looked at each other.

'Yes,' he replied bluntly. 'This is how it is in the city.'

'Isn't it easier to be alone?' I asked Ani.

'Also hard.' She fell quiet, then added in a wistful, innocent way, 'If I weren't a nun I'd like to find one man and spend the whole of my life with him.'

'Would you like children?' I asked in surprise.

'Yes.'

'Ani, can I ask you a personal question?' I hesitated. 'Do you ever have feelings of sexual desire?'

She scrunched her eyes, throwing me a slightly reprimanding look. 'Sometimes. It's usual for monks and nuns to get that feeling of desire but we know how heavy our vow is, how our family would lose face if we renounce, so when we get that feeling, when we know that any second we can lose our vows, most monks and nuns practise a special Tantric visualisation.' She paused, and then added, 'I can't say any more because it's a secret method. It isn't good if I discuss it with a lay person.'

One morning Ani, Phuntsok and I ambled along the city's outer pilgrimage circuit, dodging the human turds that littered the pavement. 'Lhasa people use toilets now,' Phuntsok said with a shrug. 'Village people who come into the city don't.' The holiday atmosphere contributed to the impression that the situation had relaxed in the capital; nonetheless I was wary about staying in the hotel, so we talked and strolled down the wide empty streets. On reaching the 'place of a thousand Buddhas', Ani looked dismayed at the rubbish-strewn entrance, and traced her finger across the faded murals.

'People care only about themselves not about their sacred places,' she said, reaching down to pick up a prayer flag carelessly tossed on the ground. 'There are more natural disasters. Strange things are happening – like the great flood [the 2004 Boxing Day tsunami]. I saw it on Pema's television. I've seen a lot in my life but it's getting worse. I think the future doesn't look so good.'

'Do you think that as people lose faith, there are more problems on earth?'

'Yes. People in Tibet and other countries only care if they have a car, a nice house, fancy clothes,' she continued, in a vein I wasn't expecting. 'With those things, they won't be spiritually rich.'

'You are like two nuns.' Phuntsok laughed, turning to me. 'Could you come and spend a few years in Tibet, travelling with Ani?'

'I dream of it,' I replied. 'But I couldn't cope with the physical hardships.'

A shiver of pain flickered across Ani's face. It wasn't the first time. She reluctantly admitted that her eyes were troubling her and she was suffering from stomach ache.

'Perhaps you need glasses,' I suggested. 'How well can you see?'

'Not so clearly.' She squinted. 'It's hard to read scriptures in the evening.'

'We'll get your eyes tested and let's find a chemist.'

After a conversation in Chinese, Tibetan and English, with a young Chinese pharmacist prodding Ani through the thick folds of her *chuba*, we bought some antibiotics. The pain had begun several weeks before, she said, and she'd been vomiting blood. I remembered that her father had died at the age of fifty from severe stomach and kidney problems, 'with blood coming out of his mouth and nose', and was worried it might be a hereditary condition. Outwardly unperturbed by her health, Ani agreed that if the medicine didn't work we would risk a visit to the Lhasa People's Hospital.

'As I get older I feel heavier.' She gave a small pout. 'I have more wrinkles. My vision and memory are deteriorating. My body can't cope with the aspirations of my mind. At least with age I'm becoming more emotionally peaceful.'

'Are you scared of dying?'

'No, I only worry that I haven't done enough practice. I had an astrological prediction from a Bonpo lama who said I'd only live until I'm fifty. Sometimes they make mistakes and then you do live longer. I don't think I will because I'm already sick.'

Hearing her talk about dying, I felt a wrenching inside. I knew it was part of her practice to overcome the fear of death. The fourth tenet for *yogis* from one text, the 'Four Jewels of the Kadampas' is, 'Not to be afraid of meditating alone in a cave and dying there with no one even knowing your name.'

'Will you get a sky burial?'

'Yes, if I die at home. If not, who knows? It depends who finds my body.'

❧

A day later, Ani and I met Uncle Norbu in a restaurant painted a jaunty tangerine orange, with low tables and cushions spread on the floor. Owned by a French doctor and a Tibetan, the menu reflected the marriage of the two – yak bourguignon, crème caramel – and over lunch silence reigned as we all got on with the business of eating. Ani and Norbu chose yak curry, I opted for ratatouille.

I was pleased Norbu, exceptionally well read in English, had been able to join us for a few days. He travelled across greater Tibet, working as an interpreter for various agencies and was rarely in Lhasa. Dressed in a rumpled black leather jacket and faded jeans, his short wavy hair the colour of pitch, he had a self-contained bookish air and a staccato laugh which always came as a surprise, erupting from left-field. In his back pocket was an English novel, in his rucksack a half-written report. He was the sort of person who tried to help everyone and for this was highly respected among friends and colleagues. Only sometimes explosions of anger would break the calm veneer, usually triggered by the relentless impoverishment among Tibetans that he witnessed on his travels.

After my high expectations of finding Ani the year before had been dashed, I was determined to make best use of our precious time together and hoped to visit her nomad village where she grew up. Ani kept finding excuses – the weather was too cold, it was several hours' walk over a snowy mountain pass – and I observed that when she was deliberating how much to tell me, she often fidgeted and her mind would wander.

I also began to notice that when Ani answered a question it was relative to space and time, and to whom she was talking. If we were in a monastery, a different answer would be given than if we were in a car. A reflection, I suspected, of whether the atmosphere was conducive to revealing personal or sacred information, and also, perhaps, if she thought I was ready to receive it. I've found this characteristic among Australian Aborigines and wonder if it's an indication that both indigenous cultures revere knowledge, holding it as a precious commodity, only to be imparted with integrity and wisdom, and at the right time.

It was striking that details pertinent to me – dates, feelings, chronology of events – were irrelevant to her. I was reminded of the words of Drubwang Konchok Norbu Rinpoche, the dreadlocked master from the film *The Yogis of Tibet*, who said, 'My mental state is different, it isn't focused on the mundane.' The cultural difference between Ani and I was epitomised by how we both processed information. In the

West there is a tendency to bisect and rationalise, with one thought connecting and igniting another like join-the-dots.

Ani, I sensed, thinks concentrically and, like a pebble falling into a pond, circles spreading outwards from the centre, her thoughts are multi-layered and holistic, intrinsically embracing the invisible, the unqualified and the unknown. When I questioned her on the validity of reincarnation, the conversation meandered like the tributaries of the Tsangpo until she clapped her hands in an ear-splitting thwack, exclaiming, 'Drolma, if someone doesn't accept reincarnation then it's impossible to be a Buddhist. There's nothing to prove reincarnation. But just because you cannot see something, it doesn't mean it doesn't exist.'

When it became obvious that Ani couldn't see a doctor until after Losar, I decided we should first make a trip out of Lhasa. Hiring a car and driver (you can't drive yourself), we sped past the final stages of the construction of the Qinghai–Tibet railway on the city's outskirts which would open to passengers in 2007. At the sight of the giant billboards with an image of a high-speed train, and mile upon mile of half-built sidings, teeming with workmen, pushing wheelbarrows and brandishing pickaxes, the driver let out a low groan. Among Tibetans there was a fear that the railway would lead to 'more thieves, more Chinese and more resources taken out of Tibet'.

Through Norbu, I asked Ani if she ever felt hatred towards the Chinese for what they had done in Tibet.

'It's Tibetans' bad karma – including my own – from previous lives that has led to the present situation,' she replied philosophically.

'But how do you deal with your negative feelings?'

'It's the hardest thing to deal with one's own mind,' she conceded, finally. 'When I find it hard, I pray to my *yidam* [meditation deity] for guidance. It takes time to control emotions, especially the three poisons – desire, hatred and ignorance. For me the worst is hatred.'

'Who do you feel hatred towards?' I am surprised.

'People say bad things behind my back.'

'Like who?'

'When I'm on pilgrimage sometimes people scold me harshly. I ask for help at a stranger's house and when they know I'm a beggar, the adults send their children out to tell me no-one's at home.'

'For me the worst is anger,' I said. 'Against myself, against others.'

'You have to think about the reason behind the anger,' Ani said kindly. 'You must bring your mind to what the Buddha's teachings say. When I'm sad or angry, I try to find the reason and understand why the feeling comes. In that way I let go of the feeling so it doesn't remain in my mind.' She paused to let Norbu translate before she continued.

'If anyone enrages you, Drolma, show compassion. You must think that every sentient being needs happiness, none wants suffering. Try not to kill any insect or hurt anybody even if they speak badly about you. Be tolerant.'

Listening to her I knew it to be true, if hard to practise. I recalled that nearly a decade before I had had to look up the meaning of compassion in the dictionary. How much had changed since then. Ani had consistently impressed upon me the sanctity of all life – however small, however ostensibly insignificant – encouraging me to question and re-evaluate my own conditioned and habitual responses.

Since my last visit to Ani's nunnery, five years before, the potholed road had improved dramatically. It hugged the bank of a river, and the valley sides began to narrow and press inwards. As we approached a cluster of small, bleak dwellings across the other side of the river, Ani indicated to the driver to stop. We got out of the car and Ani explained to Norbu and me, 'Those houses are built by the government for the nomads. We're told that we shouldn't stay up in the high places because we can't get rich. I've one elder sister living there, but my other relatives don't like it and still live up in the mountains.'

Behind the dwellings were several more plunging valleys and a path to Ani's home village, accessible only on foot over a high pass. After much deliberation she estimated that if she left early, she would arrive there in time for lunch. The raw rocky landscape in a uniform shade of dark brown, covered with a light sprinkling of snow, looked uninviting – treeless, stark, a world apart.

In her village lived two aunts and a sick uncle, whom Ani treated as surrogate parents and three of her brothers married to one wife – the system of polyandry is still practised among Tibetan nomads as a way to avoid dividing up land and assets. The rest of Ani's family consisted of two brothers and two sisters who lived in different regions, all married, and one younger brother who was a monk at a local monastery.

'So can we go to your village?' asked Norbu.

'It's a very rough place,' Ani said, blushing. 'If you come my family will think that Drolma is taking me away – to India or to another foreign country. They'd be worried, they wouldn't let me leave.' She paused, thinking about it. 'I would have to go ahead and warn them, otherwise they could quarrel with Drolma or me.'

I had the impression that behind her excuses there was a more pressing issue.

By now, we were parallel to a narrow bridge that crossed the river. Ani pointed, saying, 'That's where my mother died. She'd been sick for a month in hospital with diarrhoea after eating rotten food.' Her forehead puckered, as if reliving the events. 'As she wasn't getting better in hospital, my brother and I decided to take her back to the village in a tractor. But she died on the way. She was sixty-one. It was very traumatic, one of the saddest periods of my life.' She lowered her gaze.

'We checked the astrological calendar for an auspicious day and my mother was given a sky burial. After her death I felt so confused and disorientated. I would start going somewhere only to forget where I was going. My head always fell down.

'Months passed and I didn't get better. Only a year later did I begin to feel myself again. Afterwards I prayed that no other sentient beings would suffer the same fate as my mother.' As an afterthought, she added,

'Now I regret some of my deeds, how I always argued and wouldn't accept what Ama told me.'

I put my hand on her arm, touched by Ani's sincerity. We stood in silence, looking over the swift-flowing river, a lone eagle soaring above.

She turned to Norbu, and said, 'Drolma is one of my favourite people. She's like my parents. I think of them in the same way.'

'Thank you.' My heart lifted.

'She's very kind,' she continued matter-of-factly. 'I always feel very fortunate to be her friend. I'm just a wandering beggar and she compassionately takes care of me.'

And then, more firmly, she explained, 'But it would be a problem if you come to my village. There's lots of negative propaganda about Westerners, especially Americans and we're told by the government not to have close links with foreigners. So if I'm seen with you, my family won't think well of me. I could bring disrepute and cause them problems from the authorities.'

As the weight of the words sank in, she held my gaze. All the years I'd known Ani, the countless times I had asked if being with me could endanger her, and never once had she admitted it.

'Doesn't that mean problems for you if you're seen with me?' I said, frowning.

'You can't follow all the rules they set,' she replied, with a small shrug.

Getting back into the car, I reflected that Ani's openness indicated a new level of trust between us, illustrating how far we'd come on our pilgrimage – together and apart. Any doubts I had had fell away. I found myself recalling the words of John O'Donohue, who uses the Celtic expression, *anam cara* or soul friend, to describe 'a friendship that is not wounded or limited by separation or distance. Such a friendship can remain alive even when the friends live far away from each other. . . . When the soul is awakened, physical space is transfigured. Even across the distance two friends can stay attuned to each other and continue to sense the flow of each other's lives. With your *anam cara* you awaken the eternal.'[1]

When we arrived at her nunnery, Ani walked ahead into the courtyard in front of the temple. Within moments she disappeared into a sea of burgundy as the nuns flocked to her like baby chicks around a mother hen. They squeezed her cheeks, caressed her hair, jostling to get close amid a high-pitched chorus of laughter. Ani's stature appeared to grow among them, a measure of the respect and reverence she commands in her community.

The following morning, Norbu, Ani and I climbed past the score of whitewashed hermitages creeping up the hill to Ani's house. The stream was frozen, detritus embedded in the ice – empty noodle containers, toilet paper – and, noticing my eyes roll, Ani quipped, 'Yes, I know, Drolma. One thing I've learned from you is to pick up rubbish.'

She opened the brushwood gate into her back yard and motioned us inside the tiny cottage. As I adjusted my eyes to the darkness, I shivered. Within ten minutes, my toes were numb. After fumbling for the switch, Ani turned on a single low-wattage bulb – electricity had been installed two years previously. 'It never warms up,' said Ani cheerfully. 'It isn't well made with lots of cracks and holes.'

From one of the cupboards Ani pulled out the blue wash kit that I'd left her the year before. 'This toothpaste tastes very funny,' she said, holding a tube of lip balm. 'It tastes like butter.'

Norbu and I roared with laughter as he explained what it was. Ani joined in, her shoulders shaking with mirth.

The three of us sat down on odd stones outside in the yard. A nun friend joined us, so shy she was unable to meet my gaze, covering her mouth with the back of her hand. Before Ani settled down, she had her morning ablutions to attend to. Her friend brought some water in a pail and with a chunky brass ladle scooped out some for Ani to rinse her hands and face, which she rubbed vigorously with soap, noisily clearing her nose. Then she retired to her doorstep, sat in the sun and took out her faithful black comb – I always marvel at how she takes care of every possession, and how careless I am – to tease through her long hair, which still showed no hint of grey.

She produced a bowl of dry yak meat and dried blood sausage and offered some to Norbu. 'Don't be shy about eating food, not like Lhasa people.'

Throughout the day, the tea flowed and, by dusk, Ani and her friend would have demolished most of the blood sausage. We shared oranges and pistachio nuts, fantails ate the crumbs out of my bowl, and a shaggy dog would occasionally appear on the next-door roof skulking for scraps.

There, in her sandy back yard, it felt secure to talk and through Norbu our conversation swirled and eddied, dipping into pools of silence, broken only by the whirr from lammergeyers above. In the intervening four years Ani had, as she was accustomed, divided her time between her stone hermitage and pilgrimage. I had twice sent her some money via a couple of friends and she teased me, saying that I'd received all the good karma from her sacred journeys.

Three years before, she had joined 500 other monks and nuns for teachings and empowerments (enabling her to read and meditate on certain deities) at the foremost Nyingma monastery, Mindroling, in central Tibet. In 2004, deemed an auspicious time to go on pilgrimage to Tsari, Ani spent four months there. Considered on a par with Mount Kailash – both are said to be the abode of Demchok, the Buddha of Supreme Bliss – Tsari, some 200 miles south-east of Lhasa, is described by Dowman as 'a testing place for *yogis* . . . a place of breathtaking beauty'.[2]

When Ani's money dried up, she became keeper and cleaner of a small monastery on the edge of the sacred Lake Tsari Tsokar, which she described as the colour of milk, surrounded by glaciers and thick forest with 'colourful flowers and crystal-clear streams'. She made 117 *koras* of the lake – sometimes completing six a day – but was so busy at the *gompa*, explaining the history and significance to the pilgrims, that she barely had time to eat. Ani would have stayed longer in Tsari but with her food supplies running dangerously low, she hitched back to Lhasa, where, by chance, she met Dorje in the Barkhor.

The situation at her own nunnery had improved. 'The officials still hold "patriotic education" meetings. But for now I can stay.'

Does she still dream of going to India? 'Yes,' she admitted. 'If I had the money and a proper permit, but I don't think it's my fortune to go.'

I wanted to tell her how moved I was by the film *The Yogis of Tibet* and that the *yogis* who'd agreed to be interviewed did so because they believe their way of life is vanishing forever. I wasn't sure how to phrase it, when, overcome by a wave of emotion, I was surprised to find myself starting to cry and blurting out, 'Ani, you're the last of a generation. This is why I want to write about you, so other people will learn about your life, your aspirations and the hardships you've overcome to remain true to what you believe.'

As she passed me a tissue, Ani's face became grave. Norbu looked away, upset. Composing myself, I inhaled deeply and, looking at her, said simply, 'You're precious, Ani. There aren't many women like you left.'

'It's true this way of life is dying out and the tradition is ending in Tibet. It's true that lineages were broken during the Cultural Revolution,' she said, resting her hand on my arm. 'I hope as long as scriptures are preserved there will be monks and nuns like me. I do feel sad and worried. The main problem is because of the lack of freedom and the political situation. It makes it difficult to wander freely.'

'Will you be able to teach other nuns?'

'I have to wait until my lama says I can teach another nun. I can't do it by myself. My lama will tell me one day I'm sure.'

'Will you ask him?'

'No, he'll tell me. He knows my mind, my condition. When I'm with him it's like seeing myself in a mirror. He's a holy lama, very realised.'

A piercing bell rang out, cutting through the fine air. It was from next-door where an old nun was doing her practice.

'What do you want to do now in your life?'

'I'd like to see the relationship between people and their culture in other countries. I'd like know about different religions,' she said. 'Perhaps go to China on pilgrimage. I've heard there are many sacred places there but I don't know Chinese, so that's a problem.' She took a piece of the sausage, emptied the mixture of dried blood and *tsampa* onto her palm, then scooped it into her mouth.

'If you could visit the West, where would you go?'

'First India and then your country, England, or Australia.'

'Would you be nervous to travel abroad?'

'No, I don't think so. I wouldn't be scared. I think I'd enjoy it a lot.' A wide smile spread across her face. 'My main dream is to go on pilgrimage to different places, to different countries, taking my prayers and practice and what I've learned, to teach people about my experience of Buddhism.'

CHAPTER 18

The People's Hospital

BACK in Lhasa, Ani and I decided to make a visit to the People's Hospital, as her antibiotics had not worked. A sprawling complex in the centre of the city, with a maze of grimy green corridors, inside it was busy and chaotic. I held a scarf over my nose. The stench of sickness – sweat, shit, disinfectant – was pervasive. A young man with blood smeared across his shirt, his face a patchwork of bruises and plasters, limped into the waiting room. An elderly woman was helped to a chair, her eyes glassy with the glaze of death.

A friend of Norbu, a Tibetan doctor, promised help in arranging for Ani to be seen promptly, bypassing the long queues and bureaucracy. The young helpful Tibetan ushered us into a room where a Chinese doctor sat behind a rickety wooden table smoking a cigarette. Flakes of dandruff fell like a blizzard from his hair as he motioned Ani to take a seat.

After hearing her symptoms, he concluded that she should have an endoscopy. When the Tibetan doctor described to Ani what that would entail – sticking a thin tube down her throat to examine the stomach – Ani blanched.

'What does Drolma think?'

A lengthy discussion ensued while I enquired what other options were available, how clean the equipment was, what the initial prognosis was. The Tibetan doctor assured me that all equipment was sterilised and that this was a normal procedure for Ani's condition, 'a wound in the stomach lining'. Other patients wandered in and out, stopping to gawp and listen.

Ani reached for my hand, repeating, 'What do you think?'

'I think it'll be OK but you have to decide.'

'Will I die?' she asked in a small, frightened voice.

The Tibetan doctor roared with laughter. Ani shifted in her seat.

'No, no. You won't. You'll be just fine,' I soothed, comforting her.

I couldn't help feeling relief that for all Ani's spiritual attainments she was still human, still scared of dying.

After drinking a vial of liquid to numb her mouth, Ani was taken into the treatment room. Two Tibetan technicians wearing white face masks and surgical gloves were cleaning long black plastic tubes lying in metal trays. A Chinese doctor sat in front of a computer examining the results and Ani was invited to lie on a bed.

In the West it's usual for a light anaesthetic to be administered before the endoscope, fitted with a small camera, is inserted into the throat. No such niceties prevailed in Tibet where the tube was pushed straight down. Her eyes streaming, Ani retched violently. I gritted my teeth to avoid gagging. The first time was unsuccessful and, urging Ani to relax, the Tibetan doctor tried again.

I watched on the computer as the camera on the end of the probe disappeared into a pink spongy mass of folds – her stomach – before a cursory glance at the intestines. As the doctor wiggled it around, Ani moaned quietly. The camera illuminated several marks on the stomach lining. When I finally helped Ani off the bed, she fell into my arms in an unsteady embrace. We hugged, then I led her outside.

Our friendly Tibetan doctor explained that there were a few 'wounds' or scar tissue inside the stomach, which caused the pain and vomiting of blood. Their origin was bad food and previous infections. She was then taken for an X-ray of her other internal organs. All the results were normal. The Chinese doctor wrote out a prescription, telling Ani not to eat chilli, dry yak meat or yoghurt and, with a wave of his hand, we were dismissed.

The Tibetan doctor refused to charge me for the treatment, endoscopy or X-rays; nonetheless the medicine – a combination of antacid and imported antibiotics from Japan – cost over 400 renminbi. I was thankful to be there to cover the cost: I can't imagine how Ani would have done so otherwise. Before we left, the Tibetan doctor handed Ani a bundle of free medicine – for coughs, headache, diarrhoea – to take back to the nunnery, which she stuffed inside the bulging front pouch of her *chuba*.

Underneath her wan smile, she was shaken – I certainly was – and back in the hotel room she dozed, curling into herself in the foetal position with a hot-water bottle.

I contacted an Australian nurse in Lhasa who told me that 'wound' translated as a stomach ulcer and recommended that I see a French doctor, Philippe. It would be a couple of days before I tracked him down, an hour before he was due to leave Lhasa. He was sitting in a restaurant, tucking into a cup of coffee, a plate of apple pie and a piece of gooey chocolate cake. He had the look of someone who did not want to be disturbed. Apologising, I described Ani's condition and my concern that her father had died aged fifty of a similar complaint. He told me that ulcers caused by a bacterial infection – from poor diet, untreated water – were quite common in Tibet.

'Who is siss An-ee?' he asked.

'She's a wandering ani with long hair, who spends time on retreat.'

He took another mouthful of cake, his interest piqued.

'Ah special. Not many like 'err. Men yes. Not women. She's your friend?'

'Yes, like my sister.' I paused. 'Soon she goes to Amdo on pilgrimage, maybe she stays one year, maybe longer. I want to leave Tibet knowing that her health is all right and that she has all the medicine she needs.'

'*Mais oui*, she must get it fixed. The medicine you have is OK, but you must get her more antibiotics and be sure she finishes the course. Zat is ve-ree important.' He looked over the top of his round glasses.

'If not, *grand problème*. If she's up in a remote cave and a blood vessel breaks, she could die from internal bleeding.'

CHAPTER 19

Seeing with New Eyes

Aᴄᴛᴇʀ days floated by in a languid way, time sped up with my impending departure. The medication appeared to be working and Ani looked healthier, her eyes had regained their sparkle, her mood was buoyant. We arranged to meet Norbu in a second-floor café in the centre of the city. On stepping into the lift, Ani looked perplexed. The bell dinged and we ascended, stopping with a jolt. When the door opened, her face lit up.

'Awwooo,' she said. 'It's magic.'

The café was filled with Tibetan men playing cards, drinking green tea, smoking cigarettes. They turned to stare at the sight of a nun in a cloth crown and myself as we eased into big wicker chairs, next to a window overlooking the busy street.

Tilting her head from side to side, like a bird, Ani surveyed Norbu and me. 'It's from previous karma that we're all sitting here. One foreigner from England who's now in Australia, one from western Tibet and myself,' she said. 'We don't know where life will lead us, but I believe coming to know you, Drolma, is a result of our past good karma.'

It was my turn to look away in shyness.

'Drolma gave this to me.' She showed Norbu the rainbow moonstone ring. 'She comes into my mind when I see foreigners. Sometimes I think of her, I miss her.'

'I miss you too,' I whispered.

Before everything started to get too mushy, Ani and I made an agreement that every full moon we would think of each other and send love. It seemed a pragmatic – if somewhat sentimental – way to stay connected as it could be years before we met again.

We dawdled down Yutok Lam, which led to the Jokhang, past a string of new shops selling electrical appliances, to take Ani for an eye-test. Entering through glass doors, I was stunned by the establishment's hi-tech state-of-the-art appearance. Racks of frames – tortoiseshell, purple with wings, tinted – lined the walls and a crop of staff in white coats stood to attention. They looked taken aback when we explained the glasses were for Ani who to them, I imagined, appeared like a rustic figure from another era. While Ani had her head thrust on the equipment to examine her eyes, Norbu and I explained to the efficient Chinese optometrist that she needed bi-focals, 'for both distance and reading as she gets headaches when looking at her scriptures'.

A Tibetan assistant pulled out a pair of John Lennon-style glasses with shiny gold rims for her to try. She turned to see my reaction. They looked fabulous.

'Try a few more,' I coaxed. 'Just to compare.'

She did so, but the unanimous decision – by now half the shop had joined in – were the round glasses, which lent her an air of learned wisdom.

'In your right eye there's the beginning of a cataract,' said the assistant. 'If you wear these glasses it will help and also with the headaches.'

Ten minutes later the glasses were handed over. Tentatively Ani put them on. Confusion settled like fine dust over her face.

'Are these the same glasses I just tried?' she asked.

'Yes,' assured the sales assistant. 'Exactly the same.'

'*Ah leh.*'

Further down the street embarrassment swept over Ani. She kept putting the glasses on and taking them off, covering her mouth like a young girl.

'It's OK,' said Norbu, 'You look fine with them.'

Eventually she fixed them over her ears and looked around.

'My old eyes are gone,' she exclaimed in wonder. 'I have new eyes.'

Later that afternoon, still wearing her glasses, Ani and I made a *kora* around the Jokhang. Every time I looked at her I felt delighted – at seeing that her world had been transformed. At one point, so busy looking ahead she failed to notice the kerb, she stepped off the pavement into mid-air and landed with a bump, crumpling into laughter.

On a whim I motioned that we go inside the temple. Since it now cost seventy renminbi for tourists I'd hardly been back. I recalled on my first trips to Tibet I was forever muttering mantras, twisting the beads of my *mala* as I counted repetitions. Now I no longer carried it as a statement of belief, nor did I seek out those epiphanies when the world seemed to be redrawn in brilliant technicolour. These days I was more content with discovering the sacred moment by moment, breath by breath – in the everyday, in the details. And so it was with Ani: I didn't want us to do anything momentous, or go anywhere, just being together was enough.

Inside the inner courtyard of the Jokhang there was a queue of sprawling nomad families, a man with his ageing mother tied on his back, a daughter with her crippled father. The Barkhor police was keeping everyone in line. The sound of prayers rising, the smell of unwashed bodies and the saccharine aroma from the butter lamps contributed to the heady atmosphere. After about an hour Ani and I were squeezed through the narrow entrance and wound between the solid pillars past shrine rooms, creeping towards the main statue of Jowo Buddha in the far back recesses. The crowd swayed in unison to the rhythmic chanting from the monks sitting in rows, some rolling their eyes in trance, others bored and restless. I recognised many of the faces of the monks who I'd seen over the years and had a peculiar feeling of coming home.

Outside the Jowo shrine monks were yelling – '*Yar pheb, yar pheb.*
Welcome, welcome' – to the heaving, pushing crowd. Slipping on the
greasy metal steps up to the base of the statue, Ani and I bent down, one
by one, to touch our head against a falling snow of white scarves to
receive a blessing.

Once in front of the Buddha, Ani joined the mêlée of pilgrims
prostrating. She stood there, took off the glasses, squinted, covered one
eye to look at the Jowo then put the spectacles back on. Slowly, very
slowly, she turned to me, her face spellbound. From her expression I
understood that she was seeing it, as if for the first time.

The syrupy songs of Whitney Houston flooding our favourite tangerine-
coloured restaurant, Norbu, Ani and I sat down in a quiet corner. It had
dawned on me that as meditation was the prime focus in Ani's life, I
should try to understand what it entailed a little more. She'd said that she
was following Dzogchen meditation, which is a way to see the world
directly as it is without any judgement or mental conditioning.

To do this she had developed a highly refined appreciation of the
relationship between the movement of the mind and conceptual
thought. In the Nyingma tradition the mind is described as either at rest
or in agitation. By becoming aware of the difference between the two, the
practitioner allows the mind's movement to settle, giving rise to stillness.

When the English nun Tenzin Palmo, who spent twelve years on
retreat in a cave in India, was questioned about bliss, she said, 'Bliss is the
fuel of retreat . . . you can't do any long-term practice seriously unless
there is inner joy.' But the bliss in itself is useless, she continued. 'It's only
useful when it is used as a state of mind for understanding Emptiness –
when that blissful mind is able to look into its own nature.'

'So,' I asked Ani, with Norbu interpreting, 'have you experienced
bliss?'

After a considered pause, she replied, 'Yes, I have. I can make my mind very peaceful. All my energy is focused into one point, like it's shining so it becomes very quiet. Once you learn how to control your mind you bring it to one-pointed focus, then you can go deeper into meditation,' she continued. 'Meditating is like taking care of a little child near the road, you always have to watch it. When it grows up, like the mind, it becomes easier.' She looked hard at us both and then said, 'If you like, I'll teach you the way to meditate.'

Norbu and I sat up.

'There are seven rules. To begin you must have the left leg on the right leg, called the "thunderbolt position". This is the traditional way of sitting – in the lotus – but as it can be very hard, it's all right just to sit cross-legged. Then you place the back of the right hand on the left palm with the thumbs facing, but not touching each other.'

She counted down on her fingers. 'Number three, keep the shoulders straight like eagle's wings, not slumped.' We both rolled our shoulders back in concert. Sitting erect, Ani seemed to grow a couple of inches. 'The backbone must be very straight, the neck neither back nor forward, just a little bent. Yes, yes. That's good, Drolma-la'. She clicked her tongue like a schoolteacher.

'Sixth, the tongue should gently touch the palate behind the teeth. And lastly, the eyes must not be wide' – she exaggerated, stretching her eyes to twice their size – 'nor shut. They must look down the nose gently staring ahead in a natural gaze.'

On uttering these words, her own eyes automatically half closed, her mouth and cheeks relaxed, her lips tilted downwards. Within seconds she became like a carved marble statue, engulfed by a profound serenity. Norbu and I sat motionless, waiting, watching her gaze turn inwards, as if travelling down a well-worn path of sublime illumination. It was an entirely different expression of Ani, and one I had never seen before. More than the physical change was the warm feeling she began to radiate – heart opening, like molten honey spilling through my veins. After a few moments Ani opened her eyes and, like the flick of a switch, she was back.

'Here we are, the three great meditators,' she joked, continuing with the instructions, explaining how to visualise the three Tibetan symbols – *Om, Ah, Hung* – and methods to control the breath.

'There's a saying that the *yogi's* exhale is rarer than gold. When you hold your breath, your body becomes very light and when you're a real expert, your body becomes so light that you know how to fly.'

'So is the Tantric path the swiftest way to enlightenment?' I asked.

'Yes. It's like taking an aeroplane.'

'Do you think you'll get there in one life?'

'Unlikely, as it's much harder now than when Milarepa was alive. We're coming to the end of the Kali Yuga and it takes people longer to reach enlightenment.'

(The Kali Yuga is considered the present degenerate era. In about 300 years a new Golden Age will emerge like a phoenix from the ashes.)

The year before, Ani had gone on pilgrimage to Milarepa's famous nine-storey tower, Sekhar Guthok in Lhodrak, close to the border with Bhutan. In the eleventh century, enduring extreme physical hardship, with sores covering his entire body, Milarepa built and tore down at least three towers at the behest of his erratic, difficult guru, Marpa, who was deliberately pushing his disciple to the limits of endurance before he was deigned worthy of receiving teachings. Ani had gone on pilgrimage to the tower, she said, as it symbolised Milarepa's 'courage, commitment and faithfulness', and as she hoped 'to gain blessing, merit and inspiration'.

'Would you do such things for your lama if it meant you reached enlightenment?' I asked.

'Sure, definitely,' she replied. 'If it's that easy.'

⌒

After Losar the city was stretching into a gentle yawn. Norbu said goodbye and returned to work. The Chinese were coming back from their New Year holiday, the shuttered Tibetan businesses reopening. On this trip I had been barely aware of the political undercurrents and shadowy informers that I'd come to associate with Lhasa. I knew enough not to be fooled. A change in policy in Beijing and the chains around Tibet could be tightened overnight. And yet, I found myself wondering whether these days brute force was still required.

The tide of consumerism was washing up the beach and with it a swell of new shops and supermarkets, giant billboards of David Beckham and Chinese sylphs advertising Oil of Olay. In its wake were the marginalised and dispossessed Tibetans – the beggars, the prostitutes, the unemployed – the jetsam and flotsam of a divided society.

The stress on the Tibetans was undoubtedly more than some could bear. I saw it in the gulf between generations: between a grandmother who could remember the first waves of Communist soldiers, a mother who was brought up during the Cultural Revolution and her teenage daughter who spoke Chinese as her first language, plucked her eyebrows pencil thin and dressed in the latest Chengdu fashion. Beneath the intergenerational trauma was, I suspected, a deep-seated grief which contributed to the combination of apathy and anger, resilience and numbness.

The Qinghai–Tibet railway signified this inexorable march of Tibet's inclusion, not only in China, but also with the rest of the world. In time for the opening of the Beijing 2008 Olympics, it would be possible to go on a train from London to Lhasa. After centuries of isolation, in little over fifty years, Tibet had been forced into global participation and ubiquity.

On my last afternoon in Lhasa I asked Ani if we could meditate together once more. Yes, of course, she said. In my hotel room we sat opposite each other. My mind flickering like a candle in a gale, I couldn't stop myself from looking up to see Ani's expression. It was as it had been in the restaurant: an image of profound peace, and the sensation of looking into an inky-black starry night, eternal and vast. I closed my eyes. I turned my attention inwards. A curious stillness, palpable yet indefinable, spread through me and throughout the room.

At that moment I understood, finally, what sustains Ani when all else falls away. For in that silence, lies the fullness of existence – our deepest potential, our gift not only to ourselves, but to the world. For that space, not empty, no – full and immensely rich – is the wellspring of joy.

And it is this condition that mystics across the world have devoted their lives to, and perhaps, when I was with Ani, I came a breath closer to experiencing within myself. The words of the Dalai Lama came back to me: that you don't need to go anywhere. Ultimately a pilgrimage begins and ends in one's own heart. I knew my pilgrimage was over.

That night while I was packing for my early morning departure, Ani slept on top of the covers, her hair fanning across the pillow. When I finally crept into bed and switched off the light she woke up, turned to me and laughed. It was my last memory before sleep.

Dorje took us to the airport early the next day.

Ani showed off her glasses, and told him, 'It's like turning on a light. Everything is very clear. I feel bad without them.' She paused, her forehead furrowed. 'But I'm worried about wearing them too much, that I'll lose them, they'll get broken.'

'Ani-la,' Dorje boomed kindly, 'you must wear them. They'll be OK. It's good for your health.'

'Thank you,' she said again, turning to me. 'For the glasses and medicine.'

Leaving Lhasa in darkness, I silently repeated the words, 'safe journey, safe return' like I always did. I was not sad to leave this time, I was ready to go. The moon, almost full, hovered in the sky like a scorching white sun.

'*Tse-pa cho-nga reh-reh.* Every full moon,' I said, 'we'll think of each other.'

'*Re, re.* Yes, yes,' said Ani, her hands clasped in prayer. 'You've given me so much and I've given you nothing.'

'Your friendship is more than I can ask. Money and things come and go,' I said. 'What you've given me will stay all my life.'

'People like you are rare.' She fell silent for a moment. 'In friendship there's always peace. There's no jealousy, no loneliness, only closeness and love.'

As we drove, the dawn rays touched the pleated mountains. A soft mist hovered over the milky viridescent waters of the Yarlung Tsangpo. We passed houses built like a fortress, the colour of creamy buttermilk with clumps of prayer flags – sentinels to the gods – on the roofs. Tibetans trotted by on hardy ponies, their pillar-box red and sunshine-yellow woollen saddles a flash of vibrancy in this wintry landscape. I sighed inwardly at the beauty of this land, a place of such haunting melancholy flooded with an intense luminosity.

The airport was crowded with Tibetan students returning to mainland China after the New Year break. Mothers, fathers and grand-mothers were waving goodbye to their children. A smartly dressed mother wiped the nose of her teenage son, an old man wept silently as he bade farewell to his granddaughter. Dorje offered me a *khata*. Ani followed suit.

I bowed my head as she draped a long silky scarf around my neck, then pulled me towards her in a firm Western-style hug. Without pause to think, I tipped my brow towards hers in the Tibetan traditional greeting, our foreheads met, and for a moment we stood there as one, before the weight of the crowd prised us apart.

Chapter 1
The Pass of Sharp Stones

[1] Frank Kingdon Ward, *Riddle of the Tsangpo Gorges*, London: Edward Arnold, 1926, as quoted in Kenneth Cox, ed., *Frank Kingdon Ward's Riddle of the Tsangpo Gorges*, Suffolk: Antique Collectors' Club, 2001, p. 147.

Chapter 2
The Search for the Red Lily

[1] Eric Hansen, *Orchid Fever*, London: Methuen, 2001, p. 36.

[2] Françoise Pommaret, 'The Mon-pa revisited: In search of Mon', in Toni Huber, ed., *Sacred Spaces and Powerful Places in Tibetan Culture: A Collection of Essays*, Dharamasala: Library of Tibetan Works and Archives, 1999, pp. 52–73.

[3] Harold R. Fletcher, *A Quest of Flowers*, Edinburgh: Edinburgh University Press, 1975.

[4] Keith Dowman, *The Sacred Life of Tibet*, London: Thorsons, 1997, p. 50.

[5] Edwin Bernbaum, *Sacred Mountains of the World*, San Francisco: Sierra Club Books, 1990, quoted in Phil Cousineau, *The Art of Pilgrimage: The Seeker's Guide to Making Travel Sacred*, Dorset: Element Books, 1999, pp. 94–5.

[6] Frank Kingdon Ward, *A Plant Hunter in Tibet*, London: Jonathan Cape, 1934, p. 137.

Chapter 3
Monsoon in Kathmandu

1 William McGowan, 'Last Tango in Kathmandu', *Men's Journal*, March 2000.

2 *Tibet 2000: Environment and Development Issues*, New Delhi: Environmental and Development Desk, DIIR, 2000, p. iv.

Chapter 5
Into the Hidden Valleys

1 Norma Levine, *Blessing Power of the Buddhas: Sacred Objects, Secret Lands*, Dorset: Element, 1993, p. 109.

2 Span Hanna, 'Vast as the Sky: The Terma Tradition in Modern Tibet', in G. Samuel, H. Gregor and E. Stutchbury, eds., *Tantra and Popular Religion in Tibet*, New Delhi: International Academy of Indian Culture and Aditya Prakashan, 1994, pp.1–13.

3 Ibid.

4 Levine, op. cit., p. 106.

5 Ian Baker, *The Heart of the World: A Journey to the Last Secret Place*, New York: Penguin Press, 2004, p. 450.

6 Tsering Shakya, *The Dragon in the Land of Snows*, London: Pimlico, 1999, p. 209.

7 F. M. Bailey, *No Passport to Tibet*, London: Rupert Hart Davis, 1957, p. 18.

8 Frank Kingdon Ward, *Riddle of the Tsangpo Gorges*, London: Edward Arnold, 1926.

9 Ibid.

10 From Kingdon Ward, *Riddle of the Tsangpo Gorges*, as quoted in Cox, op. cit., pp. 146–7.

11 Dowman, op. cit., p. 220.

12 Shakya, op. cit., p. 347.

13 Tsultrim Allione, *Women of Wisdom*, New York: Snow Lion Publications, 2000.

14 McGowan, op. cit.

Chapter 6
The Essence of Flowers

1 Kurtis R. Schaeffer, *Himalayan Hermitess; The Life of a Tibetan Buddhist Nun*, New York: Oxford University Press, 2004, p. 25.

2 As quoted in Phil Cousineau,*The Art of Pilgrimage: The Seeker's Guide to Making Travel Sacred*, Dorset: Element Books, 1999.

3 Toni Huber, 'Putting the Gnas Back into Gnas-skor: Rethinking Tibetan Pilgrimage Practice', in Toni Huber, ed., *Sacred Spaces and Powerful Places in Tibetan Culture: A Collection of Essays*, Dharamasala: Library of Tibetan Works and Archives, 1999, pp. 79–81.

4 Carroll Dunham, Ian Baker and Thomas Kelly, *Tibet: Reflections from the Wheel of Life*, New York: Abbeville Press, 1993.

5 Cox, op. cit., p. 60.

6 Baker, op. cit., p. 303.

Chapter 8
Love in Lhasa

1 'The wrong side of the mountains' in the *Economist*, 10 December 2005.

2 *China's Great Leap West*, Tibet Information Network, London: 2000, pp. 30–31.

3 Steve Lehman, *The Tibetans: A Struggle to Survive*, London: Virgin Books, 1998, p. 11.

4 Shakya, op. cit., p. 402.

5 'When the Sky Fell to Earth: The New Crackdown on Buddhism in Tibet', a report by the International Campaign for Tibet, Washington: ICT, 2004, p. 49.

Chapter 9
Life in Exile

1 Allione, op. cit.

2 Janice Willis, ed., *Feminine Ground: Essays on Women and Tibet*, New York: Snow Lion, [1989] 1995, p. 104. The figures given are from T. W. D. Shakabpa, *Tibet: A Political History*, New Haven: Yale University Press, 1967. Willis suspects both figures are considerably higher than the actual number of monks and nuns in pre-1959 Tibet.

3 Nancy Falk, 'The Case of the Vanishing Nuns', quoted in Willis, op. cit., p. 160.

4 Allione, op. cit.

5 Schaeffer, op. cit., p. 54. and p. 53.

6 Ibid., p. 86 and pp. 84–5.

7 Mick Brown, *The Spiritual Tourist: A Personal Odyssey through the Outer Reaches of Belief*, London: Bloomsbury, 1998.

8 Lehman, op. cit., p.48.

9 'Tight Security in Tibet to mark 40th anniversary of Lhasa uprising', news update by Tibet Information Network, 10 March 1999.

10 Jennifer Westwood, *Sacred Journeys: Paths for the New Pilgrim*, London: Gaia Books, 1997, p. 77.

Chapter 10
Lhasa Uprising

1 Steve D. Marshall, 'Rukhag 3: The Nuns of Drapchi Prison', London: Tibet Information Network, 2000.

2 'Tight Security in Tibet to mark 40th anniversary of Lhasa uprising', op. cit.

3 Lehman, op. cit., p. 11.

Chapter 11
The Sky Burial Cave

1 Philip Rawson, *Sacred Tibet*, Singapore: Thames and Hudson, 1991, p. 21.

Chapter 12
To the Nunnery

[1] Peter Dawkins, *Zoence – the Science of Life: Discovering the Sacred Spaces of Your Life*, Maine: Samuel Weiser, 1998, p. 142.

[2] David Fontana, *The Secret Language of Symbols: A Visual Key to Symbols and their Meanings*, London: Pavilion Books, 1993.

[3] Dunham et al., op. cit.

[4] Matthieu Ricard, tr., *The Life of Shabkar: The Autobiography of a Tibetan Yogin*, New York: Snow Lion, 2003.

[5] Huber, op. cit., p. 96.

Chapter 13
Journey to the Sacred Mountain

[1] Swami Pranavananda, *Kailas-Manasarovar*, New Delhi: Surya Print Process, [1949] 1983 p. 200.

[2] In the words of Nyangral Nyima Ozer, author of Padmasambhava's hagiography, in Schaeffer, op. cit., pp. 94.

[3] Chögyam Trungpa, *Crazy Wisdom*, Boston: Shambhala, 1991.

[4] 'Wisdom Crazy: An Interview with Steven Goodman', spring 2005 issue of *Inquiring Mind*

Chapter 14
Following in the Footsteps of a Mystic

[1] Peter Gold, *Navajo and Tibetan Sacred Wisdom: The Circle of the Spirit*, Toronto: Inner Traditions International, 1994, p. 30.

[2] Huber, op. cit., p. 86.

Chapter 15
A Cloud Wanderer

[1] Alexandra David-Neel, *Magic and Mystery in Tibet*, London: Souvenir Press, [1929] 1967.

[2] John Crook and James Low, *The Yogins of Ladakh: A Pilgrimage Among the Hermits of the Buddhist Himalayas*, Delhi: Motilal Banarsidass, 1997.

[3] Baker, op. cit., p. 474.

[4] Allione, op. cit.

[5] Shakya, op. cit., p. 322.

[6] While often attributed to Nelson Mandela, I subsequently came across the proper source for this quote in Williamson, Marianne, *A Return to Love: Reflections on the Principles of A Course in Miracles*, London: Thorsons, 1996, pp. 191.

Chapter 16
A Vanishing Culture

[1] *Social Evils: Prostitution and Pornography in Lhasa*, London, Tibet Information Network, Briefing Paper No. 31, July 1999.

Chapter 17
Found Ani

[1] John O'Donohue, *Anam Cara: Spiritual Wisdom from the Celtic World*, London: Bantam Books, 1997, pp. 31 – 32.

[2] Dowman, op. cit., p. 177.

GLOSSARY

Chang	Barley beer.
Chod	Advanced spiritual practice to break attachment to powerful emotions such as desire; lit. 'cutting through'.
Chuba	Full-length Tibetan tunic.
Dakini	Goddess incarnate or female Tantric deity who upholds Buddhist teachings; lit. 'sky dancer'.
Dri	Female yak.
Gompa	Monastery.
Guanxi	Personal connections.
Inji	Western.
Khata	White ceremonial scarf.
Kora	To walk in a circular fashion around a sacred object such as a mountain, often on pilgrimage.
Mala	Rosary or prayer beads.
Om Mani Padme Hung	The most popular Tibetan Buddhist prayer for invoking compassion; lit. 'jewel in the heart of the lotus'.
Phurbu	Ritual dagger.
Sangha	Community of Buddhist practitioners.
Stupa	Circular structure to house Buddhist relics.
Tashi Delek	Tibetan greeting, lit. 'hello'.
Thukpa	Noodle soup.
Tsampa	Ground barley flour.
Tulku	Reincarnated spiritual teacher.
Yidam	Personal meditational deity.
Yogi/Yogini	Advanced spiritual practitioner who devotes his or her life to meditation.

SELECTED BIBLIOGRAPHY

Alighieri, Dante, *The Divine Comedy: I Inferno*, New York: Oxford University Press, [1939] 1961

Allen, Charles, *A Mountain in Tibet*, Calcutta: Rupa, [Andre Deutsch, 1982] 1992

Allione, Tsultrim, *Women of Wisdom*, New York: Snow Lion Publications, 2000.

Aperture Human Rights Watch, *Tibet Since 1950: Silence, Prison, or Exile*, New York: Aperture Foundation, 2000

Bailey, F. M., *No Passport to Tibet*, London: Rupert Hart Davis, 1957

Baker, Ian, *The Heart of the World: A Journey to the Last Secret Place*, New York: Penguin Press, 2004

Bancroft, Anne, *Women in Search of the Sacred*, London: Arkana, 1996

Bass, Catriona, *Inside the Treasure House: A Time in Tibet*, London: Abacus Books, [1990] 1992

Bhagavad Gita, The, tr. Mascaro, Juan, Middlesex: Penguin Classics, [1962] 1971

Bishop, Peter, *The Myth of Shangri-La: Tibet, Travel Writing and the Western Creation of Sacred Landscape*, London: Athlone Press, 1989

Brown, Mick, *The Spiritual Tourist: A Personal Odyssey through the Outer Reaches of Belief*, London: Bloomsbury, 1998

Bunyan, John, *The Pilgrim's Progress*, London: Oxford University Press, 1942

Campbell, Joseph, *The Hero with a Thousand Faces*, London: Fontana Press, [1949] 1993

Castle, Leila, ed., *Earthwalking Sky Dancers: Women's Pilgrimages to*

Sacred Places, Berkeley: Frog, 1996

China's Great Leap West, London: Tibet Information Network, 2000

Cortens, Theolyn, *Discovering Angels: Journeys through Archetypal Landscapes*, Oxford: Caer Sidi Publications, 1996

Cousineau, Phil, *The Art of Pilgrimage: The Seeker's Guide to Making Travel Sacred*, Dorset: Element Books, 1999

Cox, Kenneth, ed., *Frank Kingdon Ward's Riddle of the Tsangpo Gorges*, Suffolk: Antique Collectors' Club, 2001

Craig, Mary, *Tears of Blood: A Cry for Tibet*, London: Harper Collins, 1992

Crook, John and Low, James, *The Yogins of Ladakh: A Pilgrimage Among the Hermits of the Buddhist Himalayas*, Delhi: Motilal Banarsidass, 1997

Dalai Lama, *Freedom in Exile: The Autobiography of the Dalai Lama*, New York: Harper Collins, 1990

David-Neel, Alexandra, *Magic and Mystery in Tibet*, London: Souvenir Press, [1929] 1967

Dawkins, Peter, *Zoence – the Science of Life: Discovering the Sacred Spaces of Your Life*, Maine: Samuel Weiser, 1998

Dhondup, K., *Songs of the Sixth Dalai Lama*, Dharamasala: Library of Tibetan Works and Archives, [1981] 1996

Dorje, Gyurme, *Tibet Handbook*, Bath: Footprint Handbooks, 1996

Dowman, Keith, *The Sacred Life of Tibet*, London: Thorsons, 1997

Dunham, Carroll, Baker, Ian, and Kelly, Thomas, *Tibet: Reflections from the Wheel of Life*, New York: Abbeville Press, 1993

Edou, Jerome, *Machig Labdron and the Foundations of Chod*, New York: Snow Lion Publications, 1996

Ehrhard, Franz-Karl, 'The Role of "Treasure Discoverers" and Their Writings in the Search for Himalayan Sacred Lands', in *The Tibet Journal*, Autumn 1994, Vol. XIX, No. 3, Library of Tibetan Works and Archives: Dharamasala

Feuerstein, Georg, *Holy Madness: the shock tactics and radical teachings of crazy-wise adepts, holy fools, and rascal gurus*, New York: Arkana, 1992

Fletcher, Harold R., *A Quest of Flowers*, Edinburgh: Edinburgh University Press, 1975

Foster, Barbara and Foster, Michael, *Forbidden Journey: The Life of Alexandra David-Neel*, San Francisco: Harper & Row, [1987] 1989

Fontana, David, *The Secret Language of Symbols: A Visual Key to Symbols and their Meanings*, London: Pavilion Books, 1993

French, Patrick, *Tibet, Tibet: A Personal History of a Lost Land*, London: Harper Perennial, [2003] 2004

Getty, Adele, *Goddess: Mother of Living Nature*, London: Thames and Hudson, 1990

Gold, Peter, *Navajo and Tibetan Sacred Wisdom: The Circle of the Spirit*, Vermont: Inner Traditions International, 1994

Govinda, Lama Anagarika, *The Way of the White Clouds: A Buddhist in Tibet*, London: Rider, [1966] 1974

Govinda, Lama Anagarika, *Foundations of Tibetan Mysticism*, London: Rider, 1969

Gutschow, Kim, *Being a Buddhist Nun: The Struggle for Enlightenment in the Himalayas*, Cambridge, Massachusetts: Harvard University Press, 2004

Gyatso, Palden, *Fire Under the Snow: Testimony of a Tibetan Prisoner*, London: Harvill Press, 1997

Hall, Nor, *The Moon & the Virgin: A voyage towards self-discovery and healing*, London: The Women's Press, [1980] 1991

Hanna, Span, 'Vast as the Sky: The Terma Tradition in Modern Tibet', in Samuel, G., Gregor, H., and Stutchbury, E., eds., *Tantra and Popular Religion in Tibet*, New Delhi: International Academy of Indian Culture and Aditya Prakashan, 1994, pp. 1–13

Hansen, Eric, *Orchid Fever*, London: Methuen, 2001

Hilton, James, *Lost Horizon*, London: Pan Books, [Macmillian and Co. 1933] 1947

Huber, Toni, 'Putting the Gnas Back into Gnas-skor: Rethinking Tibetan Pilgrimage Practice', in Huber, Toni, ed., *Sacred Spaces and Powerful Places in Tibetan Culture: A Collection of Essays*, Dharamasala: Library of Tibetan Works and Archives, 1999

Karko, Kate, *Namma: A Tibetan Love Story*, London: Hodder and Stoughton, 2000

Kindred, Glennie, *Earth Wisdom*, London: Hay House, 2004

Kingdon Ward, Frank, *Riddle of the Tsangpo Gorges*, London: Edward Arnold, 1926

Kingdon, Ward, *A Plant Hunter in Tibet*, London: Jonathan Cape, 1934

Le Page, Victoria, *Shambhala: The Fascinating Truth behind the Myth of Shangri-la*, Illinois: Quest Books, 1996

Le Suer, Alec, *Running a Hotel on the Roof of the Word: Five Years in Tibet*, Chichester: Summersdale Publishers, 1998

Lehman, Steve, *The Tibetans: A Struggle to Survive*, London: Virgin Books, 1998

Levine, Norma, *Blessing Power of the Buddhas: Sacred Objects, Secret Lands*, Dorset: Element, 1993

Li, Zhisui, *The Private Life of Chairman Mao*, London, Arrow Books, [1994] 1996

Lyte, Charles, *Frank Kingdon-Ward: The Last of the Great Plant Hunters*, London: John Murray, 1989

Mackenzie, Vicki, *Cave in the Snow: Tenzin Palmo's Quest for Enlightenment*, London: Bloomsbury, 1998

Marshall, Steve D., 'Rukhag 3: The Nuns of Drapchi Prison', London: Tibet Information Network, 2000

McCue, Gary, *Trekking in Tibet: A Traveler's Guide*, Seattle: The Mountaineers [1991] 1999

McCurry, Steve, *The Path to Buddha: A Tibetan Pilgrimage*, London: Phaidon Press, 2003

McGowan, William, 'Last Tango in Kathmandu', *Men's Journal*, March 2000

Murphy, Dervla, *Tibetan Foothold*, London: John Murray, 1966

Norbu, Namkhai, *The Crystal and the Way of Light*, London: Arkana, [1986] 1993

O'Donohue, John, *Anam Cara: Spiritual Wisdom from the Celtic World*,

London: Bantam Books, 1997

Pachen, Ani and Donnelley, Adelaide, *Sorrow Mountain: The Remarkable Story of a Tibetan Warrior Nun*, London: Doubleday, 2000

Pommaret, Françoise, 'The Mon-pa revisited: In search of Mon', in Huber, Toni, ed., *Sacred Spaces and Powerful Places in Tibetan Culture: A Collection of Essays*, Dharamasala: Library of Tibetan Works and Archives, 1999, pp. 52–73

Pranavananda, Swami, *Kailas-Manasarovar*, New Delhi: Surya Print Process, [1949] 1983

Rasmussen, J., and Whitehead, J., *Himalayan Enchantment*, London: Serindia Publications, 1990

Rawson, Philip, *Sacred Tibet*, London: Thames and Hudson, 1991

Ricard, Matthieu, tr. *The Life of Shabkar: The Autobiography of a Tibetan Yogin*, New York: Snow Lion, 2003

Rinpoche, Sogyal, *The Tibetan Book of Living and Dying*, Calcutta: Rupa, [1993] 1997

Roerich, Nicholas, *Shambhala*, New Delhi: Aravali Books International, 1997

Schaeffer, Kurtis R., *Himalayan Hermitess: The Life of a Tibetan Buddhist Nun*, New York: Oxford University Press, 2004

Shakabpa, T. W. D., *Tibet: A Political History*, New Haven: Yale University Press, 1967

Shakya, Tsering, *The Dragon in the Land of Snows*, London: Pimlico, 1999

Sheldrake, Rupert and Fox, Matthew, *Natural Grace: Dialogues on Science and Spirituality*, London: Bloomsbury, 1996

Simmer-Brown, Judith, *Dakini's Warm Breath: The Feminine Principle in Tibetan Buddhism*, Boston: Shambhala Publications, 2001

Snelling, John, *The Sacred Mountain: The Complete Guide to Tibet's Mount Kailas*, London: East-West Publications, [1983] 1990

Teasdill, Wendy, *Walking to the Mountain: A Pilgrimage to Tibet's Holy Mount Kailash*, Hong Kong: Asia 2000, 1996

'Tight Security in Tibet to mark 40th anniversary of Lhasa uprising', news update by Tibet Information Network, 10 March 1999

Tibet 2000: Environment and Development Issues, Dharamasala: Environmental and Development Desk, DIIR, 2000

Trungpa, Chogyam, *Shambhala: The Sacred Path of the Warrior*, New Delhi: Rupa, [1978] 1984

Trungpa, Chogyam, *Crazy Wisdom*, Boston: Shambhala, 1991.

Vreeland, Nicholas, ed., *An Open Heart: Practising Compassion in Everyday Life by the Dalai Lama*, London: Hodder and Stoughton, 2001

Westwood, Jennifer, *Sacred Journeys: Paths for the New Pilgrim*, London: Gaia Books, 1997

'When the Sky Fell to Earth: The New Crackdown on Buddhism in Tibet', a report by the International Campaign for Tibet, Washington: ICT, 2004

Williamson, Marianne, *A Return to Love: Reflections on the Principles of A Course in Miracles*, London: Thorsons, [1992] 1996

Willis, Janice, ed., *Feminine Ground: Essays on Women and Tibet*, New York: Snow Lion, [1989] 1995

'Wisdom Crazy: An Interview with Steven Goodman', spring 2005 issue of *Inquiring Mind*

Yun, Xu, *Empty Cloud: The Autobiography of the Chinese Zen Master*, tr. Luk, Charles, Dorset: Element Books, 1988

ACKNOWLEDGEMENTS

This book has been many years in the making. I would firstly like to thank my family: my parents, Tony and Patricia, for their boundless love, patience and counsel; both sisters, Jane (for the title) and Sarah (for going to Lhasa first and inspiring me with her photos); their husbands, Tris for his keen interest and Pete's perceptive editorial suggestions; Aden, for his loving support in the final stages of the journey.

A special thanks to the following for their friendship, guidance and encouragement over the years – particularly Nicki Kempston, Julia Thomas and Jane Walker, who've always been there when I lost my way – Michael Amendolia, Tattwa Bodha (Dominique Bechet), Dorset Campbell-Ross, Anna Davidovich, Will Ellsworth-Jones, Tashi Gyatso, Marie Hayes, Luke Hey, John Hutchin, Paul Kennedy (Sarito), Sophie and Tim Knock, John Lazarus, John May, Swami Nischalananda Saraswati, Gina Offredi, Suzy Parker, Amanda Perry-Bolt, Carol and Karma Phuntsok, Ali Reynolds, Michael Sexton, Tracey Sims, Bernadette Vallely, Alan Wherry and Belinda Wiggs.

I'm profoundly grateful to Ken Cox for inviting me to search for the red lily and for his patience in explaining all things botanical and careful reading of earlier chapters; Jane Bradish-Ellames for helping make an idea into a reality; Mick Brown for always believing the book would come to fruition; Kate Saunders for her time, advice and critique of the manuscript; Kats Edwards for friendship, forbearance and surviving the rigours of the road; Charles Manson (Yeshi) for generously sharing his Buddhist knowledge; David Burlinson for helping me first get to Tibet and Ian Baker for the opportunity to go to Pemako; to both His Holiness the Dalai Lama and Jean Rasmussen for agreeing to be interviewed.

I would like to acknowledge Emma Soames, former editor of the *Telegraph Magazine*, and Sarah Miller, editor of *Condé Nast Traveller*, where versions of the article about the red lily and Pemako first appeared.

I'd also like to recognise the contribution of the Tibet Information Network (sadly no longer in operation); Tibetan lessons from Ani Dawa in Dharamasala and Tinley Dhondup in Kathmandu; the Tibetan Centre for Human Rights and the following, whose suggestions and contribution to the manuscript have been invaluable: Dhondup Chophel, Gil Gillenwater, Norma Levine, Michele Martin, Tenzin Palmo, Tsering Shakya and Jan Willis.

A particular note of thanks to Toby Eady for his initial interest; and above all, to my agent, Jessica Woollard, for her conviction from the beginning, astute corrections and unflagging enthusiasm, and my editor, Judith Kendra, for championing the book, sensitive editing and intuitive understanding of Ani and me. Thanks to Sue Lascelles for shepherding the manuscript through the final stages, Morag Lyall for copy-editing and all at Rider.

Finally, I am humbly indebted to all those Tibetans who've assisted and supported my journeys – in ways both seen and unseen – and who, often at personal risk, translated for me, travelled with me and entrusted me. In order to protect their identity they cannot be named; but Lucky, Sunny and Uncle will know who they are. Thank you to all other Lhasa friends and strangers whose experiences and stories have found voice through my book. And of course, to Ani, for her blessings, courage and generosity of spirit which has been – and continues to be – such an inspiration.